THE COMPLETE GUIDE TO THERAPEUTIC PARENTING

also in the Therapeutic Parenting Books series

The Quick Guide to Therapeutic Parenting
Sarah Naish and Sarah Dillon
ISBN 978 1 78775 357 0
eISBN 978 1 78775 358 7

Therapeutic Parenting Essentials
Moving from Trauma to Trust
Sarah Naish, Sarah Dillon and Jane Mitchell
ISBN 978 1 78775 031 9
eISBN 978 1 78775 032 6

The A–Z of Therapeutic Parenting
Strategies and Solutions
Sarah Naish
ISBN 978 1 78592 376 0
eISBN 978 1 78450 732 9

THE COMPLETE GUIDE TO THERAPEUTIC PARENTING

A HELPFUL GUIDE TO THE THEORY, RESEARCH AND WHAT IT MEANS FOR EVERYDAY LIFE

JANE MITCHELL and SARAH NAISH

Jessica Kingsley Publishers
London and Philadelphia

First published in Great Britain in 2021 by Jessica Kingsley Publishers
An Hachette Company

1

A CIP catalogue record for this title is available from the
British Library and the Library of Congress

ISBN 978 1 78775 376 1
eISBN 978 1 78775 377 8

Printed and bound in Great Britain by Clays Ltd

Jessica Kingsley Publishers
Carmelite House
50 Victoria Embankment
London EC4Y 0DZ

www.jkp.com

Contents

Welcome!

Welcome to the wonderful, exhausting but ultimately fulfilling world of the therapeutic parent! Whether you are a parent (foster, adoptive, biological or family member), social worker, teacher or other supporting professional, we hope that you will find within these pages some helpful insights and solutions.

Throughout this book we refer to parents – because whether you are a biological parent, a foster parent, an adoptive parent, a special guardian or a kinship carer you are definitely a parent, and what you are doing is parenting your child or the child who is in your care.

The legislation and procedure referred to is the English system, my apologies for being unable to supply relevant information for individual countries. However the broad concepts of Therapeutic Parenting given throughout the book are being used effectively worldwide.

In the book you may encounter unfamiliar terms – we've tried to explain these on first mention where possible, but if you need a reminder, do please check the index, which has an entry in bold for where a technical term or piece of jargon has been explained.

A note about the case histories

Each case history is based on a combination of real life stories drawn from my long career as a trainer and supporter of families. These have been anonymised to protect the families involved.

About the authors

Jane Mitchell

My whole life has been centred around children, from the time my first sibling arrived (I am the oldest of five), through to my first jobs in babysitting, then creating my own family and working in childminding, before studying for a degree in early years childcare and education. I am now Director of the National Association of Therapeutic Parents, and an adoptive parent myself as well as a birth mother of three. I specialize in developing resources and training for the Centre of Excellence in Child Trauma around attachment, developmental trauma and related neuroscience. I have been involved in running a Diploma in Therapeutic Parenting and have worked with adoptive and foster families for over 15 years.

Sarah Naish

I am an adopter of five siblings and a former foster parent, social worker and owner of an independent fostering agency. I work full time in training and consultancy within adoption and fostering and am also the CEO of the Centre of Excellence in Child Trauma, which encompasses the National Association for Therapeutic Parenting.

About our books

This book is part of a series of books on therapeutic parenting – we will start by briefly describing each book in the series to give you a sense of where this books fits, and its particular strengths.

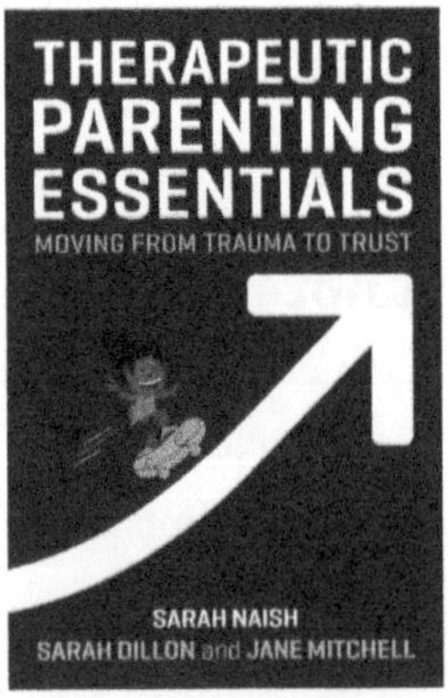

The Quick Guide to Therapeutic Parenting by Sarah Naish and Sarah Dillon is a visual introduction – perfect for newcomers who want to grasp the essentials or to give to grandparents or teachers who just want a simple explanation – with cartoons, easy-to-understand information and inspirational quotes throughout.

The A–Z of Therapeutic Parenting by Sarah Naish is, as the title suggests, an A–Z of really useful strategies to help therapeutic parents with common everyday challenges.

Therapeutic Parenting Essentials: Moving from Trauma to Trust by Sarah Naish, Sarah Dillon and Jane Mitchell is a book which describes the real, lived experience of therapeutic parenting – what it looks like in practice, and how it feels not only from the parent's perspective, but also from the child's.

The Complete Guide to Therapeutic Parenting by Jane Mitchell and Sarah Naish – this book, which aims to look under the bonnet of therapeutic parenting to explain how and why it works, including the theory and research that lies behind it. It's been written to be accessible and informative, but also based on the latest findings about trauma, the brain and therapeutic parenting. Throughout this book Jane has used examples from her own experiences of parenting to highlight certain issues. For that reason, although Sarah is a co-author due to her outstanding contribution to how we understand childhood trauma and because of the material used within the book as well as our past collaborations, in this book Jane has taken the lead on the written material and for that reason has written in the first person singular. Where Jane writes 'I' or 'my' she is referring to her own experience and knowledge.

The journey to therapeutic parenting

In training about therapeutic parenting, people often say that they wish they had had access to this knowledge years ago – such is its power.

But of course, the information about developmental trauma and the role of an attuned adult in the neurological, physical and emotional development of a baby is relatively new. It has been evolving over the past 20 years as science and psychology have combined to give us greater information about neurological development and original thinking about the importance of emotional literacy. It has deepened our understanding of the ways in which our earliest relationships shape the way we interact with others and how we approach life. The application of theory and research to understanding and parenting children who have suffered developmental trauma is still a work in progress, and we continue to learn more about this fascinating subject.

I remember bringing my adopted daughter home, so vividly! I had birth children and had been a childminder for several years. For the last four of these, I had been working with the local authority and supporting vulnerable families. I met my daughter while childminding her, and after the usual process I was able to adopt her 18 months later.

Like so many of us working with children in childcare, education or social work, I thought I knew the answers to my daughter's behaviour. It did not take me long to find out I was wrong, but finding out what on earth was happening was a much longer process!

Back in 2003, when I was trying to find some answers, I started with Daniel Goleman and his writing on emotional literacy. Daniel wrote a book called *Emotional Intelligence* in 1996 which explored how the architecture of the brain underlies emotion and rationality, and how emotional intelligence can provide a basis for self-awareness, empathy and social skills – qualities which are found in individuals who have positive relationships and successful careers.

This made sense to me as a starting point – it was clear that helping a child to understand their own needs and feelings by developing their emotional language would help them to learn to ask for help and manage those feelings, but it didn't give me the answers I needed to help a child who showed behaviours that were off the scale – beyond anything I had encountered before that point.

Over the following years I attended seminars – the best were at the Centre for Child Mental Health in Islington organized by Margot

Sunderland – and I took whatever training I could find and read everything I could get my hands on. I discovered books by Dan Hughes, who writes about child trauma with insight and humour, and was able to give some strategies to help – a revelation to me back then!

Other great sources of information were Margot Sunderland, Karl Heinz-Brisch, Daniel Siegel and Sue Gerhardt, all of whom brought new ideas and information. If these names are not familiar to you right now, don't worry – this book will introduce you to some of these people and explain some of their ideas in greater depth. The book also includes a bibliography designed to help anyone looking to deepen their knowledge.

As I learned more, I started delivering training to families about attachment and managing challenging behaviours, studied for a degree and a PGCE, and started to see references to therapeutic parenting in books and journals.

One day in 2015 I received a message from Sarah Naish asking if I would be interested in delivering training for her Inspire Group. Meeting Sarah was like finding a long-lost sister who just understood everything I was saying.

So began a lasting friendship, and a working relationship that has involved working with Sarah to bring support to families in need through different associated elements: Inspire Group – developing training and resources to meet the needs of parents and agencies; the Diploma in Therapeutic Parenting for parents and professionals who wish to gain a deeper skill set; the National Association of Therapeutic Parents or NAoTP (which I have the pleasure of being a founder member of), which brings together peer support, training from Inspire Group and skilled advisors to help families as well as providing services to schools and professionals working with children; and overarching everything, the Centre of Excellence in Child Trauma, which brings together information and also holds an annual conference.

We have seen huge expansion, with local authorities, independent fostering agencies, schools and parents (adoptive, bio, foster or kinship/special guardian) taking up membership of the NAoTP and/or buying the expertise of Inspire Group training. In 2020 this expanded at an incredible rate as we were able to identify support needs and find ways to continue support over virtual platforms almost immediately. This proved to be an incredibly valuable service and saw our membership triple in a month.

In this book I present my own experiences as well as drawing on the incredible knowledge, experience and writings of Sarah Naish.

1

Why Do They Do That? Developmental Trauma

In this first chapter we are going to start talking about what 'developmental trauma' means and why it has such an impact on all aspects of our children's development. We will look at the ways that our children build their understanding of the world around them, and how this can be disrupted with far-reaching effects on children. We will identify some of the ways we have come to understand why it is that any trauma in early life (even in the womb) can have such far-reaching effects on the social, emotional, cognitive (learning and communication) and even physical development of the child and introduce the idea of therapeutic parenting as the best response to help children and families heal.

What is developmental trauma?

Developmental trauma can be understood as any condition or event occurring during pregnancy or the early years which has an effect on the neurological development of the child and therefore their physical, emotional, social or cognitive development.

In 2005 the Dutch psychiatrist, author and educator Bessel van der Kolk suggested a diagnosis of Developmental Trauma Disorder (DTD) where early development has been absent or insufficient:

> The symptoms of DTD include disruptions of affect regulation, disturbed attachment patterns, the rapid behavioural regressions and shifts in emotional states, the loss of autonomous strivings, the aggressive behaviour against self and others, the failure to achieve developmental competencies; the loss of bodily regulation in the areas of sleep, food and self-care; the altered schemas of the world; the anticipatory behaviour and traumatic expectations; the multiple somatic problems, from gastrointestinal distress to headaches; the apparent lack of awareness of danger and resulting self-endangering behaviours; the self-hatred and self-blame and the chronic feelings of ineffectiveness. (van der Kolk 2005)

What this means is that children who have suffered early trauma may have some or all of the following issues:

- Have extreme difficulty or even unable to manage their emotions
- Find it very hard to bond with parents and form positive attachments
- Show aggressive behaviours
- Show regressed behaviours (act much younger than their years)
- Have developmental delay across some or all areas – physical, emotional, social or cognitive
- Have difficulty sleeping
- Have difficulty managing food issues (stealing or hoarding food is a very common example)

- Have a negative concept of themselves, the world and adults including an expectation of rejection and punishment
- Suffer from self-hatred and exceedingly low self-esteem
- Are unable to control impulsivity and risk-taking
- Are unable to link cause and effect and therefore cannot understand consequences
- May have multiple sensory processing issues.

What causes developmental trauma?

Developmental trauma can be caused by many things – here are some examples:

In utero trauma

This is damage sustained in the womb. We now know that damage sustained in the womb can have long-lasting and sometimes permanent effects on the neurological development of the child.

In utero trauma can be due to maternal illness; due to stress on the part of the mother such as a hidden pregnancy or domestic violence; or due to a mother who is struggling with an addiction and therefore exposes the developing embryo to the harmful and damaging effects of drugs or alcohol. Developmental trauma can also occur as a result of illness during pregnancy. We will examine some of the most common causes.

Medication

The effects of prescribed drugs – a very famous example being Thalidomide in the 1960s leading to marked physical abnormalities.

Maternal illnesses and conditions

Hyperemesis Gravidarum (HG)

A condition which affects around 1 per cent of pregnant women. It is an extreme condition:

- There is relentless nausea and/or vomiting. This is very different than the 'morning sickness' experienced by many women in the first trimester of their pregnancies, and can cause rapid weight loss, malnutrition and dehydration.
- The symptoms of HG are relentless – the person might be sick many times a day, and be unable to keep down food or drink.
- There is significant risk to mother and child, and over a third of HG babies are premature.
- HG babies have increased risk of low birth weight and small size.
- HG babies have an increased risk of emotional, behavioural and developmental disorders.

(Adapted from https://helpher.org)

Preeclampsia

This is a complication of pregnancy, the symptoms of which are high blood pressure, signs of damage to organ systems such as liver and kidneys, and accompanying blurred vision, dizziness and headache. However, preeclampsia may also develop without symptoms. Preeclampsia can have fatal complications for mother and child. Causes seem to be as a result of compromised blood supply to the foetus. Early in pregnancy new blood vessels develop specifically to supply the placenta. Preeclampsia occurs when these fail to develop properly, causing an abnormality of the blood vessels, which limits blood flow.

The complications can include foetal growth restriction because of lack of nutrients and oxygen, pre-term birth, low birth weight and placental abruption where the uterus separates from the inner wall of the uterus before delivery (www.mayoclinic.org/diseases-conditions/preeclampsia/symptoms-causes/syc-20355745).

Gestational diabetes

This is a type of diabetes that occurs as a result of high levels of hormones produced during pregnancy that have an effect on the action of insulin, normally resulting in a net mild increase of blood sugar. In gestational diabetes blood sugar increases to a level which can affect the growth and wellbeing of the baby. Risks for the baby include:

- excessive birth weight, making birth injuries more likely or requiring a **'C Section'** (caesarian section where the baby is delivered via an incision made in the abdominal wall of the mother)
- preterm (early) birth and respiratory distress syndrome
- low blood sugar (hypoglycaemia) because the baby has high insulin production
- higher risk of type 2 diabetes.

(www.mayoclinic.org/diseases-conditions/gestational-diabetes/symptoms-causes/syc-20355339)

Maternal stress

Severe stress during pregnancy has been shown to have an effect on foetal development. For example, maternal depression or high anxiety due to hidden pregnancy or involvement in an abusive relationship could lead to increased stress and therefore increased production of cortisol on the part of the mother. Sue Gerhardt explains that 'as early as pregnancy, the stress response is already forming within the foetus... In particular her high cortisol could pass through the placenta into his brain' (p.67). She reminds us that this is unsurprising, as for the duration of the pregnancy they are in a shared body, with the same diet and the same stress levels, and in the case of alcohol or drugs these will also enter the system of the developing baby. High levels of cortisol can affect the developing brain over time with specific effects on the hippocampus, reducing the number of cortisol receptors so that circulating cortisol remains high. This can also affect the growth of the hippocampus (affecting memory) as well as the part of the prefrontal cortex of the brain which enables us to recognize social cues and adjust behaviour (Gerhardt 2004). The ability of the parent to nurture and provide regulation for the child will then affect the eventual outcome – 'a well-resourced and well-regulated infant becomes a child and adult who can regulate himself or herself well, whilst a poorly resourced and poorly regulated infant becomes a child who cannot regulate herself well' (Gerhardt 2004). **Cortisol** is the hormone which is produced in response to chronic long-term stress, whereas adrenalin is produced in response to sudden acute stress and is part of the fight–flight response that occurs in the presence of a risk to survival.

Recreational drug use

A baby may be born addicted and in unbelievable pain as they undergo a process of withdrawal, making their earliest experiences of the world terrifying and painful. Unfortunately, the impact of narcotics on the developing embryo can also lead to other neurological and physical complications as the developing baby is at risk of damage to the complicated structure of the brain. The term for this is **neonatal abstinence syndrome** or NAS. Information about NAS from the Lucile Packard Children's Hospital, Stanford, states that in addition to the issues connected to withdrawal there may be low birth weight, premature birth, seizures or birth defects (www.stanfordchildrens.org/en/topic/default?id=neonatal-abstinence-syndrome-90-P02387).

Alcohol abuse in pregnancy

Foetal alcohol syndrome disorder (FASD) has been associated with many symptoms which show impaired development. These include cerebral palsy, learning difficulties, social communication difficulties, damage to liver, kidneys or heart, and sensory issues.

Domestic violence

The developing baby is exposed to all of the terror and fear that the mother endures and receives their stress hormones directly through the bloodstream, which alters their genetic expression. The baby is like a witness to the events, and can 'hear' the aggression and shouting; this can lead to fearful reactions once born.

Stability and consistency of homelife

Imagine a child who has been born into care, or who has been removed as a result of an investigation into abuse.

First of all, their understanding and expectation, based on their experience, is that the abuse will continue because this is the only way of life that they have known. This leads to behaviours which may be very challenging; for example, the child may be controlling, refuse nurture, distrust adults, tell lies and be violent or aggressive verbally and/or physically.

How the child will respond and heal will depend on the quality of the placement (empathy and understanding of the foster or adoptive parents or family member), whether they are re-traumatized by contact arrangements or by unsuitable parenting, and how many times they are moved around the system.

Every time they are moved there will be an impact on the way they feel about themselves, and because where there are frequent moves there is also a lack of consistency and reliability, it will be hard for them to internalize a clear set of rules to follow.

Medical issues

There are many issues that can affect a child at birth that will impact on their early life and experiences due to separation from parents disrupting the essential early bonding experience and bringing painful intrusions into their life or making survival harder for them from the outset. These may include:

- premature birth
- congenital heart disease
- medical conditions, syndromes or disorders
- disability – sensory or physical
- physical abnormality
- repeated hospitalizations

- chronic unrelieved pain
- repeated procedures/operations.

Abuse – direct or witnessed

Physical abuse

Beating, biting, burning, use of weapons to cause injury... sadly there continue to be cases around the world where such abuse results in the death of the child, but we should also remember that being a witness to extreme violence is also terrifying and of course has an adverse effect on the development of the child.

Emotional abuse

This form of cruelty impacts on the child's view of themselves, leaving them feeling worthless, unlovable and, as one parent recently put it, 'disposable'. And it can place them in positions where in order to get a little bit of kindness they have to agree to be party to additional abuse, perhaps sexual in nature.

Emotional abuse invariably is present alongside other forms of abuse. Forms of emotional abuse are belittling or maligning the child; ignoring the child; withholding love and nurturing; or giving negative messages to the child about their expectations, capabilities, appearance, usefulness or importance.

Imagine how this would affect a very young child or growing child who has no other way of knowing what kind of person they are apart from what they are told by adults around them.

Neglect

Now that we have a better understanding of how the brain develops in response to experience (forming neurological connections which give the child their template of the world they live in and how to manage this), we know more about the far-reaching implications for overall development.

Neglect is essentially a failure to provide appropriate stimulation, safety, food, warmth, comfort or medical support. Failure to feed appropriately causes malnutrition or starvation. Failure to stimulate or provide a suitable environment to explore causes physical issues and sensory impairment. Failure to interact causes social, emotional and cognitive issues.

Children may suffer neglect for a variety of reasons – there may be deliberate neglect on the part of the caregiver (for a first-hand case history you could read *A Child Called It* (1995), a memoir of childhood abuse by Dave Pelzer). Neglect rarely occurs in isolation, but is generally found in addition to other forms of abuse, whether emotional, sexual or physical, or may be due to adverse mental health such as chronic depression or postnatal depression on the part of the parent.

Sexual abuse

Sexual abuse happens across all cultures and across all social environments. It happens to children of all ages, including very small babies, and has a horrific impact in terms of emotional and physical development, including physical damage which may cause medical problems for life. Sexual abuse is exposure to or involvement in sexual activities including penetration, either penile or with implements, vaginally or anally, oral sex, child prostitution, taking photographic images of young children for distribution, and exposing children to sexual activity via images, films or direct observation.

Adverse childhood experiences

Adverse childhood experiences (ACEs) is the term used to describe all types of abuse, neglect and other potentially traumatic experiences that occur to children (under the age of 18, after which time they are legally adults). The term was coined by the CDC-Kaiser Permanente Adverse Childhood Experiences (1995–1997) study, which identified that ACEs can lead to poor outcomes for children and have a lasting impact on health as well as being an underlying factor for aggression and violence (www.cdc.gov/violenceprevention/childabuseandneglect/acestudy/about.html).

ACEs as an acronym has been used to stand for a range of different terms as well as adverse childhood experiences (including abuse, neglect and chronic illness), but others have used it to describe adverse community experiences or adverse climate experiences.

> ACEs are adverse childhood experiences that harm children's developing brains and lead to changing how they respond to stress and damaging their immune systems so profoundly that the effects show up decades later. ACEs cause much of our burden of chronic disease, most mental illness, and are at the root of most violence.

There is also therefore a link to epigenetics – the way that our experiences, community and climate can change the way that DNA is expressed in a developing embryo in order to face the challenges of the environment they are being born into. This means that if, for example, the mother is in an adverse environment and so has high circulating levels of cortisol in her bloodstream, the developing baby will undergo changes in the way their DNA is expressed in response. As a result, a baby may suffer the damage that is caused by high levels of maternal circulating cortisol and also be born with abnormally high circulating cortisol themselves. Where a child has high circulating cortisol, the effect of adrenalin on their system will be more pronounced more quickly, triggering what look like disproportionate responses to situations, which can be incomprehensible to the person trying to care for the child.

One result of ACEs can be that we find that we have a child who can react explosively to ordinary life events – such as the frustration caused by an adult saying no. Dan Siegel (2015) states that:

> The patterns of particular states of mind in an infant can be seen as an implicit form of memory. Repeated experiences of terror and fear can be engrained within the circuits of the brain as states of mind. With chronic occurrence, these states can become more readily activated (retrieved) in the future so that they become characteristic traits of the individual. In this way our lives can become shaped by reactivations of implicit memory, which lack a sense that something is being recalled. We simply enter these engrained states and experience them as the reality of our present experience.

It appears that repeated traumatic childhood experiences form an implicit (state of mind) memory, with the result that children can be very quickly and easily triggered into trauma memories and trauma states.

Public Health England 2008 cites three direct and six indirect experiences that have an impact on childhood development:

- *Direct*: Verbal abuse, physical abuse, sexual abuse
- *Indirect* (household/environment): Domestic violence, parental separation, mental illness, alcohol abuse, drug abuse and incarceration.

The greater the number of ACEs experienced, the more likely that mental and physical health will be affected, with correspondingly poorer outcomes for health and increased risk of premature death in adulthood.

IN YOUR FAMILY...

- What do you know about your child's medical history?
- If a birth child, what was happening during or just after pregnancy?
- Were there complications with the birth?
- What do you know about reasons for removal from family?
- Do you know if children were subjected to abuse?
- How many placements has the child had?
- Are there any questions you now need to ask?
- Professionals – do you need to check the information you hold?
- Have you made full disclosure to families?

Early neurological development

Development of the neurological system begins in the first few weeks of pregnancy with structures becoming visible during the first **trimester** (the first three months) with the development of the neural tube, which will later differentiate into the spinal cord, cerebellum, limbic system and prefrontal cortex of the brain. The specialized cells of the brain – **neurones** and their synapses (connections) – begin developing after around seven weeks. Clearly this means that these structures are vulnerable to toxic substances such as alcohol, recreational drugs, tobacco and some foodstuffs. However, the developing brain is also susceptible to the effects of cortisol. Sue Gerhardt (2004) states that:

> too much cortisol early on – in the first three years in particular, when the daily pattern of cortisol is established – can even affect brain structure. In particular, it can damage those areas of the brain that are developing rapidly in the early years, because it can be toxic to the development of neural connections just at the time when the connections are being made and the pathways established.

Sue Gerhardt also says that the prefrontal cortex and the social brain develop as a result of the social interactions and experiences of the developing child. These incidents shape the pathways which are established and are then confirmed and strengthened by repeated experience, forming the mindset of the child. This is what leads to what we often refer to as the 'hardwired' perceptions and responses of the child. In a 'good enough' family, where there is a minimum standard of parental care which will ensure that the child is able to grow into a healthy and well-adjusted individual, parents help the child to develop appropriate strategies and responses enabling the child to be resilient and manage ordinary stress through their co-regulation (supporting the child to manage their big feelings using empathy) and modelling. Unfortunately, if the opposite situation occurs and a child suffers humiliation, lack of responsiveness, neglect and other abuse, not only is it impossible to learn an appropriate stress response, but also the environmental factors and lack of emotional availability of a caregiver mean that the child has increased stress.

After birth, the child's sensory experiences stimulate specific regions of the brain which then activate pathways. The more frequently the activity is repeated the more the pathway strengthens, until in the end this will become the default response. So for example, exploration of movement activates motor regions in the prefrontal cortex; speech and language – the baby talk and running commentary parents often employ with their children – activate communication-related regions of the brain. Synaptic strength – i.e. strong pathways formed by repeated consistent actions with consistent consequences, stability and routine – contributes to the efficiency of the neuronal networks that enable cognitive functions such as learning and working memory. This has implications for cognitive functions and ability to manage school, which we will discuss later.

During the first few years, and then again during adolescence, there is rapid growth of the brain, and pathways that are less utilized are 'pruned' away. Therefore 'if as babies and young children we live with angry, aggressive people, we will keep pathways that help us to be alert to anger and aggression' (Gerhardt 2004). Traumatized children display exactly this type of response; alternatively they may be overcompliant, or they may abscond from stressful situations. Our brains are formed to enable us to adapt to survive in the environment and culture we are born into, and the result of this is that our early formative experiences shape us in a profound way. If we are born into a stressful environment then we have two choices in order to survive – fight or flight.

For further information, we recommend two books by Sue Gerhardt – *Why Love Matters* (2004) and *The Selfish Society* (2010) – and Dan Siegel's *The Developing Mind* (second edition 2015).

Three parts of the brain

The model of the triune brain was first proposed by Paul McLean in the 1960s to show how the human brain developed as part of an evolutionary process.

The innermost structure, which also includes the spinal cord, is the **reptilian brain** or central nervous system (CNS). Not under conscious control, this ancient structure is responsive to feedback from the body and the environment to regulate and ensure that survival needs are met. The CNS maintains life – regulation of breathing, maintaining heartbeat, blood flow (circulation), appetite, temperature moderation, etc. None of this happens consciously, although we may be consciously aware of the effects, so we notice if we are shivering, or if we have palpitations or if we are hungry. This system will respond to survival threats – the fight or flight response. In a dangerous situation, the brain will prepare the body for one of two responses – running away or fighting. In extreme stress you will also see the 'freeze' response.

The middle part of the brain, wrapped around the CNS, is the **mammalian or limbic brain** – a subcortical structure associated with emotions, memory (the hippocampus) and arousal or stimulation levels (the amygdala, a structure which is sensitive to stress – like a stress smoke alarm receiving sensory data from the thalamus). Again, these are ancient structures responsible for primitive interpretations of data.

The outermost part of the brain is the **cortex** (the rational brain) – the conscious part of the brain. The function of the cortex is to expand knowledge and understanding – make sense of the world and inform our responses to people and situations. The frontal lobe of the cortex is where such higher brain functions such as planning, organization, impulse control and emotional regulation can take place. Any or all of these functions may be reduced as the brain is re-shaped during the pruning process, which takes place during adolescence as part of a secondary phase of neurological development. Other lobes give meaning to visual input (**occipital lobe**), auditory input (hearing – **temporal lobe**) and voluntary or intentional movement (**premotor cortex**). At different stages of the restructuring process it makes sense to imagine that we may be clumsy, unresponsive, uncommunicative or oversensitive.

Dan Siegel has developed a simple model to help us to understand the brain – the hand model. This model allows us to think about the structure of the brain, where if you clench your fist over your thumb, you end up with a reasonable working model of how the brain is structurally arranged. Siegel also uses this as an explanation of what happens when stress causes the cortex to 'disconnect' from the limbic and reptilian areas, making us 'flip our lid'. Put simply, the organized cortex is able to regulate stress and enable the individual not to become overwhelmed. However, when overwhelm does occur, part of the response of the reptilian brain is to divert blood from the brain to the large muscles of the body, increase heart rate, enhance sensory organs and put the individual in the best state to fight for survival. Effectively the rational capacity of the brain is disengaged. Too much thinking can prevent the immediate response that might save your life. It is vital to remember that once you are in fight or flight, which is a state of overwhelm, you are not consciously in control of your thoughts or actions.

Attachment – helping to build healthy brains

Attachment theory was first proposed by John Bowlby. Having served in the Royal Army Medical Corps in World War II, John Bowlby was appointed Director of the Tavistock Clinic and in 1950 became a mental health consultant to the World Health Organization. He became interested in how children reacted when separated from their parents, and this then led to his work on the importance of attachment in child development. The theory states that the nurturing and reciprocal bond between a caregiver and a child is essential for growth of emotional and social ability – 'Attachment is a deep and enduring emotional bond that connects one person to another across time' (Bowlby 1988).

Our understanding of the importance of a strong attachment to a responsive caregiver has evolved considerably over the years since this theory was first proposed in the late 1950s, and with the emergence of neurodevelopmental knowledge we now have a greater understanding of the importance of what seems like a simple cycle.

Healthy attachment cycle

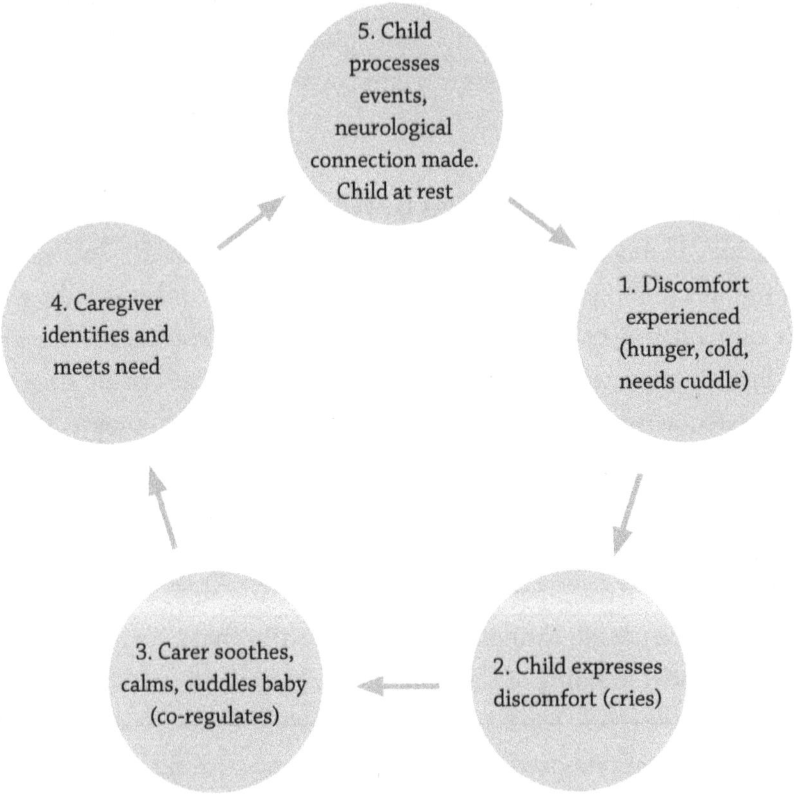

Figure 1.1 Healthy attachment cycle

1. The child experiences discomfort – they are cold, wet, lonely, hungry, bored or scared. (The world is, after all, a big unfamiliar place which is confusingly full of multiple sensory stimuli – sights, smells, sounds, tastes, feelings.)

2. The child expresses their discomfort in the only way they can and cries. For the child, they are expressing a survival need which they are unable to fulfil for themselves. Human babies are completely vulnerable and dependent at birth. Their life depends on their parents or other responsible adult and so discomfort is perceived by their brain as a threat to their existence.

3. The parent responds to the baby's distress. The first thing that happens is that the child is picked up and calmed by the physical contact and soothing noises of the parent. This is a very empathic response, and it soothes both the baby and the parent, so we call this co-regulation.

4. The parent identifies what the issue is, and feeds/changes/cuddles/plays with the baby. Both baby and caregiver experience pleasure in their interaction, whether calming, playful or relaxing, and this is conveyed by tone of voice, eye contact, facial expression, etc.

5. The baby returns to a resting state and processes (unconsciously). A neurological pathway is established which records this interaction and forms part of the baby's emerging knowledge and understanding of their own unique experience of the world.

From this we can extrapolate the following:

- *Baby's emerging experience of the world*: caring, safe, loving, welcoming, stable, fun and consistent – predictable
- *Baby's sense of parents and adults*: safe, comforting, trustworthy
- *Baby's sense of self*: loved, wanted, beautiful, engaging, worthwhile, important, confident, emerging, positive self-esteem.

Where there has been a positive attachment experience, needs are perceived as being met by the individual. They are confident that they will be cared for, fed and nurtured and have been able to engage with their parents in a wonderful way that has enabled them to build an expectation based on love and security. They have a core knowledge that their needs will be met, enabling them to be resilient and tolerant if they are occasionally hungry, cold, upset, have an argument, etc. They are able to manage social interactions and make connections readily. Their experience of the world as accommodating means that they can take risks, are able to bear the disappointment of being wrong and explore different avenues. These individuals will be able to embrace a challenge, whether this is academic, physical or emotional. We call this developing perception the internal working model.

These repeated experiences create the architecture of the child's cortex – the part of the brain that is concerned with conscious choices, voluntary movement, self-regulation and how we view the world, our view of ourselves and our expectations of others. These vitally important early experiences will colour all of the child's interactions with the world.

Deficient or unhealthy attachment cycle

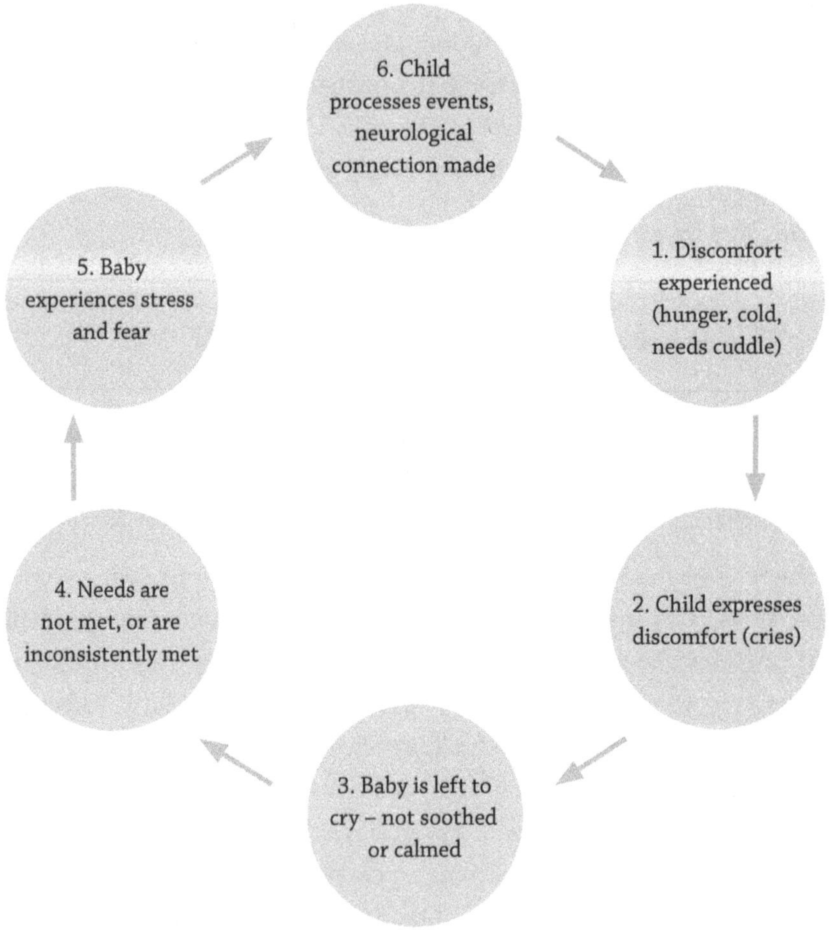

Figure 1.2 Deficient or unhealthy attachment cycle

1. The baby experiences discomfort – they are cold, wet, lonely, hungry, bored or scared. (The world is, after all, a big unfamiliar place which is confusingly full of multiple sensory stimuli – sights, smells, sounds, tastes, feelings.)

2. The baby expresses their discomfort in the only way they can and cries. For the child, they are expressing a survival need which they are unable to fulfil for themselves. Human babies are completely vulnerable and dependent at birth. Their life depends on their caregivers and so discomfort is perceived by their brain as a threat to their existence.

3. The parent fails to soothe and regulate, or shows an angry response, or gives inconsistent responses, leading to stress, confusion and fear for the baby. Some babies are punished physically by their parents or caregivers.

4. Needs are not met, are inconsistently met, or are inadequately met. The baby does not have the wonderful experience of joyfulness in their parents' presence and does not have that experience mirrored back to them or it is inconsistent, leading to stress and anxiety.

5. The baby's experience is inconsistent and is frequently stressful.

6. Processing occurs and neurological pathways are established, which inform the baby's emerging sense of themselves, adults and the world.

In this instance, we can extrapolate a different set of outcomes for the child:

- *Baby's emerging experience of the world*: unsafe, lack of love, hostile, dangerous, need to fight to survive, inconsistent, unpredictable or predictably dangerous

- *Baby's sense of parents and adults*: unsafe, unpredictable, untrustworthy and, in the worst cases, may bring pain and terror

- *Baby's sense of self*: unloved, unlovable, unwanted, horrible, bad, worthless, unimportant, no confidence, low or absent self-esteem.

In this case, the internal working model of the child which becomes hard wired is very different, leading to a survival-based approach to the world and adults, and a self-image which is extremely negative, based on their belief that they are 'bad'.

Where there has been an insufficient, absent or disengaged attachment or other developmental trauma, the individual will be focused on getting their survival needs met – they have to have food, air and shelter.

The stress created by this existence will disrupt the healthy development of the brain. This baby may filter most of his experience via fear of being unable to survive in this hostile environment. It will be hard to connect and engage with others. The baby may have issues with their self-esteem as well as finding it hard to trust or maintain a positive outlook. In this case the executive function is largely shut down, or depends on information that will feed into **adaptive responses** (a response which has evolved to ensure survival) based in fear and presenting possibly as anger or withdrawal that will reinforce the fearful outlook of the baby.

Resilience, trust and hope may well be alien emotions. This child may be resistant to and fearful of change, and if this is the case they will need to have patient and repeated positive messages to enable them to rewire and move past the block caused by their developmental trauma. In addition, the focus on survival and lack of an attuned relationship may lead to developmental delays in all or any areas: physical, emotional, social or cognitive.

This situation may be further compounded by multiple placements and placement breakdowns and lack of understanding by professionals who perceive that the child's needs are now met, without considering that it will take time, commitment and patience on the part of the caregiver and repeated consistent positive messages to enable the traumatized child to develop a more positive mindset.

THINK ABOUT IT...

The brain is built by repeated experience.

- What might the formative experiences have been for your child or children?
- Does this give some insight as to why it is so hard for children to 'move on'?

The internal working model

The process we have been talking about forms our **internal working model** – a kind of an idea or representation we carry around with us that is our understanding of the world and how it works. In a nutshell:

Internal working model	
Child with secure relationships (secure attachment)	**Child from unsafe, traumatic care (insecure attachment)**
Sense of self: valued, important, loved, safe, worthwhile, beautiful, confident	Sense of self: unworthy, unlovable, stupid, worthless, invisible, unsafe, scared
Sense of parents/adults: safe, secure, loving, consistent, reliable, helpful, trustworthy, caring	Sense of parents/adults: scary, unreliable, unpredictable, untrustworthy, cause pain
Sense of world: safe, welcoming, fun, safe to explore and learn	Sense of world: unsafe, terrifying, need to fight to survive (some children learn to be 'invisible' and excessively compliant to avoid drawing attention to themselves, which is also a survival response)

CASE STUDY 1.1 – INABILITY TO PARENT A CHILD

Amelia was born to a mother who had mental health issues and had been unable to parent previous children. Within a month she had been placed in foster care but was then returned to her mum. By three months of age she was back in foster care, where she stayed for several months.

Additional provision was put in place to help her mum cope, but she was again returned to care at age two and then placed for adoption when she was three years old. She had suffered extremes of neglect during her times with her birth mum as well as being witness to verbal and physical abuse. She had multiple moves and received inconsistent parenting; additionally there was concern about the care provided by one of the foster families.

THINK ABOUT IT...

- What potential elements of developmental trauma can you identify in this case?
- How do you think this child may approach the world?
- What might this child's mindset be with regard to a family environment?
- What associations might this child ascribe to 'Mum'?
- What challenges might the adoptive parents face?

Fight–flight response

What actually happens?

The fight–flight response occurs as a result of activation of the HPA axis (hypothalamus–pituitary–adrenal axis). This happens when the amygdala, which has several functions including emotional-based survival reactions, activates hormonal changes which enable us to survive by responding very quickly to danger. So the sequence goes like this:

- A stressor representing the survival threat is received in the limbic area of the brain.

- The amygdala is activated strongly by the threat to survival and fires, activating the hypothalamus.

- The hypothalamus secretes corticotropin-releasing hormone (CRH) which in turn triggers the anterior pituitary gland.

- The action of CRH on the pituitary triggers release of adrenocorticotrophic hormone (ACTH).
- ACTH acts on the adrenal glands, causing a surge of adrenalin, cortisol and endorphin.
- Adrenalin then prepares the body for action: increased heart rate and blood flow bring oxygen and glycose to the muscles. In addition, the pupils of the eyes dilate.
- Cortisol causes an increase in amino acids and sugars in the bloodstream, and the amino acids aid repair and recovery of damaged tissues, while blood sugars ensure that there is sufficient energy to deal with the situation.
- Endorphins act as a natural tranquillizer, blocking pain and inducing euphoria.

The main structures responsible

- *Hypothalamus*: Situated in the middle of the brain, the role of the hypothalamus is to keep the body in balance. It does this by connecting the nervous system with the **endocrine system** (which produces hormones to maintain stability by acting on key organs). These systems are working all the time in the background, and are not under conscious control. Some of the functions that the hypothalamus has a role in are body temperature (causing sweating and dilating blood vessels to cool us, or causing shivering to warm us), thirst, appetite, sleep cycles, blood pressure, digestion and sex drive.
- *Pituitary*: Like the conductor of the endocrine system, the pituitary gland directs organs or endocrine glands to suppress or induce hormone production. The pituitary itself responds to the hormones produced by the hypothalamus. The pituitary gland orchestrates many important functions in the body including

fluid balance, fight–flight response, maturation of reproductive systems, and growth.

- *Adrenal gland*: There are two adrenal glands, situated on top of the kidneys. These glands affect metabolism, blood pressure, immunity, sex hormones and response to stress and fight–flight response. When responding to a fight–flight survival situation, the adrenals flood the system with hormones such as adrenalin and cortisol, which in turn increase the heart rate and therefore blood pressure, slow down unnecessary functions and increase awareness of surroundings.
- *Amygdala*: Two small almond-shaped structures situated in the temporal lobe process react to sensory input and act as a 'smoke alarm', initiating the hormonal sequence which occurs when we are under threat.

Behaviours resulting from intense anxiety states

- *Controlling behaviours*: The child has had to exercise control over their environment in whatever way is available to them in order to survive.
- *Defiant or oppositional behaviours (often linked to transitions)*: The child will refuse to follow instructions and be demand avoidant. However, remembering the fear that can be induced by their experiences, we can develop strategies to help this.
- *Parentified*: Seen in sibling groups, one of the children takes the role of parent, directing the others and not trusting the parent to remember to change clothes or nappies or feed the other siblings.
- *'Jekyll and Hyde child'*: High circulating cortisol means that this child is always alert, hypervigilant and susceptible to stressors. This makes the amygdala very sensitive, so that the adrenalin surge of a fight–flight response can occur much more readily – especially where the child has been trying to contain their escalating stress all

day due to their anxiety of what will happen if they are 'naughty'. They therefore 'put a lid' on their growing anxiety and work hard to present an acceptable face; however, the anxiety increases and eventually becomes too much to bear and then there is an emotional explosion. This often happens when the child returns to their safe place (home), and is often directed at the person they feel able to trust to show their trauma to (a parent). Unfortunately, because the behaviours happen at home, this is frequently misconstrued as being a parenting issue. We frequently hear about these situations in relation to the school day – the child seems fine at school, but comes home unable to suppress their emotional state any longer. The analogy that is often used is a bottle of fizzy pop that is shaken up all through the day – as soon as the top is taken off the fizzy drink sprays absolutely everywhere, it can't be held back.

- *Aggression and violence*: High anxiety quickly results in an overwhelmed child, and the poor internal working model means that they will quickly fall back into their old patterns of feeling worthless and helpless. There is a difference from when they were helpless babies though – they can feel powerful by physically taking control.
- *Self-harm*: In an attempt to distract from anxiety, or gain some control over their lives or to distract from psychological pain, children (even very young children) can resort to self-harm. The behaviour can help for a while, but is temporary, and then gives rise to intense feelings of shame. This will often take the form of cutting, or inserting objects into the skin – even pushing staples into flesh to induce infection. Self-harm should not always be regarded as a suicide attempt (although this may be the case) but is likely to be a way to manage to keep on living.

To understand the experience of the child and to retain our own empathy when faced with extremely challenging behaviours, it is useful to think of the child as 'falling back' into trauma.

The Trauma Room

Dan Siegel (2012) asserts that 'experiences of pain and terror can be engrained within the circuits of the brain as states of mind'. These states of mind, which are often repeated, become characteristic of the individual so that they easily enter these feelings and experience them as reality in the here and now. Sarah Dillon (2019) calls this process of falling back into their trauma 'falling back into Room 1'. She explains how and why children can so readily flip into a trauma state due to overwhelm or even a small stressor acting on a beleaguered and stressed system, and this is underpinned by her own experience as a child in care – she speaks with authority as the voice of the child.

THE TRAUMA FROM ROOM 1 SARAH DILLON (2017)

Imagine two rooms separated only by a paper thin wall.

ROOM 1 represents the trauma history of the child. What might we find in room 1?

- Unmet basic needs (Neglect)
- Domestic abuse
- Addictions
- Scapegoating
- Violence
- Chaos
- Ignoring
- Screaming, shouting, swearing
- Abandonment and rejection
- Unavailable adults
- Unsafe and terrifying adults
- Unmet educational needs
- Unmet medical needs
- No play or adult interaction
- Wee and poo issues if not potty trained
- No co-regulation
- No predictability

- No routines
- No boundaries
- No affection
- Sexual abuse
- Physical abuse
- Emotional and psychological abuse
- Lack of food or incorrect food
- Not weaned properly
- No fun, day trips or holidays
- No one attending to child at night
- Threats
- Dangerous animals
- Hygiene needs not met
- Lack of medical care
- No clean clothes
- No dentist
- Inappropriate access to internet, phones and games

In Room 1 ALL adults are unsafe and won't meet your needs. In Room 1, all you can do is survive (STAY ALIVE).

ROOM 2 is where they live now (with you) What might we find in room 2?

- Warmth, Care, Love
- Predictability
- Stability
- Food
- Boundaries
- Routine
- Nurture
- Parental engagement and supervision
- Play
- Needs met
- Safe and available adults
- Acceptance

- Predictability
- Affection
- Structure
- Educational and medical needs met
- Fun, day trips and holidays
- Clean clothes and bed
- Toys and appropriate games
- Hygiene
- Medical needs met
- Dentist

In room 2 adults are safe and will meet your needs. In room 2 a child will THRIVE .

How does a child leaving room 1 and moving into room 2 feel?
Answer: PETRIFIED/TERRIFIED (they are NOT grateful and we should not expect them to be).
ALL CHILDREN SHOULD BE BORN IN ROOM 2. This is a human right!!

Most brain development happens after we are born. This happens when a child feels safe enough to attach to a responsive and available care giver who consistently meets their needs between the age of 0-3yrs.

During this time 1000 cells per second develop in the baby's brain. When this doesn't happen, the child will find maladaptive ways to get their needs met In order to stay alive.

Due to the lack of development of the frontal lobe, and associated underdeveloped hippocampus, the child has tremendous difficulty in transferring short term memory into long term memory.

As a result, the child lives In an almost 'Groundhog Day' situation and struggles to differentiate between past and present.

The paper thin wall separating ROOM 1 and ROOM 2 represents the above memory issues.

Further to this the child is conditioned to believe that what happened in ROOM 1 is normal and is how ALL adults behave!

The paper thin wall has pores in it and experiences from ROOM 1 seep through the pores into ROOM 2.

What might this look like?

Some examples:

A chid might recreate the literal chaos of ROOM 1 in their own bedroom. They may have wee and poo issues due to not being potty trained or as a communication of abuse and other trauma.

If the child has lived with domestic abuse they will befriend the parent/caregiver In ROOM 2 who they perceive as the inevitable perpetrator. They will also likely reject the other parent as the nurturing enemy. The one who didn't keep them safe or meet their needs in ROOM 1.

Some may be completely shut down as a way of surviving whilst others keep running away.

Due to the negative repetitive conditioning in ROOM 1, the child feels comfortable behaving this way. They therefore stimulate the environment in ROOM 2 (behave in controlling ways etc.), to elicit the same response they would have received in ROOM1. They unconsciously recreate the chaos of ROOM 1 In ROOM 2. This could include pushing your buttons to get you to reject them, scapegoat one child, hit them, take everything away from them, abuse them, ground them, scream, shout and swear at them etc. etc.

NB: THE CHILD IS NOT DOING THIS TO YOU, THEY ARE CONDITIONED TO BEHAVE THIS WAY!

Imagine being left handed (like me), and someone telling you to now be right handed at all times.

Pretty impossible to do! You would quickly resort to using your left hand again at any opportunity but this would obviously be an unconscious response.

In addition to the paper thin wall where stuff seeps though, there is also a trap door. The child can fall through the trap door at any time and land straight back into ROOM 1 emotionally, psychologically and on a sensory or visceral level even though their body is still with you in ROOM 2.

They can be triggered by something known or unknown in ROOM 2 and reexperience something historical in the here and now. The child experiences this as if it's actually happening again!

This can result In recreating actual historical events in the present. It can also lead to allegations where the child re-experiences a traumatic experience at the hands of an unsafe adult and accuses you of actually doing it. When this happens, the child IS NOT deliberately blaming you, They are caught in a time warp and truly believe it's actually happening!

Finally, the child will subconsciously draw or pull you through the trap door into ROOM 1 and you will quickly find yourself reacting in ways you wouldn't normally behave. This in turn will push you into compassion fatigue and sadly the child will either move on or the experience of an unavailable adult will quickly become the child's reality once again!

Please use this analogy to help you depersonalise your child's behaviours.
It's not you, it's what they've been through.
It's not me, it's what's happened to me.

Childhood trauma, traumatic memory and false allegations

Childhood trauma

Experience shows us that early disruption of attunement and lack of an attachment figure or abuse of a child has a direct effect on the development of the child's brain – specifically in relation to the internal working model discussed previously in which they view themselves as unlovable, worthless and disposable, adults as untrustworthy and terrifying, and the world as a hostile place. Children who have experienced relentless and repeated trauma such as violence, neglect and physical or sexual abuse are likely to form these core beliefs about themselves. We are now finding that science and research endorse this:

> Children exposed to ongoing stress and trauma such as that associated with exposure to community violence may develop schemas of the world

> as a hostile place and experience changed attitudes about people, life and the future. (Cichetti and Lynch 1993; Terr 1991; in Siegel 2015)

Our children from care have a very negative internal working model, which results from their experiences and has been hardwired into their brain from their earliest age. Their expectation is that the new adults they encounter will behave like the abusing adults, as this has been their primary experience. It takes a lot of time and patience to turn the situation around, and the more placements they have had the harder it becomes. Children also tend to subconsciously recreate their chaotic previous life by their actions – they are highly rejecting as a result of their fear of abandonment, and this is a strategy which enables them not to get too close and avoids being vulnerable and feeling powerless or the pain of rejection. At least they have rejected you first! Attempting to build a relationship with such a child is hard, as in their earliest days they did not have the experience of 'serve and return' communication where adult and child are able to communicate backwards and forwards by words, actions and facial expressions, showing their delight in the unfolding of their relationship. When families are disrupted by false allegations the child unwittingly replicates their own trauma and consolidates their negative internal working model. Paradoxically we often see that these disruptions occur at a point when the child is beginning to attach and feel that they are claimed by and belong to a family. This experience of being claimed can make the child feel very vulnerable and produces intense fear of rejection, causing the child to speak from their fear of what will happen (i.e. they will be abandoned and rejected again). This is classic fear-based anxiety-driven behaviour, which we see over and over again.

Bruce Perry states:

> In the traumatized child, the narrated words are mere shadows of what is being communicated as they recall the event. The child's recall of a traumatic event involves not just the narrative shards as recalled using cognitive memory but also the intense fear of the emotional memory, the motor agitation of the motor memories and the physiological arousal (or dissociative response) of the state memory. Yet the syntax,

semantics and grammar of these non-cognitive narrations do not yet have the standing in court that the syntax, semantics and grammar of verbal language does.

Learning the language of trauma and translating the verbal and non-verbal elements of this language will require many more years of investigation. Yet, as this investigation is underway, it is the task of all of us working with maltreated children to educate our peers and the rest of society that this language exists (e.g., Briere and Conte, 1993; Ceci and Bruck, 1993). To educate our society that traumatic events, like other experience, change the brain. Further, that the brain stores elements of the traumatic events as cognitive memory, motor memory, emotional memory and state memory, altering the functional capacity of the traumatized individual. And, in the end, by robbing the individual potential of millions of children each year, childhood trauma and neglect robs the potential of our families, our communities and our societies. (www.healing-arts.org/tir/perry_memories_of_fear.pdf)

Effect of trauma on memory states

Dan Siegel (2015) suggests that physiological elements occurring during an overwhelming event such as amygdala discharge and noradrenaline secretion in response to massive stress may increase encoding of implicit (subconscious) memory. Explicit memory may be inhibited by cortisol, blocking hippocampus functioning and therefore affecting subsequent recall. Memories of trauma may be triggered by sensory input which will activate the firing of the amygdala and the fight–flight response. For the child suffering from developmental trauma with memories of abuse, this can mean that specific sensory triggers will immediately activate their amygdala and initiate a fight–flight response which will feel as though it is happening in the present.

Sarah developed an analogy for this – imagine yourself filing – and this stands for encoding memories in your hippocampus. The items you are filing are date stamped, sequential and in a system that allows them to be retrieved. (This is your day-to-day experience of encoding memory in your explicit memory.) Suddenly there is a major incident, and the fire alarm goes off (a trauma occurs, and your amygdala fires, which sends the hippocampus offline). Unable to remember how to file, you stuff all the papers in the safe (implicit memory) and run. Later, after the event, you cannot remember what you did with those files, they are not accessible. However, the next time the fire alarm goes off, the implicit memory is once again triggered and you retrieve the information.

Naoki Higashida describes how this feels for him in his book *The Reason I Jump* (2013):

> We do remember what we did, when, who we did it with and things like this, but these memories are all scattershot and never connected in the right order. The trouble with scattered memories is that sometimes they replay themselves in my head as if they had only just taken place – and when this happens, the emotions I felt originally all come rushing back to me, like a sudden storm.
>
> I know I have lots of pleasant memories, but my flashback memories are always bad ones, and from out of the blue I get incredibly distressed, burst into tears or just start panicking. Never mind that it's a memory from ages ago – the same helpless feeling I had then overflows and floods out and it just won't stop. (p.62)

Talking about narrative memory, Naoki says, 'I imagine a normal person's memory is arranged continuously, like a line. My memory, however, is more like a pool of dots. I'm always "picking up" these dots' (p.24). Sarah refers to this as a memory carousel, capturing the essence of the memories which flit into consciousness only to become inaccessible once more when the moment has passed.

False allegations

The significance of this for children who are in care is that sensory data which is imperceptible to others may literally cause them to feel that they are back in the situation of trauma, and this will be exacerbated when the child has high circulating cortisol due to stress such as approaching an anniversary (for instance, of a move or transition, birthday, Christmas, anniversary of a traumatic event). In that moment, a fleeting facial expression, a sound, a smell or an action may be misinterpreted. The child remembers the incident but experiences it in the present and makes a disclosure such as 'My mum hits me'. However, they may be referring to a historic incident, which may or may not be previously known.

Sympathetic face

Children from trauma have learned to survive against the odds, and one thing that they respond to is a sympathetic face. In order to maintain the soothing feelings produced by being presented with this expression, they may also invent things to maintain that feeling – for instance, maybe they eat all their food on the way to school because they are having a worry that day. They saw someone who looked a bit like a member of their birth family on the way and it got them feeling stressed, so they ate all their lunch because food is a way for them to regulate themselves. When they get into school the teacher notices that they are stressed, and the sympathetic-faced teacher asks if they are OK. 'No,' they say, 'I am really hungry.' They go on to say in answer to further sympathetic questions that they are never given breakfast, and have not been given lunch, keeping that attention centred on them as long as possible and possibly earning a food reward in the form of a snack.

Clearly, allegations must be investigated, but by following a process, understanding the history, working in partnership with parents and social workers and understanding trauma and the child's history, many cases of false allegations which lead to family breakdowns and further trauma for the child and the families involved can be avoided. This is not conscious or malicious on the part of the child, who is simply trying to stay alive. That sounds rather extreme, but for the child it is literally all about survival. This is easier to understand if you imagine the plight of the baby whose needs are rarely met, and who is unable to do anything for themselves. Their survival absolutely depends on somehow getting the attention of an adult to help them and they will do whatever required to achieve this. If smiles and cooing don't work, then screaming until you are hoarse might; negative attention that ensures you survive is better than no attention at all, and so the lesson is learned and this strategy is hardwired into the developing brain.

Helping children to recover: developing a narrative

It is a good idea to have a narrative to use with children to help them understand why they can suddenly get overwhelmed by emotional states that they are scared by and have no idea where they came from.

For instance, an adoptive mum, Zoe, whose adopted daughter Mary has problems every Christmas, explained that she remembered that Mary was removed from her birth home in mid-December, moved to foster parents and then moved on to the adoptive mum in January. Zoe realized that this was significant despite the fact that Mary was only around a year old at the time. She suffered the loss of her birth mum, a major transition, the loss of her foster parent and a further transition all around Christmas time when the sensory elements are at the highest point of the year with the sound of bells and carol singing, smells, tastes, etc. which will all serve to trigger her intensely painful implicit or 'state' memories of this time. There will almost certainly have been additional trauma even before this happened. Zoe developed a narrative to help Mary to understand:

> A lot of bad things happened to you when you were a baby, and your baby brain could not cope with what was happening, so it hid the memory deep in your mind where you did not have to try and manage it all the time. But memory is strange, and if you see, hear, smell or taste something that reminds you of that time in your life it wakes your baby brain up again, and makes you feel the same way that you felt when you were going through it as a baby. You were moved from your home, into foster care, and then to me over Christmas time. I think that every Christmas your baby brain gets woken up because of all the lights, sounds, smells and tastes, and you feel like you did back then – scared, angry and powerless. I am so sorry that you felt so helpless and were

so unhappy and scared. I am so sorry that I cannot take that hurt away from you. But I do love you.

This can be amended to include relevant history, if known, in a sensitive and developmentally appropriate way.

Neuroplasticity – the light at the end of the tunnel

Before we go any further, it is important to remember that the brain is a very 'plastic' organ; in other words, we can create new understanding and learning despite hardwired concepts and behaviours – it just takes time. In *The Developing Mind* Dan Siegel reminds us that the human brain can change its response as a result of new experiences throughout life, developing new synapses and even making new myelin and growing new neurones; we see this in action every time we acquire new knowledge, a new skill, or when we are able to regain skills that are lost – for instance, as a result of a stroke. The key is the repeated therapeutic intervention, which activates and then strengthens the new neuronal pathways and synaptic connections. The principle of how the brain develops remains true throughout life – as Dan Siegel says, 'neurones that fire together, wire together'. It is also true that on the 'use it or lose it' principle neuronal connections which are not active will over time disintegrate. The Brainworks website (https://brainworksneurotherapy.com) reminds us that repetition and practice of thoughts, emotions or movements create and strengthen new connections and pathways, and that these lead to changes in how our brains work, and therefore how we receive and respond to information and sensations.

We call this process and the constant repetition necessary to implement these psychological changes 'CPR for the brain' – where CPR stands for consistency, predictability and reliability. The good news is that all the time you feel like a broken record, repeating the same things, reminding and reassuring on a daily basis you are in fact creating a new way of thinking in your child's brain which is based on the attachment and attunement principles where the survival needs – physiological, safety and belonging – are met.

CPR for the brain

We know now that our experiences build our ideas and our internal working model (our way of understanding ourselves, others and the world). Our earliest experiences received through our senses activate pathways in our brain and give us survival information. For children who have suffered abuse and trauma, this can lead to a brain wired to survive:

- *I am* bad, worthless, unlovable, stupid, rubbish, lonely, scared, invisible. My life is in danger.
- *Others (adults) are* scary, dangerous, untrustworthy, unreliable, unpredictable. They cause me pain.
- *The world is* dangerous, hostile, unwelcoming, scary. I have to remain alert all the time to stay alive.

Introducing *c*onsistency, *p*redictability and *r*eliability into our routines and responses and approaching our children in a caring, empathic and therapeutic manner activates different pathways. They are not as strong as the old ideas, but gradually they take hold. At first this feels very hard for our children, and it's hard for us too because it feels like we are banging our head against a brick wall. Actually, our feelings start to mirror our children's:

- *I am* confused. This doesn't fit. I feel wobbly and out of control. I have to take charge.
- *Others (adults) are* confusing. They seem to care. That can't be right; it's probably a trick. It will all change. I must keep my guard up.
- *The world is* not how it used to be. I don't understand. I think my head will explode while I try to make sense of it.

Try not to worry, it's a sign of connection to your child.

Over time, as we keep to our routines and boundaries, and provide a nurturing therapeutic environment, the new pathways become stronger, more resilient. The old pathways remain, but they are activated less frequently and usually under extreme stress or as a result of an early memory/feeling triggering a response. It is hard, but children can resolve their conflicts with support, and this will enable them to have a different kind of life and relationships from the one they were stuck in through no fault of their own. Then:

- *I am* OK. Pretty good actually. I am learning that I am lovable, I have skills, I am caring. Sometimes I still feel bad.
- *Adults are* usually loving and helpful, especially my parents. It can be hard to work out if strangers are trustworthy or not. My parents can help me sort things out.
- *The world is* not so scary. I know I can have help to work things out. Parts of it are even quite fun!

Parents feel much the same, but as parents and children continue the process they can find joy in each other.

Observed behaviour and the importance of modelling appropriate responses

We have discussed how environmental factors and experience shape the brain from conception. Observation also plays a significant part in the development of the baby and infant. One of the main ways in which we learn roles, behaviour, social norms and skills is through observation, and clearly this will start with the immediate family.

Social learning theory

Albert Bandura (1925–), in his social learning theory, suggests that learning takes place in a social context – i.e. by direct observation of the individuals around you. Children copy their parents or family members first, and this then extends to other members of the community. In this way children will be best adapted to mature in a way that reflects the social and cultural structure, values and beliefs of their community. We learn to behave in the ways that we observe in our home environment. This is an important consideration when we consider the many and varied environments, cultures and communities a child could be born into, from famine or war-torn situations to the relative stability of Europe and North America.

Mirror neurones

In the early 1990s Giacomo Rizzolatti, a neuroscientist, found in Macaque monkeys neurones which fire both in the brain of the monkey performing an action and in the brain of the monkey observing this action. The existence of mirror neurones in humans would explain the processes which enable an individual to learn by observation, allowing actions to be understood and replicated – for instance, learning to ride a bike, dance or drive a car. However, it is also suggested by Christian Keysers, a psychologist studying the human mirror neurone system at the University of Groningen, that mirror neurones enable us to understand social situations and are important for development of empathy. This research has implications when we consider the behaviours that are exhibited by children who have been subjected to adverse childhood experiences and the intense fear and anxiety states experienced by them as 'normal' (www.apa.org/monitor/oct05/mirror).

Understanding others

An example of how a child explores how it feels to be another person is in the area of make believe and role-play – maybe the child sees a TV programme or has a book read to them, then they try to experience the feeling by replaying the scenario in play.

For example, my grandson had early play where he wanted to act out the roles from *Toy Story* and required me to be Buzz Lightyear to his Woody. This gave us opportunities to reflect on the experience of role-play and how it felt in a simple way – 'That was fun!' – providing the building blocks for further development of role-play and therefore understanding others by approval and encouragement, and participation in the process.

These simple games can therefore become the foundation for understanding others and becoming socially able – pretending to be someone else helps us to imagine how they might think and feel. Again, we can see that not having these opportunities may impact on the ability of the child to imagine the experience of someone else.

Therapeutic parenting and the child with developmental trauma

It is easy to see why a child with a traumatic background needs specific parenting. A parent in these circumstances needs to have patience, compassion, flexibility and the ability to learn new skills, reflect and in many cases manage lack of understanding and support. They will need to be able to reframe their child's behaviour and seek therapeutic parenting strategies to help the child form new perceptions and build a different brain. Thanks to brain plasticity, this is possible. However, it requires massive commitment, and an ability on the parent's part to identify and utilize support and to take care of themselves. These are themes that will be developed throughout this book.

2

What Is Therapeutic Parenting?

In this chapter we are going to talk in more detail about what therapeutic parenting is and why it can be so powerful in helping families that are re-parenting children who have experienced trauma in their early life.

Therapeutic parenting is a unique approach to parenting, or re-parenting, children who have suffered from developmental trauma and who may struggle with aspects of development, whether this is physical, cognitive, emotional or social, or indeed any combination of these. Therapeutic parenting offers an opportunity for a unique perspective on childcare that is focused on the relationships within the family unit and is child centred. The Centre of Excellence in Child Trauma uses the following definition:

> [Therapeutic parenting is] a deeply nurturing parenting style, with a foundation of self-awareness and a central core of mentalization, developed from consistent, empathic, insightful responses to a child's distress and behaviours; allowing the child to begin to self-regulate, develop an understanding of their own behaviours and ultimately form secure attachments. (www.coect.co.uk)

In this chapter we explore knowledge and understanding of child development and the effects of developmental trauma and continue to think about attachment theory and neurodevelopmental science. With this information and with new strategies we hope that parents will be able to develop new strategies and have a deeper understanding of the issues at the root of the difficulties faced by families parenting children affected by trauma. Therapeutic parenting is not solely a technique for traumatized families however – all children, whatever their circumstances, can benefit from the nurturing and child-centred parenting strategies that are discussed here.

IN MY EXPERIENCE...

Most of this chapter contains information that only became available to me gradually as my own journey with my adopted daughter progressed. I remember vividly reading, attending workshops and seminars and embracing the new knowledge as it became available to the general public – especially when I started learning about the aspects which explained the neurological development of the child and how this affects their psychology and the way they interact with their families, the wider community and the world. I wish that I had had access to all of this at the outset – my journey with my own daughter is still in progress, in the most positive way possible, but it would have been so nice to have the advantages that I hope I can now offer to you!

What is therapeutic parenting, and why do we need it?

Therapeutic parenting is necessary when a child has suffered trauma – through physical illness, or if they have been subjected to highly addictive and harmful substances in utero (e.g. recreational drugs, alcohol or even prescribed medications), or if they have suffered abuse or domestic violence. Any of these events (sometimes called adverse childhood experiences or ACEs) will be sufficient for them to suffer from developmental trauma. As we discussed in Chapter 1, children can also suffer trauma as a result of maternal illness, and of course trauma occurs in homes where children are subjected to or witness domestic violence (even if they are eventually removed to safety by the abused partner). Likewise, when children are removed and cared for within the extended family, as is the case with special guardians or kinship carers, their trauma will remain.

In the most extreme cases of neglect and/or abuse, children are removed from the family home and placed in care, and may be placed for adoption in due course. It is worth remembering that children who have experienced sufficient trauma to merit a removal from the family home will have suffered extreme forms of abuse in most cases.

A very common misconception held by professionals, parents and the general public is that if the child is removed from their toxic environment and transferred to a stable and loving home – where they are safe from abuse and have regular meals and receive warmth, care and nurture – this is some kind of magic wand which means all their needs are now met and they should be fine. Such a belief does not take into account the history of the child and the parenting they have received, or how this will have affected the way the child's brain has been built as a result of their experiences. The expectations and reality of the child and the way they approach adults, siblings and indeed the world can only be based on their past experiences. Their understanding of what to expect from adults, professionals, schools and the world around them may be fixed in a negative way, and of course their interpretations of the actions of their new families, being based on past experiences, have been developed to manage the adverse circumstances they were in. These children, who were powerless as babies and young children, can refuse to feel vulnerable and powerless any more and turn to aggression, which is based on fear and triggered by their own stress response, and is a way for them to finally feel that they have power.

The tragic thing is that these responses are based on previous experiences which act as a distorting mirror, causing the child to be in a perpetual state of stress. Furthermore, due to early trauma and failure to meet developmental milestones socially, cognitively or emotionally, these children can often display behaviours which are far more typical of a much younger child. The whole situation is compounded when the **adaptive strategies** adopted by the child in response to an abusive environment – strategies that enabled them to survive – trigger the adults around the child to respond in a negative or punitive way – for instance, shouting, giving a consequence that the child does not understand, or sending them away (time out). This is a shameful experience for the child and can inadvertently reinforce the negative view that the child has of the world and themselves.

Dan Siegel (2012) states that 'The initial sharing of mental experiences therefore lays the groundwork for the rest of mental development'. Childhood experiences directly impact on the essential 'reflective' functioning of the brain where child and parent co-create ideas. What this means is that the baby expresses an interest by cooing, smiling and using other engaging behaviours, and the parent joins in with the process, using simple words and facial expressions to follow the curiosity of the baby and then extending this experience by repeating actions and sounds that produce this wonderful interaction. Of course, this also introduces aspects of communication and physical development as parent and child play, move and communicate together. They are learning about each other, and the parent is gradually gaining an understanding of the different ways that their baby communicates their need to play, to eat, to rest.

The ability of the parent to enter into the play and exploration of the child develops the ability of the child to see the adult as a thinking, feeling person – an early exploration of **mindsight** (being able to understand our own and others' minds). For example, the baby may link a movement they make with a responsive movement or expression on the part of their parent, such as smiling, cooing or reaching out for the parent. They discover in this process that they can have an effect on their parent's responses, and as time goes on they will learn that some of the parental responses feel better to the child and then seek to reproduce the behaviour that ensures the positive attention. However, we also have to remember that it is essential for survival that the baby or young child somehow manages to get their needs met. Any attention is preferable to no attention. So if the only way their needs are met and ensure survival is to shout, scream, grab, pinch or kick, then the child will adopt these behaviours instead.

A child's development can be impaired by early relationship histories. We will be discussing how these developmental issues affect the behaviours shown by the child as well as strategies to manage as we continue through the book.

Why do we need therapeutic parents for children with developmental trauma?

In Figure 2.1, a basic developmental wall is shown, where a child has a 'good enough' stable upbringing in which there is security, engagement, play, time to rest, and the right amount of disappointments, disagreements and arguments to enforce social standards, but due to parental support, relationship repair and 'making up', the child also develops resilience, learns that it is OK to make mistakes and learns to take acceptable risks both physically and in their learning, which in turn creates confidence. Because they trust and love their parents and feel loved in return, they have the ideal situation – what John Bowlby (1988) called 'a secure base'. Home and family for this child are likely to mean a safe place that they can return to and that they will use as a template for future parenting. This child can grow and develop in a home with 'standard' parenting, because from an early age their needs have been consistently met within a secure attachment relationship with their main carer, and they know that occasional disruptions when their parents become angry with them will not destroy their relationship. In this developmental wall, the basic foundation of love, safety, nutrition, stimulation and rest becomes part of the secure base from which the other layers can develop as part of healthy development. Hence, although there are clearly common factors – the need for food, love and rest for instance is still as relevant at ages 7–11 as it was at ages 0–1 – as skills develop within this structure there is a consistent movement towards acquisition of necessary emotional, social, cognitive and physical skills. This is possible because the adult provides an appropriate role model and also what Sarah calls the 'unassailable secure base', where the adult maintains appropriate levels of nurture, control, structure and routine.

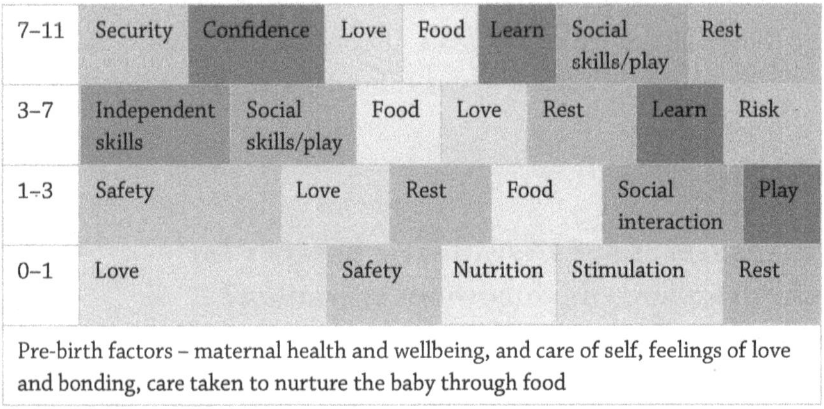
7–11
Security
Confidence
Love
Food
Learn
Social skills/play
Rest
3–7
Independent skills
Social skills/play
Food
Love
Rest
Learn
Risk
1–3
Safety
Love
Rest
Food
Social interaction
Play
0–1
Love
Safety
Nutrition
Stimulation
Rest
Pre-birth factors – maternal health and wellbeing, and care of self, feelings of love and bonding, care taken to nurture the baby through food

Figure 2.1 Developmental wall 1

We should now consider what happens within a toxic or abusive environment when a child has not received some of these important foundation factors of love, safety, nutrition, stimulation and rest, or has only had these experiences unreliably. Care has been absent or inconsistent and, depending on which foundation factors have not been available to support early development of skills and knowledge, there will be corresponding difficulties on the part of the child.

In Figure 2.2 we see that if some of the foundation factors are withheld, we get a different picture, and the resulting structure – ability to develop by building on a solid foundation – is not stable; there are too many gaps. If we remove love and nutrition – two elements which are often missing from a traumatic background – immediately we can see the effects.

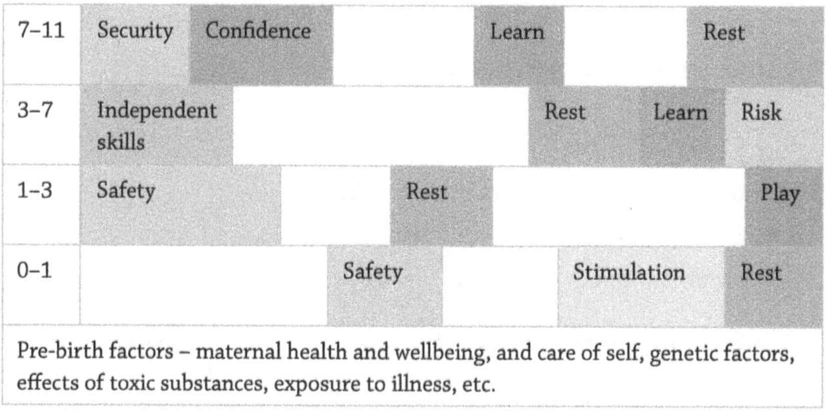

7–11
Security
Confidence
Learn
Rest
3–7
Independent skills
Rest
Learn
Risk
1–3
Safety
Rest
Play
0–1
Safety
Stimulation
Rest
Pre-birth factors – maternal health and wellbeing, and care of self, genetic factors, effects of toxic substances, exposure to illness, etc.

Figure 2.2 Developmental wall 2

This is a very threatening situation for a child. If they feel unloved, unworthy and unsafe, and they are neglected and deprived of food (a common example), then they are in a survival crisis. Food is one of the most basic physiological needs along with air and water, and a child who is not fed will be driven to try and find nutrition, resorting if necessary to inedible substances such as carpet or cardboard in order to survive. Their survival need will be focused on food, and this driving force will occupy them to the exclusion of any other developmental need.

One way to understand this is to think of our own response to hunger. When we are approaching a mealtime, the beginnings of hunger gnawing at our stomach sharpens our appetite, making us think of the meal we are anticipating and reducing our ability to concentrate and focus. This happens despite our knowledge that there will definitely be food forthcoming in the near future. We have even coined a word 'hangry' (mixture of hungry and angry) to describe how some people feel when they are hungry and not able to immediately get hold of food. How much worse is this experience if your earliest experiences were of severe neglect or irregular meals? We can suppose that the feeling of hunger is an intense trigger for that child, causing them to quickly become very distressed or even overwhelmed because this is a threat to their very survival. Once a child becomes overwhelmed by a survival need or a toxic memory, they are not connected to their thinking brain any more. They are instead driven by the much more primitive areas of the brain responsible for survival, fight or flight.

Maslow's hierarchy of needs

Another way to understand the effect on childhood development of neglect and trauma is to look at Maslow's hierarchy of needs (see Figure 2.3). It is important to understand that Maslow sees this as working from the foundations up – i.e. until physiological needs (air, water, food) are met, safety is not a priority. Unless you feel safe, belonging is not a priority. Once you have love, and belonging and social needs are met, then you are able to reach for higher goals – because we all operate best from a secure base. We see this principle in action when refugees flee their homes, their country, their culture and their friends and families and pay to get into overcrowded, unsafe boats with their children, heading for an uncertain future and possible death, because it is safer than staying in the situation they were in.

Maslow's hierarchy of needs states among other things that meeting physiological, safety and belonging or family and social needs (also known as deficiency needs) is crucial to the development of the individual if they are to achieve their full potential (**self-actualization**). It is important to remember that (in the case of children with developmental trauma) these needs must not only be met, but the child must perceive that this is their new reality, requiring the brain to form new pathways and connections, which takes time, patience and repetition. These ideas are reflected in outcomes for children which underpin legislation around adoption and fostering in the UK: being healthy (**physiological needs** – air, food, water, exercise); staying safe (safety needs); enjoying and achieving (belonging needs); making a positive contribution (esteem needs); and enjoying economic success (self-actualization).

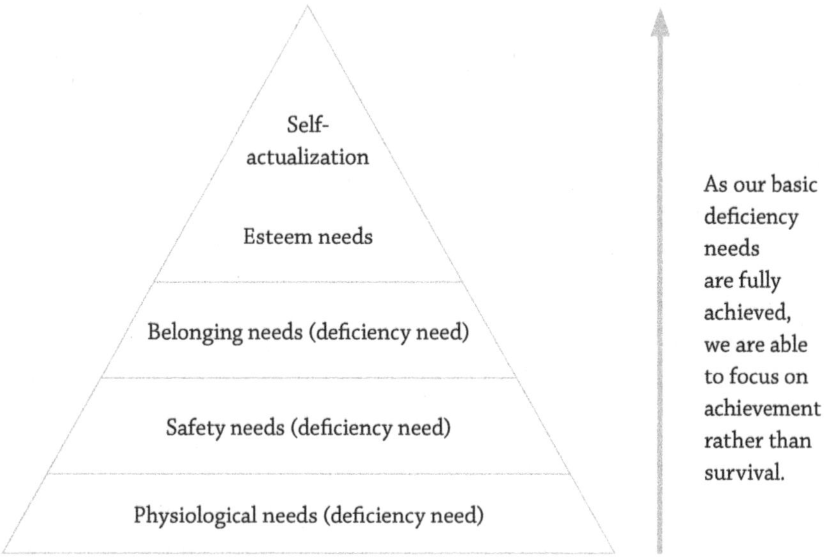

Figure 2.3 Hierarchy of needs

However, we have seen that it is not enough for needs to be met; they must be perceived and understood as being met by the individual for progress to be made. In other words, moving a child from a harmful home and placing them in a safe and secure home where their needs will be met means that as adults we know those deficiency needs are met, improving outcomes for the child. For the traumatized child, it will take time, patience and repeated experience before they are able to move on from their sense of danger – their development may be delayed or arrested; and the process of rewiring the brain to accept a different perspective than that which their experiences lead them to expect is a difficult and uncomfortable process. It is possible, as our brains are highly **plastic**, which is to say that we have an ability to learn and adapt throughout life within our individual limitations. But it is hard, and it is easy to slip into the old patterns. Try writing with the opposite hand you usually use – you can do it, but it is frustrating, slow and feels inefficient. And that is only a physical skill, relatively easy to master. We are asking children to change their whole emotional and social perception, which is hard for them and also for us as we support them through the process.

Maslow's hierarchy of needs – deficiency needs and attachment

Please refer to Figure 2.3 again for an explanation of deficiency needs.

- *Deficiency needs met*: This leads to a positive sense of self and abilities. Where there has been a positive attachment experience, needs are perceived as being met by the individual; they are confident in the provision of physiological and safety needs and have been able to engage in a loving, reciprocal relationship that has enabled them to build an expectation based on loving, attuned interactions. They have a core knowledge that their needs will be met, enabling them to be resilient and tolerant if they are occasionally hungry, cold, upset, have an argument, etc. They can manage social interactions and make connections readily. Their experience of the world as accommodating means that they can take risks, bear the disappointment of being wrong and explore different avenues. These individuals will be able to embrace a challenge, whether this is academic, physical or emotional.
- *Deficiency needs not met or, importantly, not perceived as met*: The child has a negative perception of themselves that is reinforced by their environment. Their behaviour is dominated by survival and fear-based systems engaged as a result of stress. Where there has been an insufficient, absent or disengaged attachment and/or other developmental trauma, the child will be focused on getting their survival needs met. They may filter most of their experience through fear of being unable to survive in this hostile environment. It will be hard to connect and engage with others. The child may have issues with their self-esteem as well as finding it hard to trust or maintain a positive outlook. In this case the child may rely on adaptive responses that have helped them to survive so far. These responses are based on fear and may present as anger or withdrawal that will create difficulties in their relationships. Resilience, trust and hope may well be alien emotions. They will be resistant to and fearful of change, and will need to have patient

and repeated positive messages to enable them to rewire and move past the block caused by their developmental trauma.

THINK ABOUT IT...

It is hard for anyone to read things which give an insight into the child's history. It is so painful to think that your child has been subjected to emotional and physical pain and humiliation. Children cannot be protected from events which have already occurred, but they can be helped to recover from them and move on. Understanding, knowledge and empathy, however painful the process, are necessary for parents to reclaim compassion. Children are survivors, and humans have evolved to enable new information and skills to be added throughout life – it is never too late to learn. Current research indicates that the brain is very plastic. Our experiences change our attitudes throughout life, and if traumatized children are given therapeutic parenting then they do have the capacity to change their concept of themselves, adults and their environment.

I have given below the deficit needs shown along with a description of how these unmet needs may present. Thinking of your own child or children, which of these may apply?

- *Physiological needs*: Commonly unmet due to neglect as food may not have been regularly available or suitable. The child is always hungry, steals food, secretes food in their room, or craves and steals sugar. This behaviour persists despite the easy accessibility of food and is a source of huge frustration if the parent cannot access empathy for the cause.
- *Safety needs*: Commonly unmet due to neglect and/or physical abuse. The child may be hypervigilant, unable to focus and fearful of change, or may test boundaries and take inappropriate risks

– but the underlying reason is that they need to feel safe. They are seeking safety, checking that you will keep them contained within a routine, structure and boundaries. Such a child may also show signs of their fear and anxiety of change and transitions by being oppositional or defiant, or by refusing to hear you.

- *Belonging needs*: Commonly unmet due to lack of attuned consistent caring, frequent moves or issues of rejection. The child may be resistant to affection and praise, may be very scared of being in touch with their feelings, and very scared of separation. They may seek to fight and push boundaries to test their belief that you never loved them and never will. In fact, they feel unlovable, worthless – they have not been valued and may find connection with you very scary as it makes them so vulnerable. Despite this, the road to recovery is through creating connection and supporting the child as they learn to trust, remembering that this is a very difficult thing for them to do. There will be disruptions along the way but that is OK. That is how we show a child how to repair a relationship – that it can withstand a few 'bumps' and that relationships can be resilient and lasting.

Parenting techniques

Parenting is the process whereby we develop the independent, social, moral, emotional and cognitive skills that a maturing young person needs in order to develop independence – to leave the parental home able to support themselves and with the social skills required for everyday interactions, as well as having sufficient emotional maturity for self-regulation and to be able to form a new family unit.

An attuned attachment to a significant adult forms the basis for this and begins the process of informing the development of the child, as we have seen. The child who has had 'good enough' parenting will be able to meet age-related expectations as they grow and develop and will be expected to be able to manage sanctions which are based on this secure base – the child is expected to be able to cope and rationalize and therefore learn a lesson and not repeat the behaviour. This works well where there has been consistent structure, values and rules, where there has been a loving relationship, and where ruptures (arguments, 'bad' or unsociable behaviour resulting in parental displeasure) are followed by repair, reconnection and support. The following table gives some examples and effects.

Standard parenting techniques

Technique	Effect – secure child	Effect – traumatized child
Time out	Able to self-regulate, calm down, stop and think, feel appropriate guilt, apologize, repair	Unable to calm down, escalates into fear, triggers feelings of abandonment and rejection. Unable to rationalize. May feel dreadful shame. Reverts to default feelings of worthlessness
Rewards and sanctions	Child is able to work towards a reward because they have reasonable self-esteem and confidence. The child is able to understand that if they step out of line there will be a sanction, which may not be connected to their action – e.g. the child shouts at their parent, has favourite game removed as sanction	Child does not have a sense of self that allows them to accept praise. Does not expect to be rewarded – this is not in their understanding of themselves or the world. Sanctions which are not connected directly to actions cause confusion, frustration and underline the fact they do not deserve anything
Star chart	Child is able to accept praise, feels proud of achievement, works hard to maintain approval	Child is unable to accept praise, and seems to deliberately sabotage attempts to use this technique
Planned ignoring	Child may be upset or worried, but has resilience due to previous experience	Child is likely to be triggered into stress as previous trauma or neglect is replicated by current carer's behaviour

Age-appropriate expectations	A child who developed in a loving environment with their needs met to a 'good enough' extent is likely to hit cognitive, emotional, social and physical milestones within the 'normal' range and therefore act in an age-appropriate way	A child who has lived with trauma is likely to have had experiences which will affect their functioning age. It is common for such children to display cognitive, social and emotional behaviours of a much younger person. They need support to enable these developmental gaps to be filled

Therapeutic parenting techniques

Parenting technique	**Effect on traumatized child**
Time in	Child is contained and kept safe by the presence of their parent, who will also give them a narrative explaining that they need to stay close for now, so that the parent can help them make good choices
Empathy	The child has their feelings (not behaviour) validated and reflected back to them in a caring way – 'Wow! That must have made you so angry!' or 'You must have been very scared about that. How horrible for you!' This allows a child to understand that their emotional reactions are understandable and do not mean that they themselves are 'bad'. (Adverse behaviours are not ignored – see 'Natural consequences')
Co-regulation	Parents are mindful of their child's emotional state, identifying triggers and helping the child to calm by being close, using physical contact if tolerated, and soothing noises – like the early interaction between parents and baby. This builds capacity for attachment
Naming the need	As the carers get to know their child, they help them to understand their feelings by explaining them – 'I expect you are really hungry. I have a snack for you!' 'It is very cold. Let's put your scarf on.' 'You look cross. Did you have a tough day? Maybe you are afraid that I will be upset with you. Perhaps you need a big hug!'

Natural consequences	The child learns by not being rescued (the adult will remember to regulate the ensuing distress, and not be annoyed by it!) – 'If you do not wear your coat, you will get cold.' 'If you break your phone (because you are cross), you will not have a phone for a while.' 'If you cannot stay safe when using the computer, you will not be allowed to use it, or you will have supervised time only.'
Acceptance	The adult accepts the child as they come to know and understand them, and this includes accepting their difficulties and differences. This implies that the parent has come to terms with their own losses and wishes and has engaged with their new child – a fabulous thing for everyone concerned.

These strategies have hugely beneficial effects for the child and for the parent.

Positive impact of therapeutic parenting

Neurological development of child	• Brain rewiring through positive experience • Accessing higher part of brain when asked the right questions • Strategies to reduce stress and fear-based actions – e.g. fight and flight • Ability to accept co-regulation
Emotional development of child	• Ability to develop secure attachments • Development of strategies to facilitate self-calming • Resilience • Exploration from a 'safe base' • Promotion of self-esteem, confidence and self-worth • Emotional literacy – appropriately naming own feelings and developing regulation techniques
Overall impact on child	• Positive outcome for child/change in learnt behaviour encouraged by technique • Positive outcome for parent and family • Increased self-esteem • Ability to learn • Development of social skills • Development of executive function • Development of skills for life • Stability of families • Positive outcome for child in future

Outcomes for parent	• Reduced stress • Enhanced understanding of child • Feeling of empowerment • Loving relationship with child • Improved relationship with partner • Relaxed • Validation • Increased self-esteem • Confidence in knowledge and abilities

PACE – the attitude of therapeutic parenting

Dan Hughes founded Dyadic Developmental Psychotherapy (DDP) when he was searching for a way to help children who had suffered from neglect and abuse and their families. His search led him to consider attachment theory and intersubjectivity theory and think again about the implications for a child who had suffered from lack of an attuned attachment figure at birth and the difficulties they would face as a result. The aim of DDP is to create a new healthy attachment based on increased security with a parent who is attuned to the child, compassionate, empathic to their needs and able to withstand the emotional onslaught of a child who has such difficulties with adults and trust that they resist attempts at connection, with an internal working model that they are unlovable. Over time the aim is to facilitate the growth of a secure, trusting and loving relationship.

Parenting with PACE

Much traditional day-to-day parenting assumes that the child feels safe at home, and trusts their parents and their motives when they discipline him. It also assumes that children learn from consequences, are able to function well with an age-appropriate degree of independence, and have come to accept their parents' values, ideals and goals. When these assumptions are not valid, other day-to-day parenting strategies are likely to be more effective.

Parenting using the attitude of Playfulness, Acceptance, Curiosity and Empathy helps the parent connect with their child, based on enjoyment of the relationship and an ability to understand and accept the inner experience of the child. The parent is curious about the child's inner world of thoughts, feelings and beliefs, and accepts this experience as not right nor wrong. It just is. This acceptance is conveyed to the child with empathy, showing that the adult can understand the meaning of their child's behaviour and stay calm and emotionally regulated as they talk with their child, even at very difficult times. This, in turn, helps the child calm and helps the parent remain emotionally available to the child. The capacity for emotional regulation and reflection on the part of the parent is important to the attitude of PACE, allowing the parent to remain open and available to the child and to be mindful of their own response to the child so that if they become defensive they can move back to becoming open and engaged once more. This requires support, self-care and self-compassion to achieve.

This parenting attitude creates a relationship and environment which make the world feel a safer place to the troubled child. Using PACE, the parent is able to create for their child the experience of their parents being deeply interested in them and enables them to make sense of the child's experiences. The child is able to experience unconditional love and security, providing a foundation for behaviour support, helping the child to make sense of their experience and regulate their emotional states and express these through acceptable behaviours.

Parenting that includes an attitude of PACE helps a parent see the strengths and positive features of their child that lie underneath their negative and challenging behaviours. It helps children learn to trust their parents.

PACE is an attitude of thinking, feeling, communicating and behaving that aims to make the child feel safe. It is based upon how parents connect with their very young infants. As with young toddlers, with safety the child can begin to explore.

With PACE, the troubled child can start to look at himself and let others start to *see* him, or get closer emotionally. He can start to trust.

- *Playfulness* – bringing humour and a light touch into the relationship. Connecting through fun and finding joy in the relationship:
  - Physical interactions (if tolerated – the parent needs to be aware of previous history before engaging in physical contact) – tickling, unexpected hugs
  - Games – ideally, these could be instigated by the child and might include hide and seek, catch, recreating early experiences like making cakes, drawing, reading together, joining in their play, allowing them to direct you and having pleasure in their exploration, pushing on swings, etc.
  - Playful response – 'Looks like you really need a hug!'
  - Developing family jokes
  - Repeating fun experiences or revisiting through photo albums, etc.
  - Celebrate even small achievements (remembering to bring coat home, getting a mention at school) with fist pump, 'Yay! Well done!', victory dance, etc.; be sure to explain what the achievement was at the same time to reinforce that behaviour
  - Dance and sing along to favourite music of the child's. Ham it up!

  These experiences help the child to manage positive feelings – which sounds strange, but such feelings may be alien or painful because of the constant fear of rejection. It is necessary to be observant and go carefully, as the child may wish to shut out the new feelings of closeness and fun.

Note that many children who have suffered developmental trauma play at a younger developmental age than their chronological age. The younger play experience enables them to recreate a more positive childhood experience, filling some of their developmental gaps.

PAUSE FOR THOUGHT...

After a positive experience, the child is likely to need some time to relax and enable them to process the information to facilitate the new information and create a new pathway. Be sure to keep stimulation periods followed by relaxation. Reflect on positive interactions with the child to reinforce the experience – this can be a simple 'We had great fun today, didn't we? We should do that again!'

- *Acceptance* – unconditional acceptance of a child is a great gift: an explicit expression that the child's inner life of thoughts, feelings and beliefs is accepted unconditionally and without evaluation, and means that you are able to carry some of your child's painful feelings and maintain connection and empathy. Also this means acceptance that maybe you did not end up with the family that you thought you would have, but are celebrating the one you have – an explicit expression that the child's inner life of thoughts, feelings and beliefs is accepted unconditionally and without evaluation. The child's experiences and therefore their belief about their new family is accepted with empathy and may be (if appropriate) reflected on with the child using curiosity. The parents need to have separate support to manage their natural emotional responses to a child who may be relentlessly rejecting of them. This does not mean ignoring harmful or dangerous behaviours, but accepting the reasons for this and continuing to help to change the behaviours by maintaining a safe, secure and loving environment whilst supporting the child to explore strategies to understand and manage their emotional states and therefore support new behaviour that increases safety for the whole family. One such example would be the use of natural consequences to manage behaviours. Acceptance in my view also means accepting our own limitations and what we are and are not able to manage, and accepting that we will make mistakes from time to time.

- *Curiosity* – parents help the child to understand their feelings by showing curiosity, not blame. This underlines the experience of the child that the parent is deeply interested in the child's experience. It is a tentative approach which suggests ideas but does not state these as absolute. Very importantly, the stance is non-judgemental – the parent conveys that the child's inner world (fears, anxieties and successes equally) is safe with them. This may well be linked to naming the need where a parent wonders what emotion or need was driving the behaviour – hunger, fear, rejection, trigger from the past. Such curiosity can be expressed as 'I wonder whether...? Looks like you are feeling...? It must be hard to feel like that. I am here if you would like to talk about it?' Remember that it may take time for the child to process and talk. That is OK – the important action is showing your interest and care. This lets the child know that you can 'see' them and that they are important to you.

- *Empathy* – allows the child to have the experience of having their emotions witnessed, contained and understood by someone who will help them to learn how to regulate their huge and overwhelming, often frightening feelings. The child does not have to be alone in their distress. Empathy can be hard – and there is no place for 'but' in an empathic exchange. It is a validation of the feelings of the child – other conversations about behaviour, etc. need to take a step back until the child is regulated and able to access their thinking brain again.

  Sometimes this attitude will be referred to as PLACE – as you might expect, the L stands for LOVING and of course refers to the child's experience of love which is constant and resilient, and given unconditionally; however, Kim Golding explains that PACE is an attitude whereas love is a state. Thus the attitude of PACE is surrounded by unconditional love, which of course adds an additional dimension to the approach. Utilizing this attitude in our day-to-day lives allows the child to gradually be able to integrate their experiences in the perspective of a new context – that of a secure and loving relationship.

Appropriate strategies

Strategy	**Impact**
Structured routine	Repetition builds stability. Develops new pathways in brain
Strict boundaries	Repetition builds stability. Develops new pathways in brain
Empathic response	Reduces fear and anxiety. Repetition builds stability. Develops new pathways in brain
Consistent use of strategies	Encourages understanding of cause and effect. Repetition builds stability. Develops new pathways in brain
Empathy for child's perspective and difficulties they face	Supports child in recovering from trauma
Supporting self-regulation	Reduces fear and anxiety
Containing child's overwhelming feelings using time in or naming the need	Enables child to accept co-regulation, helps them to understand their feelings and emotions

Develop a narrative

It can feel as if we say the same things again and again – and we do! Just try to remember that saying the same things again and again is a useful thing to do, activating the same neuronal pathways and strengthening them. Your children may seem to be ignoring you, or they may seem to have little effect; but remember, your child cannot stop their ears from hearing and their brain from processing what you say to them. Keep messages simple, and repeat them often:

- 'It must be hard learning how to live in a new family. Don't worry, we can keep practising, and I am here to help you.'

- 'I am your mum/dad, and I will always keep you safe.'
- 'I love you to the moon and back!'
- 'Looks like you are having some hard feelings. I am happy to talk to you whenever you want.'

Remember, trust takes time and patience. To begin with, being open to trust and love can make a child feel very, very vulnerable and scared, prompting a firm rejection of the parent, which can feel terrible for the parent concerned. It is really important then to empathize with the child's difficulties, be patient, and get some loving support from someone else – a partner or a friend, or a supportive professional.

An excellent resource for parents who are welcoming a new member of the family to start the process of talking about feelings, providing a narrative and starting your therapeutic parenting journey is Sarah's William Wobbly series of books. These offer explanations to children and strategies for parents.

We will continue to explore and expand all of these issues in the following chapters.

3

Reflective Parenting

Why We Need to Be Able to Understand Ourselves to Understand Our Children

> In this chapter we examine the reasons why parents have such difficulties in coming to terms with the challenges they face in helping their children overcoming trauma, and consider how these difficulties may have roots in the parents' own childhood experiences.

Before we go any further with the strategies that we can use to help our children, it is useful to stop and think a bit about our own triggers and responses. We all learn our parenting skills from our parents – sometimes we imitate them, sometimes we deliberately take a different approach, but essentially the way we were parented gives us a template which we subconsciously use to parent our own children. This chapter tries to help identify where some of our own triggers may lie. To understand this we need to reflect on our own actions and think about the reasons why certain behaviours just make us see red and how this allows our children to take control by escalating situations that cause us to lose our temper, which means we also lose our connection, our empathy and our compassion for our children. When this happens children replicate their trauma and confirm their adverse version of the world (think back to Chapter 1 and the internal working model). Of course, all parents 'lose their rag' from time to time – we are only human! So, we will also be talking about the importance of relationship repair. Finally, we will examine the reasons that parents can get so disconnected, exhausted and isolated as a result of the behaviour of their children and the responses from family, friends and professionals that they fall into compassion fatigue (or blocked care, an additional term that may be used), and feel that they are no longer able to continue. This is a truly horrible place to be, but we will also talk about the ways in which compassion fatigue can be averted, overcome or at least ameliorated by appropriate learning and support.

IN MY EXPERIENCE...

It's not easy being a parent! I remember with my birth children making many mistakes, reflecting, trying to learn and trying to parent in a caring and empathic way – and that was not always easy! We had our own trials with a separation and divorce from my first husband (the father of my oldest two children), the negotiations around sharing parenting and weekends and holidays, and I know my two eldest found this to be extremely difficult at times, as did I, not helped by the very different environments in our separate households. I always seemed to be re-instating boundaries and managing meltdowns after weekends away.

Then I remarried and had another child. I really congratulated myself – bringing up my daughter in a secure relationship was so easy! Finally we adopted another daughter who turned all my ideas and perceived knowledge upside down and set me on the road to therapeutic parenting. What a journey! I always seemed to be shouting. Everything was so hard, I was exhausted and no one seemed to understand, or dismissed my difficulties as being due to my parenting – too strict, not strict enough, you know the story.

I was always reflective, but my adopted daughter prompted me to use a reflective process to try and be a better mother. I started to keep a diary, and this formed the basis of the reflective practice which I followed thereafter and which is one of the key components of effective therapeutic parenting. I believe that the truth is that I was highly triggered by the behaviours demonstrated by my child, and that in that state I was not able to access the conscious therapeutic parenting skills that my daughter needed. Dan Siegel (Siegel and Hartzell 2004, p.247) reminds us that "unresolved" and leftover issues can impair our ability to offer our children joyful connections and secure attachments'. However, I believe the crucial factor is not the prior experiences of the adult, but the fact that they are unresolved. Such experiences can trip us up, and have an impact on our interactions with our children, taking us into a place where it is hard to maintain the high functioning, mindful and connected state that is necessary to have positive interactions (**high road**) and instead cause us to enter a reactive state where we are responding to our own emotional memories and triggers (**low road**). By engaging in reflective practice we are able to unpick the cause of our own behaviours and stop being triggered by the behaviours demonstrated by our children. ('High road' and 'low road' are the terms coined by Dan Siegel to describe respectively flexible, considered and emotionally integrated responses versus automatic reflexive responses prompted by unresolved experiences.)

The first task on the journey to becoming a reflective parent is to think about how to apply knowledge in a personal way to help us to gain greater understanding of our own reactions to and interactions with our families. To begin with, it is necessary to reflect on our thoughts and feelings. So here is a little exercise for you.

Active reflection

We considered in Chapter 1 how our perceptions are built as a result of our experiences. To be able to manage effectively to parent therapeutically, or to support a family in this task, it is first necessary to be very aware of our own learned preconceptions and how they affect us.

THINK ABOUT IT...

Take some time to consider your experience of parenting; for instance:

- What memories do you have from your childhood?
- What family activities did you have?
- When did you feel most connected to your parents?
- What rules were there?
- What sanctions did you incur?
- Is your perception that you were good? Bad? Getting into trouble?
- Why do you feel this?
- If you were punished, did you feel this was just, or unjust?
- How would you describe your own parenting style?
- Are there similarities between your own parenting style and your experiences of being parented?
- What behaviours on the part of your child trigger your anger?
- Do you sometimes feel you are letting your child 'get away' with bad behaviour, or do others tell you this?
- Do you know why?
- How does this feel? (raised heartbeat, blood pounding...)
- What behaviours engage you (make you feel responsive and enjoy the child)?
- Do you know why?
- How does this feel? (warm, loving, want to hug...)
- How do you feel most of the time at present?

In order to be able to make the changes necessary for effective therapeutic parenting, we first of all need to be aware of the impact we ourselves have on the situation. To understand this we need to consider our own perceptions and how they arise.

Our early experiences can give rise to certain assumptions and perceptions about behaviour and responses. Some common perceptions are that:

- children should understand and follow our rules
- the adult *must* remain in control of the child
- adults do not make mistakes (or do not admit to this)
- parents who do not ensure their children meet social expectations (age related, usually) are bad parents
- children need to be punished (have sanctions applied) to learn responsibility and consequences
- children should be obedient and reasonably compliant.

Unfortunately, our children, as we discussed in Chapter 1, have a different view of the world, of adults in general and parents in particular. This is not their fault, or their parents' fault. It is simply a reflection of their previous experience. The table that follows contrasts the usual attitudes associated with parenting with those of therapeutic parenting.

Standard viewpoint	**Therapeutic parenting viewpoint**
Children should understand and follow our rules	Children may have suffered multiple rules in multiple homes. There has been no consistency. Everyone's rules are different. Furthermore, it is likely that in one household the rules (however trivial) were enforced in inappropriate ways or were a danger to the child or even reinforced their sense of shame or fear ('Don't tell or else everyone will know how bad you are'; 'Don't tell or you know what will happen...')
The adult *must* remain in control of the child	The child may have learned that the only way they can survive and get their needs met is to control their environment by whatever means are available to them. This may involve lying, stealing, grabbing attention in any way they can, or generally disruptive behaviour, and is completely at odds with the standard perception that the adult is always in control, always right, must not be argued with
Adults do not make mistakes (or do not admit to this)	Adults are strong enough to admit when they are wrong, and model ways to say and show that they are sorry. Some parents may feel that this shows weakness, but it actually builds resilience and an understanding that we can have a relationship that survives despite the bumps
Parents who do not ensure that their children meet social expectations (age related, usually) are bad parents	Children who have suffered developmental trauma may well have developmental delay in all areas (physical, social, emotional, cognitive) and especially in the social and emotional domains. They have not necessarily had good enough parenting or consistent parenting and stability to enable them to develop these very important areas. This will mean that they are easily overwhelmed, and when in this state are likely to act out the age when trauma occurred. They require therapeutic parenting to help them 're-wire' their behaviour, and to do this we have to 're-think' our parenting

Children need to be punished (have sanctions applied) to learn responsibility and consequences	Very often, our children are punished and given consequences or sanctions for behaviour that occurs when they are out of control. This means they are not deliberately acting out, but are in a state of overwhelm because an intense stress reaction has been triggered by an event. Natural consequences should be allowed, with the child being helped to reflect with support after the event (strategies to support this are discussed fully in future chapters)
Children should be obedient and reasonably compliant	Children who live in fear from past experiences are unlikely to be compliant to requests. Rephrasing requests into statements may be useful (e.g. 'Time to find your coat, we need to leave in five minutes!' whilst getting your own coat on (modelling behaviour). Parents find disobedience to be disrespectful and intensely triggering, but it is important to be mindful that this is almost always due to intense anxiety

THINK ABOUT IT...

Think of a recent interaction between you and your child that made you angry, embarrassed or feel out of control.

- Are you aware of what triggered the behaviour? Could you have reacted differently?
- If you feel your response was inappropriate, are you able to apologize?

Now, think of a recent interaction between you and your child that made you feel connected and happy and gave you real enjoyment in their company.

- Reflect on the activity and the situation.
- Could you replicate this experience?

Blame and responsibility

Very often, when faced with difficult circumstances where we may feel out of control or out of our depth, we shift the blame onto another person. 'They made me so angry!' 'If they would just do what they are told, for once!' 'You are driving me nuts!' This also happens sometimes when professionals feel overwhelmed by a situation that is unfolding in a family – they blame the parents. 'It must be the parenting that is at fault, the school has no difficulty!' or 'I don't know what the parents are talking about. The child is lovely whenever I come to see them!' This is a very easy trap to fall into – when things go wrong it makes us feel bad (ashamed, guilty and disempowered), and a way to deal with this is to take that pain and try to give it to someone else. Our children do this a great deal – telling us we are rubbish, that we never loved them, or that they never wanted to be in our family. This is a way of expressing their deepest fears, and so we can find ways to reframe this by responding in an empathic way.

They say	They fear	Try this response
You are rubbish!	It makes me feel too vulnerable to admit I care about you. I am going to push that feeling away!	Wow! I am sorry you feel that way! I am going to keep trying to be the best parent I can be for you
You never loved me!	I think I am unlovable. It's scary to be loved. I don't think I deserve love	It's hard to think your (mum/dad/parents...) never loved you. I always love you, and always will
I never wanted to be in your family!	I am scared you will get rid of me. I am going to reject you first!	It is difficult, I know. But we are family

It is much harder to manage if we get caught in a cycle of blame between parents, social workers, support workers, teachers and other professionals – when this happens the family gets derailed because parents lose confidence in their support structure; they become exhausted and isolated and find it harder and harder to cope. The structure of the support framework around the family is weakened and in the end the child or children sense the discord, become scared and tell everyone a different story in an attempt to control (triangulate), causing further confusion – the end result can be the disruption and breakdown of the family unit. We explore this whole subject in greater depth later on in the book.

THINK ABOUT IT...

If parents are blaming the child, and professionals are blaming the parents, then:

- Who is supporting the family?
- Who is helping the child?
- Is anyone taking responsibility for making necessary changes?
- Who can do this?

Take a look at this famous poem while you are thinking!

Children Learn What They Live

If children live with criticism, they learn to condemn.
If children live with hostility, they learn to fight.
If children live with fear, they learn to be apprehensive.
If children live with pity, they learn to feel sorry for themselves.
If children live with ridicule, they learn to feel shy.
If children live with jealousy, they learn to feel envy.
If children live with shame, they learn to feel guilty.
If children live with encouragement, they learn confidence.
If children live with tolerance, they learn patience.
If children live with praise, they learn appreciation.
If children live with acceptance, they learn to love.
If children live with approval, they learn to like themselves.
If children live with recognition, they learn it is good to have a goal.
If children live with sharing, they learn generosity.
If children live with honesty, they learn truthfulness.
If children live with fairness, they learn justice.
If children live with kindness and consideration, they learn respect.
If children live with security, they learn to have faith in themselves and in those about them.
If children live with friendliness, they learn the world is a nice place in which to live.

Child-behaviour-based triggers

Parents who are re-parenting traumatized children can find that their child's behaviour triggers very intense personal responses in them. To understand this we need to think first about the human physiological response to stress (see Figure 3.1). The stress response is activated to protect us and ensure survival when we are threatened by aggressive behaviour or a hostile environment. It is a physiological and unconscious response to a threat and is triggered at an unconscious level, sometimes by stimuli we are unaware of – traumatic memories can be held 'in the body' and trigger a stress response via any of our sensory organs. (Think phobia.)

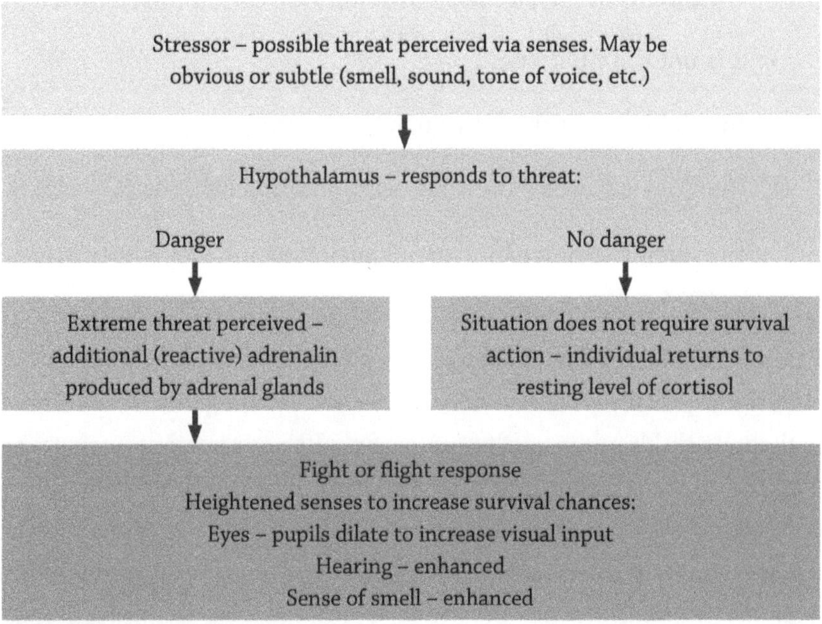

Figure 3.1 Stress response

Commonly the fight response leads to physical and verbal aggression; flight leads to withdrawal or actual running away.

Bloom and Farragher (2010) stated that 'fear and anger are dominant emotions when under threat'. In addition, if the stressful situation is maintained, the individual's memory, perception and identity are affected. This is known as **disassociation**. Pitman (1977) states that 'children who are exposed to traumatic events are particularly prone to disassociation'. This means that cognitive function, **executive function** (ability to have impulse control, self-regulate, understand situations in context, predict consequences) and memory all alter under the influence of acute stress. Dan Siegel in his hand model of the brain refers to this flight into survival mode as 'flipping your lid' (see the YouTube section in the Bibliography) – when faced with an immensely stressful situation we are not rational. The implications for this when faced with a child who has suffered developmental trauma are profound:

- The child is not acting maliciously.
- The child is not deliberately winding you up.
- It is not the child's fault.
- The child cannot think through their actions.
- The child is scared – the underlying emotion behind anger is fear.
- The child is driven by their experiences and by subconscious triggers.

Parents face incredible challenges in giving appropriate care to these children, especially since emotional states are 'catching'; what this means is that our children can easily wind us up, push our buttons – whatever way you choose to express it. The importance of this is that we have a connection with our child. The good news is that if they can wind you up, you can help them to regulate themselves by calming yourself, for example by mindfulness or breathing techniques. One simple technique that can help is simply to practise pausing – literally for a second or so – to let your brain engage before you react. The act of pausing can remind us that the reason you are doing this is to remember the child's point of view and their inability to be rational. By doing this and having a conscious rather than an emotional or stress-based response, we find that carers are able to calm down, think clearly, maintain safety for self and child, and develop the child's understanding through parental presence, narrative and empathy.

Parental presence

> Simple physical presence can convey a world of meaning to a child that does not have trust in adults. If a child is overwhelmed, your calm presence can calm them down. If a child is unhappy, your empathic presence (including appropriate physical contact, if the child will accept it) will reassure them. If a child feels worthless, then spending time with them lets them know they are important to you. As a therapeutic parent, we can use our body language, our facial expression and proximity to convey emotional messages of acceptance, love, empathy, calm and reassurance. This is the essence of co-regulation – words should be kept to a minimum. During the attachment cycle, when a baby has a need the first job of the adult is to regulate the baby's emotional state, calming and reassuring them and this is what we still need to do for our challenging children. This then allows movement into meeting the need. (Jane Mitchell from article posted on Therapeutic Parents Facebook Page, summer 2016)

Over time, the child experiences the adult as trustworthy and able to parent using containment and acceptance. This is further helped if the adult and other supporters develop a narrative for the child to support their new experiences.

Developing a narrative

Whilst children are still in their first stages of life, operating at a physical and sensory level, we automatically fill in the gaps for them by providing a constant narrative. Whether it is discussing with a baby whether they need feeding and reassuring them about each step you take, or teaching a child about appropriate clothes by reminding them to get their wellies on because it is raining, we constantly give information.

Remembering that our children may not have received this important developmental information and letting them know that we can 'see' them (which in itself conveys a message that the child is important, held in mind and loved) is a massively important intervention. This can mean a simple addition to ordinary conversation – instead of 'here's your snack' when the child arrives home from school, you might say, 'I know you are hungry when you get out of school, so here is a snack for you.' The same applies to giving them information about their emotional state – 'Looks to me like you are feeling angry/sad/happy. Are you OK?/Do you want to tell me about that?' The child receives the information about their emotion but also about your concern. They may or may not choose to talk, but that does not matter. Sometimes children (and adults) need time to process before they talk. The underlying meaning conveyed to the child is that they are important to you, that you care about them, that you have thought about them even when they are not with you (kept them in mind). Many children will then give you a negative response – and this is especially common as children approach adolescence – but here is the good news! Whatever their mouth is saying as a defence, they cannot stop their ears from hearing and their brain from processing and experiencing what you have said. So be a broken record, repeat the same thing often and ignore the poor responses.

Empathy

One of the most effective tools we have is empathy (our golden bullet!). It allows us to join the person in their emotional state and express how this might feel for them – for example, a friend tells you about a row they have had with their partner. Maybe you identify with their anger – 'You must have been furious!' You might express indignation on their behalf – 'How dare they? I can't believe they did that!' – and then you might express concern – 'Are you OK? Can I help?' Typically, the validation of the feelings really helps the friend to talk about the experience, reflect on it and decide on an action for themselves. Empathy is not about making judgements or about finding solutions (although that might be a result). It is about identifying the underlying feelings and giving a safe place for these to be explored. The hardest part of empathy is keeping it simple and centred on the experience of the other person, and knowing when to keep quiet and just listen.

Dan Hughes uses the term "Affective- Reflective Dialogue" to express the way in which a therapist can help the family to hear each other in a different way, matching the affect – level of feeling or arousal – and enabling a greater understanding. Instead of separate and disjointed versions of events, the therapist helps the family to co-create a new story. Dan states that "the therapist strives to initiate and maintain matched affect, joint awareness or attention, and a complementary intention throughout the dialogue" (Hughes 2011, pp. 48, 49).

Who is pressing your buttons?

What can sometimes further muddy the water is that our own experiences of being parented or parenting interfere with our perceptions – hence the activity earlier in this chapter. Reasons for parents to be triggered into stressed states include:

- childhood relationships with own parent
- childhood experiences
- relationship with spouse/partner
- significant life experiences
- self-esteem and confidence issues
- judgements or perceived judgements of family, friends, professionals
- personal levels of resilience
- personal attachment style
- compassion fatigue.

Once we are sufficiently stressed, we follow the same physiological route as our children, and our underlying fear and fight–flight response can be easily activated. Unfortunately, this can lead to ruptures in our relationships both at home and at work, and leave us feeling unsure of ourselves and our abilities as parents, spouses, professionals – a generalized feeling of shame and disempowerment.

Compassion fatigue

'Compassion fatigue' is the term Sarah Naish uses to describe the emotional and physical burnout which can be experienced by adoptive and foster parents who are attempting to re-parent some of the most traumatized children in the care system. This group of people reported symptoms including exhaustion, lack of motivation, family breakdown and failure in being able to continue to find the levels of empathy and energy required to continue.

We can use the analogy of the carer as a jug of water containing elements of therapeutic parenting – compassion, nurture, stability, consistency, natural consequences, curiosity, playfulness, love and acceptance – which are the elements needed to help to re-wire the child who has suffered trauma and consequently is distrustful of the world in general and adults in particular, especially carers and professionals. This child is like a leaky cup (punctured by experiences), whereas the carer is like a jug of water aiming to replace the child's previous experiences by providing nurturing, loving, consistency and stability (among other strategies); repeated pouring will help the child to move forward, but the caring jug will empty unless there is recognition of the immensity of the task and appropriate support is given – refilling the jug. When their caring jug empties, the parent can get so stuck that they create a barrier to help and support because they do not believe anyone wants to know or that anyone can understand. It's like putting a watertight lid on their empty jug, preventing it from being refilled. It becomes easy for some professionals to blame the parent because they 'won't accept support', isolating them still further. To relieve this situation requires time, patience, empathy and unconditional support. Gradually as the parent experiences the empathic support of other parents or professionals who 'get' it, they are able to lift their lids, and take on board the support, strategies and knowledge that are on offer. With help the family can emerge stronger and more resilient, massively reducing the risk of a family breakdown.

To make matters more difficult, the child is likely to be resistant to accepting the new style of parenting due to their own experiences. It is usual for parents to have to manage a range of adverse behaviours including violence and aggression. Under this kind of pressure, it is not surprising that we see parents move from a positive emotional response where they are regulated, empathic and loving to a negative emotional response where they are dysregulated, stressed and therefore angry and fearful. This is also unsurprising if the child's emotional state is dominant. An article in *Psychology Today* illustrates this:

> Studies have found that the mimicry of a frown or a smile or other kinds of emotional expression trigger reactions in our brains that cause us to interpret those expressions as our own feelings. Simply put, as a species, we are innately vulnerable to 'catching' other people's emotions. (Sherrie Bourg Carter)

This would suggest that it will be easy to engage in a negative feedback loop emotionally (see Figure 3.2).

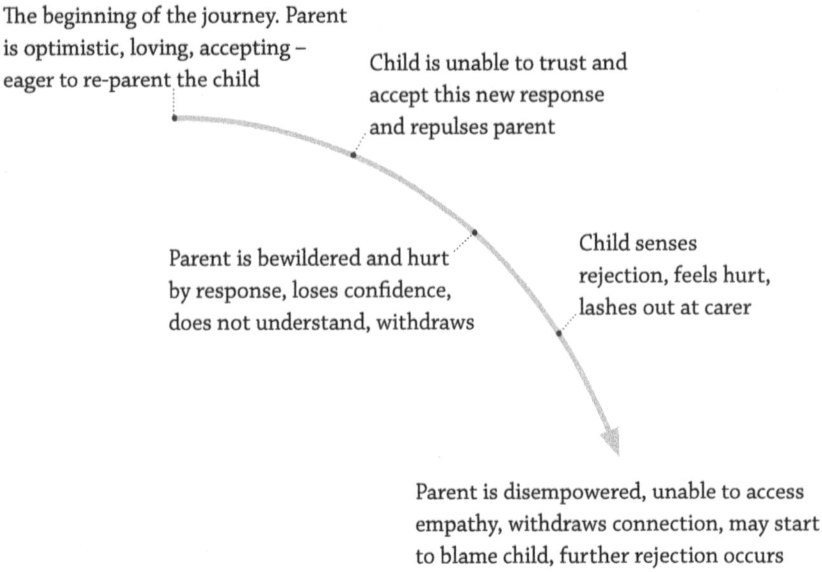

The beginning of the journey. Parent is optimistic, loving, accepting – eager to re-parent the child
Child is unable to trust and accept this new response and repulses parent
Parent is bewildered and hurt by response, loses confidence, does not understand, withdraws
Child senses rejection, feels hurt, lashes out at carer
Parent is disempowered, unable to access empathy, withdraws connection, may start to blame child, further rejection occurs

Figure 3.2 Disrupted relationship

At this point, the parent may decide that they are unable to manage the emotional and physical burden any longer and the placement may break down. It will take care, support and education to rebuild the relationship.

In a national survey of foster carers and adoptive parents (Ottaway and Selwyn 2016) carried out by the University of Bristol's Hadley Centre for Adoption and Foster Care Studies, 77 per cent of the 546 carers in the UK surveyed reported symptoms of compassion fatigue. One foster carer for ten years said, 'If we dare talk about it we're seen as failing – only we're not failing, we just need a bit of help', and that:

> There used to be more support when I started out but a lack of funding, among other things, means there's a flow of social workers these days who don't get to know you. It's not their fault, it's the way the system works.

Carers also reported feeling judged and blamed by social workers and agencies – 'The social workers and their lack of training cause me far more problems than the children I care for.' Lead researcher Heather Ottaway commented, 'Foster carers who were affected reported only being able to meet children's basic needs, and could not meet their often-considerable emotional needs.'

What about me? – The importance of self-care

Parenting a traumatized child is tough, and can be a relentless 24/7 task. It can feel as though you stop being the person you were and become somebody's parent instead. Worse, you may find the person you become is unrecognizable to you – you may feel very lost. This loss of personal identity can be linked to feelings of being unable to cope, and loss of confidence and self-esteem, which can be exacerbated by lack of support from family, friends or professionals and the consequent sense of isolation and lack of personal time, emotional support and money. The way to empowerment is through gathering information about your child's background and your child's medical history, including mental health issues, and accessing appropriate therapeutic support for your child. This might include:

- education and training for you and your family
- identification of educational needs
- identification of therapeutic input – life story therapy, family therapy, cognitive behavioural therapy, etc.
- personal and professional support and validation.

For you, there are a variety of strategies which can be explored:

- *Respite*: think friends, family, after-school club, extracurricular clubs as well as respite organized via your agency (foster child) or post-adoption social worker (adopted child). Also, if your children are at school, take days off (with your partner if appropriate) and just have time for you and each other.
- *Mindfulness exercises*
- *Breathing exercises*

- *Physical exercise*: promotes endorphins (natural feel-good factor), helps with energy and provides a welcome distraction whilst keeping you fit
- *Support groups*
- *Time out for self*: bath, coffee with friends, shopping trip, spa date, walks, swim, dance, sharing a glass of wine – whatever gives you total respite for even a short time
- *Be kind to yourself*: being a perfect parent is neither possible nor preferable. Your child needs you to model making mistakes, apologizing and moving on whilst keeping the relationship intact to develop their trust in you and your relationship with them.

The importance of self-care cannot be stressed enough. This is not selfish or 'nice if you can get it' but essential to enable carers to maintain the high levels of therapeutic parenting on practical and emotional levels which are necessary to children who have suffered developmental trauma. Bear in mind as well the lessons of this chapter – emotional states are catching, so make time to have fun, to relax, to bring those feelings into your home.

Reflective practice

The ability to reflect is a crucial factor in re-parenting traumatized children, giving us an opportunity to look back at incidents and review them in a calm and objective way. This can be done individually or as part of family therapy, individual counselling, chatting within a support group or a cuppa with your mum. There are no rights or wrongs, except that you do need to be in a calm state for this to be effective. The technique is largely observational and depends on your ability to take a step back and describe a situation in a very factual way. You then look at the environmental and other factors – including, of course, your own state of mind. Finally, you assess whether there is any action which can usefully be taken. Reflective practice as an integral part of therapeutic parenting is a very empowering tool which requires the parent to place their experience in context, to put new ideas and interventions into effect, and then to evaluate the impact on the family situation. There is no judgement: something works, something does not work – it all adds to the overall picture and gives additional information which adds to the learning curve. Or you might fine tune something which did not quite fit. As an illustration, below are two examples from my 'Reflecting on chaos' (June 2007) in *Adoption Today*. The first example:

Date and time	Event description	Reflection on event	Action to be taken
Sunday 25 February, morning	On request to go out to walk, J displayed extreme opposition, defiance, refusal to put shoes on. On insisting, screaming and difficult/ dangerous behaviour in the car, kicking at window, etc. On arrival at walk kicking up mud deliberately	Did not give J warning to enable time to get used to idea of going out, interrupted play	Make sure adequate warning given in future to give time to adjust

As you can see, this is a pretty standard occurrence where you give an instruction or make a request, and your child immediately says no. This probably happens several times a day. Whilst I was in the moment, I probably had a thought very much along the lines of 'Here we go again' and a dialogue explaining that I was in charge; I needed to make decisions for her as she is still too little. I would have held her hand to keep her by me. The difference was writing this down – obviously you are not in the moment, and therefore more able to see around the situation. I started getting into my stride with the idea, and so my entries became more complex, as can be seen in the much more extreme example that follows.

Date and time	Event description	Reflection on event	Action to be taken
Thursday 1 March, 4.30pm	J became angry and jealous due to two minded children being present, especially when A needed nappy change. Shouting, running away, grabbing at wipes and towel- etc., shouting at A. Sent J upstairs to calm down, settled boys to watch CBeebies as v. tired. Tried to talk to J – shouting, screaming, hitting, kicking and spitting – I hate you, I hate your stupid childminding. Left her to it, went back later. J was still throwing things around, screaming, very angry. Picked up video case and hit me hard enough to cut my brow. I realized I was bleeding and went to get tissue. J realized I was bleeding and immediately panicked about consequences, shouting I hate you, I don't want to be here, I want to go to Mummy J [birth mum] or Nanny C [foster mum]. Left her to calm down, went back up when heard her crying, she started shouting as soon as she saw me, but as I reassured her, her shouting turned into tears and she started saying I'm very very sorry. She was extremely distressed for the next hour. Read *No Matter What*.	Jealousy and anger over childminding and hitting out gave rise to event. J panicked, fear of abandonment and rejection coming up causing her anger and extreme distress. Talked through issues leading up to event – i.e. jealousy and anger, talked about how things went wrong, and how she felt afterwards (very scared, thought I would run away). I talked through how she can trust me not to leave, reassured her, and pointed out that hitting can lead to bad result so best not to do it. Resolution? I felt at least we were able to repair our relationship and talk through some major issues. This may turn to my advantage. I cannot get rid of the cut, and that will remind her and enable me to reassure for a couple of days. This episode reminded me that underlying all of J's worst behaviour is her terror of being abandoned and rejected.	Deal with the fear and anxiety. Remember how scared she is when she is at her worst – it is easier to deal with a scared child and empathize, than a raging one. Remember reassuring books – *No Matter What* (Debi Gliori), *Guess How Much I Love You* (Sam McBratney).

Interestingly, reading through this several years after the event, it screams out to me that I made a classic mistake in employing time out, rather than time in! I was early in my journey at that time. To be honest, I probably would have had to send her to her room anyway as she was posing a danger to the other two children – she would have lashed out at them. As time went on, the consequences of J having such difficulty with sharing (as a result of her issues with interpersonal relationships as a whole) meant that I had to stop childminding for the two very young children mentioned above as this was untenable for me and detrimental to all of the children's needs.

4

First Steps and Transition Planning

In this chapter we examine the process of bringing a child or children into our family: how it feels for us, how it feels for them and how these two perspectives may be a complete mismatch. We will also consider the difficulties our children have in managing change and transitions – why is it so hard for so many children and what can we do to help them? The chapter builds on the previous chapters and is an opportunity to look at this specific area in more depth.

One of the very important factors to be borne in mind is to remember that in order to effect change in the behaviour of our children and create a nurturing and supportive environment we first of all need to look at our own perceptions and our own behaviour, and think about how to use techniques that will create a therapeutic attitude and environment at home. Our children cannot simply change their behaviour. They are playing out old scripts according to the expectations that they have as a result of their earliest experiences. In order to change the behaviours and the outcomes for the whole family, we have to change the way that we approach the child and follow natural consequences that allow children to make direct connections between their actions and the results of those actions through direct experience. This is backed up by narratives and by reflecting with the child to make meaning.

IN MY EXPERIENCE...

When I brought my adopted daughter home (I have older birth children), I really tried to think about how it was for her, and even so I underestimated the grief that she would feel on being separated from her foster mum. I thought that our long knowledge of each other would lessen the impact; also I was desperate to claim her as my own and so I suppose I minimized the attachment she had formed. (I had been her childminder for a year and a half, a foster parent to her for a few weeks while a long-term family was found, and had provided brain breaks and maintained contact with her throughout the year and a half she lived with her foster family.) The foster mum and dad and I tried to plan a really robust transition, with a gradual move over at a pace we felt was appropriate, and we talked to her about this, but of course at three years old and with developmental delay, these were concepts that were far too tricky for my daughter to grasp. We all decided that we would keep in contact, and explained to my daughter that her foster mum and dad were too old to be parents but that they would be her 'grandparents' – Nanny and Grandpa. I so vividly remember the day they came to visit for the first time after she moved in permanently and of course did not take her home – my daughter literally threw back her head and howled with grief. It was absolutely heartrending to witness, and all I could do was to be with her, offering comfort and empathy.

My daughter already had a bed, bedding, toys and even clothes at my house, so in that respect there was familiarity, but in 2003 the importance of the transition was not well understood

– we did the very best we could between us, and I looked forward to my daughter being a settled, happy member of the family in a few months' time. How wrong I was!

Transition planning

First steps

There can be no doubt that transitions – change of any sort – are hard for most children in the system, whatever their care structure. Whether the child is entering the system for the first time, or moving on to an adoptive family from foster care, or moving as a result of a breakdown of a foster family, this is likely to mean trauma and triggering of fearful reactions on the part of the child. Our aim is to be mindful of their experiences, both past and present, and to create an environment of safety and belonging which has elements of familiarity. We need to have a range of skills, strategies and understanding to enable us to support the child or children.

We need to remember the very different perspectives as a child moves into care or transitions within the care system.

The child

First, consider what the child's experience may have been.

In the time that I have been working in the field, I have heard awful stories – children who have suffered sexual abuse as babies, who have been left in their cots for years and therefore deprived of processes of attunement and the necessary stimulation to encourage movement and physical development; children who have been beaten; children who have witnessed severe domestic violence, even including death or serious attack on a parent or death of siblings. One case I heard of was of a toddler who had to be cut out of the pushchair that he was sitting in and was welded to with filth including his own faeces. These are clearly not experiences that you can 'forget' and we know now that even in cases where the perceived knowledge was that the child was 'too young to remember' this is not the case. Dan Siegel (2012) explains in his definition of 'memory' that 'what we usually think of as "memory" refers to the way in which events can influence the brain and alter its future activity in a specific manner'. Memory incorporates several interconnected sensory impressions around any specific event – in other words it is not just what you see but what you hear, smell, touch, taste or feel emotionally that are interwoven in the same experience. Hence a piece of music may remind you of a specific occasion which you may associate with feeling intense happiness or sadness or which you may associate with a certain person or set of events. Siegel calls these 'associational linkages'. A baby or young toddler may not have words to explain or express what they have experienced, but these memories are held as implicit memories and may be triggered by sensory stimuli at any time. **Implicit memory** is based around behaviours, body sensations and images and is not consciously activated, as implicit memory is held in ancient structures in the brain's limbic area. Dan Siegel suggests that the infant's brain can create a model of the world from birth, and furthermore that babies' brains are capable of creating generalizations based on their experiences. This is the basis of the internal working model which we have discussed previously.

Explicit memory develops alongside language and the development of the cortex. Explicit memory is factual and autobiographical, and can be consciously accessed. It is also linked sequentially – i.e. it follows a kind of timeline which helps us to place our experiences in place and time.

To consider all of this as it affects the child entering a new family, we have first of all to wonder how this may feel for them. The child is entering an unknown, unfamiliar environment. They are extremely likely to have had experiences which lead them to mistrust adults and be inappropriately self-reliant. The terms 'Mum', 'Dad' and 'family' may have fearful associations for them. Change itself may be terrifying. Their feelings may be:

- ambivalent
- fearful
- angry
- excited

- passive.

They may:

- have low expectations
- expect failure
- feel shame
- feel responsible
- have a sense of betraying their parents
- miss their family (even after abuse)
- mistrust adults
- need to control (to get needs met).

It is really easy for us as adults to forget that the rules of our own home, which we feel are obvious and more or less similar to everyone else's, are in fact quite individual and a minefield for the child to understand and negotiate. We can start with the fact that children do not just enter care – there have to have been strong reasons why this would be in the best interest of the child before they can be removed. Some children coming into care have had horrendous experiences and, as we have already discussed, these experiences will have shaped the architecture of their brain, in terms of both their expectations and their responses.

Expectations of new parents

There may be a range of ideas associated with adoption and fostering and our own perception of what this may mean for us:

- Parenthood
- Family
- Desire to make a difference
- Excitement

- Anxiety
- Love or expectation of a loving experience
- Caring
- Expectation of happiness
- Feeling complete
- Recreating our childhood
- Fun and adventures
- Parental expectations.

Looking at this in the light of what we have already discussed in relation to the child entering the system and being in need of a family, it is clear to see that there is a huge potential difference, and although prospective adopters and foster parents are given training, it is not always sufficient to explore the core issues and that these will continue to affect the child over time. As Dan Siegel (2012) says, 'experiences of terror and fear can be ingrained within the circuitry of the brain'. Parents need a new way of managing, and to be helped to adjust to having a different kind of family from the one they expected and wished for.

It is useful to bear these points in mind as you go through the process of transition, whether you are an adoptive parent, a foster parent, an agency or a social worker.

Steps in transition

Step 1: build familiarity

Remember that this is a process, not an event.

- Create a welcome pack for the child with your photos, photos of your home, things you like, any pets, garden, etc.
- Allow the child to build their trust in you. This is highly unlikely to be automatic, as their experience will necessarily be one where

adults are not trustworthy and are possibly very scary. Find ways to engage in play and activities with them, and try not to overwhelm them with your own excitement. Be gentle and calm.

- Talk to the child about anything and everything. Show them your interest in them and that they are important to you.
- Get as much background information as you can from previous foster parents, as well as background and history of the child from their social worker. It is unfortunately quite common for information to be withheld (presumably so that prospective families are not put off), but the more information you can get the better. A chronology of dates the child was taken into care (if applicable) and any further moves, major events, birthdays of birth family members and any information about trauma that is known to have happened (such as hospitalizations or known abuse) will help to predict times of year that may trigger a trauma memory for the child or give you an idea of why specific behaviours are emerging. This will be essential in developing strategies and maintaining stability.
- Take your time with introductions (where this is possible), gradually increasing the length of visits.
- Ask about favourite items – toys, food, games to play, TV programmes, activities.
- Is the child used to a routine? What is it? Follow the structure as closely as possible. It will be easier for your child if you fit around their needs for now. This will help them to feel more secure in their new home.
- Children enjoy sensory familiarity – what are their favourite tastes, smells (including smelly old blankets, toys, etc.)? Hold off on washing these items. Use the same detergents as the previous placement if possible. Get some menu ideas. What are their

favourite clothes? Do not be in a hurry to replace items; allow this to happen naturally as the child grows.

- Be consistent! Every house has different rules, so be patient – it is hard to adjust. Pick your battles wisely and give the child time to settle.
- Create a timetable so that the child knows what to expect and when. Many children find it easier to manage pictures than words, no matter what their age, so use pictures and have pictures of the time as well. Keep this simple, and stick to it. Remember that consistency, predictability and reliability are key to building a sense of security and being able to predict what is likely to happen next. Imagine how this can feel very secure and safe for a child who has experienced chaos. It is also likely to be very helpful for you to have this timetable so that you can start to frame a routine.
- Keep it simple. There is a lot for you all to remember. The first steps need to be baby ones – getting to know each other and trying to form connections. Your child does not need to be introduced to everyone all at once. As with a small baby, they need to start by being sure of their relationship with you, and gradually assimilate new members of the family and make new friends. Imagine how hard this is for the child who has lost their family, friends, school, community – everything that they thought was theirs. Maybe the only point of consistency for them is an old toy or blanket. You all need time and practice at how to manage this new situation.
- Keep activities low key and ensure that you are part of the activity. Walks in the park, playing catch or other ball games, joining in with their play – all of these things will be more beneficial than expensive and overwhelming outings.
- Be patient with the child and yourself – this is a time of massive adjustment.

THINK ABOUT IT...

Whatever the situation, the previous foster family or social services should have some ideas about familiar items for the child. Gather as much information as possible and try to maintain as much consistency as you are able to. Allow transitional objects to comfort the child, irrespective of their level of tattiness, smelliness, etc. These items (which may be toys, blankets or even clothes) may be the only stable thing in the child's scary and unpredictable life. Introduce changes gradually. The child does not have your concept of 'better' to enable them to understand or feel grateful for the things that are happening to them, and they may simply feel isolated and adrift in a strange place.

Step 2: routines and boundaries

Structure, boundaries and routine are part of the scaffolding which first starts to build our understanding of the world around us, and indeed lay the foundation for our cognitive and social capability. Sue Gerhardt (2004) reminds us that out of countless pathways forged by experience, only the pathways which are strengthened by repeated experience are maintained. Unused pathways are pruned away. This means that in the brain of the child who has 'good enough' attuned parenting, the strong connections of confidence in adults, being able to get needs met and feeling loved and important are retained. Where there has been deficient parenting, trauma or abuse, the brain retains patterns of how to respond to adults in ways which are possibly inappropriate and may be controlling, due to lack of predictability of care.

In the book *Therapeutic Parenting in a Nutshell* (Naish 2016) Sarah talks about the necessity of a routine in establishing an inflexible, safe and consistent framework within which the child can experience predictability and over time develop trust in what comes first and what happens next. In the case of children who have suffered neglect, for whatever reason this may well not have been a feature. The child may have been fed inconsistently, been cuddled, beaten or ignored in a confusing way, and may never have felt a sense of importance or belonging in their own home. I suggest some simple ideas to follow to reinforce a sense of belonging – personal place settings, cutlery and crockery, even table mats; having mealtimes and snack times that are absolutely fixed. (This last reminds me so strongly of my daughter, who had to have breakfast at 7, lunch at 12 and supper at 5 with additional snacks literally for years!) Always being seated in the same place, always having the same place in the car, perhaps with personal transitional items in those places – all these things create a sense of being seen, being important and having worth in the eyes of the parent.

I also advise keeping firm fixed boundaries around the child – these are not relaxed for 'special' occasions but are absolutely adhered to. The child will not be forbidden to do something today and allowed to do it tomorrow. The purpose of this is to create a very clear idea of expectations and safety, which enables the child to feel very safe and contained.

In many ways, in adopting this stance, we are recreating the firm routines that we adopt with a tiny baby, who is unable to self-regulate or to let us know what their needs are. This is intentional as we need to bridge the developmental gap that occurred alongside the trauma that was experienced.

Top tips

We need first to remember that our child or foster child, having grown up elsewhere, will not immediately know or understand our rules and boundaries. First, prioritize what are the most important things to you, and then work out which of them you can let go of – just for now.

- Where you need to correct a child – do it gently, explaining what the preferred behaviour is, rather than using disciplinary language such as 'Do not...' or 'Don't you dare...!', so we might instead say, 'In this house, we use kind words'; 'In this house we do not swear. I know this is all new to you – don't worry, we will keep practising together!'; 'I know there is a lot to remember. Don't worry, I will keep reminding you.'

- De-escalate – step back from unnecessary conflict. If you ask a child to brush their teeth and they refuse, don't make a battle of it. Just keep trying again the next day, and the next, and the next. Repetition builds brains, but arguments create huge divides. Parents get locked in an idea that they need to be in control (i.e. win battles) when sometimes you can make a different parental choice that recognizes your child's need on a more empathic level.

- Use empathy to help the child manage their feelings in disputes. This also names the need and lets the child know you can 'see' them and that they are important to you – 'I can see this is very hard for you...'; 'I can see you are very angry about this...'; 'It looks like you might be very scared...' At these times, quiet, calm 'time in' may work better than punitive measures or sanctions – this is because using time in regulates and calms. Punitive measures feed into the child's sense of failure and shame and cause escalations. Punitive measures work where children have a secure emotional bond which enables them to manage the shame and disappointment with help from their parents. They will also have experienced relationship bumps and will know that they are still loved even if a parent has been annoyed and shouted at them. This has not been the case with children from trauma – their expectation, which is often quoted by foster parents, is that if they do anything wrong they will be sent away.

- To help with routines, create a visual timetable to help them keep track. Encourage them to help choose activities, but build in plenty of rest and processing time, which should also be a time for you to remain quietly with the child so that they get used to your safe parental presence. Remember that it is hard for children to disengage from any activity they are fully engaged in. Remember to give your child a reminder when time is nearly up. For teens, give a broad structure with some more flexibility but be clear about times that you expect the child to be there.

- Use natural consequences – try not to rescue the child. If they will not wear their coat, they will get wet. If they are not getting ready for school, they will be late.
- Parents often say that their child will deliberately sabotage if they know the parents have to go somewhere by a certain time. This is a great way of maintaining your attention, and if it is angry attention that does not matter! Have a 'plan B', such as more flexible working hours. Employers have to consider requests for flexible working. Or if you have an appointment, leave ludicrous amounts of time – if you are early you can always get a quiet coffee or tea and have some 'me' time! This will help you to remain calm, which will mean that situations resolve more quickly.
- Avoid overwhelm – keep things simple, and introductions few and far between. Avoid huge welcoming parties.
- Be proud of your child, thank them, notice them doing things well or helping out and be specific about why you are feeling proud. 'Thank you for bringing the cutlery. That will help us all to be ready to eat more quickly!' Praise should be given for even very small things that you might think a child of that age 'should do'. Remember that these are likely to be new skills, and praise can be very connecting, helping a child to feel valued.
- Not all children are able to accept praise, as it may not agree with their internal working model of themselves. If this is the case, talk to someone else – a friend, a partner, the family dog or goldfish; be very specific: 'I was so proud of John today, he was so helpful and cleared up his plate after dinner.' The child will hear, and their brain will process, but they will not be worried by the intensity of the situation.
- Give them regular small chores to help them to feel they have responsibilities in the home. We only (unusually) do chores in our own homes, not other people's!

- Keep your boundaries and expectations developmentally appropriate. If your child has an emotional or cognitive age of six, then even if they are 15 they will only have the understanding and emotional capacity of a six-year-old, and this needs to be taken into account in your dealings with them.

Margot Sunderland (2007) says that lack of parental boundaries increases a child's insecurity, giving the idea that adults are not in control of the situation. The challenge according to Margot is to communicate clearly when behaviour is unacceptable in ways that do not shame or engage primitive systems of fear and rage. The way that this can be achieved is by being very matter of fact, by being clear about the unacceptable behaviour, *not* the unacceptable child (you can't change who you *are*, but you can change what you *do*).

Remember, we are creating a new environment for a child who has no trust in reliability or security from their experience. Think carefully about what your rules are, limit the number of rules to be remembered and keep them simple. For example, in our house we...

- stay safe
- have kind hands
- use kind words
- have fun!

Step 3: care plan and therapies

It seems evident that these items should be in place and, in the case of fostering, the agency should have information for matching purposes with the details of the child needing placement. However, it is worth having your own checklist unless (as can be the case for special guardians) you have close knowledge of the history – for example, due to proximity to the family.

- Is there ongoing medical care? Medications? Are there any medical conditions, and if so, what are they? Is there ongoing therapy that needs to be transferred to the new area?

- Schooling provision? This will need additional transition planning. School staff will need to have an understanding of the effects of trauma on the child and suitable approaches to take, and be prepared to fully cooperate with the family to ensure that the child has a successful experience.
- Is there a care package (grant, adoption allowance, professional involvement) which will be ongoing?
- Have any needs been identified for ongoing therapy? Has any assessment of the child's needs been undertaken?
- Are there any aids in use or which might be helpful? (For example, an alternative communication system for children with communication difficulties, visual timetable, weighted blanket, sensory jacket, sensory toys.)
- Is this child entitled to Disability Living Allowance for children? Are they on a disability register?

Step 4: settling in

- If possible, familiarize the child with their new home. Use photos or a video to create a virtual 'walk through' of your house. Include photos of any pets and a few of the people they may meet immediately, but keep the list very small.
- Take adoption leave, and do not immediately start school transition. Take some time to allow your child to settle in and for you to get to know them.
- Plan a transition into the new school, which is gradual and child focused.
- Manage your excitement; attend first to the child's need to settle and familiarize themselves – think baby!
- Be patient. This is all new to them (and to you).

- Don't be in a hurry to replace clothes, toys, etc. – let them tell you about their possessions. Let them help unpack – that way they can go at their own pace and tell you more about themselves, why things are important to them and what memories they have.
- Give the child a say in the colours and decoration of their room, bedding and so forth. Do not be tempted to decorate and fill the room with toys before they arrive.
- It may feel strange and overwhelming for you at first, dealing with a child 24/7. Remember they are also experiencing these same emotions. Forming a new relationship is a process; it takes time and patience.
- Have a structure in mind but be prepared to adapt it as you get to know and understand the needs of your child.

It may be useful to you to have some examples of narratives that you can use with your child. Sarah suggests the following for a dispute between siblings:

> I know it's hard for you when you hit your brother and I ask you what happened. I wonder if you're forgetting that I won't hurt you [hit you/reject you/leave you...whatever fears you think there might be from the past].

Later, at a calmer time:

> I know you want to do the right thing [not hit your brother/not get angry, etc.] but my guess is your birth family didn't help you to manage this. Guess what? This is something I can help you with. I know that we can work this out together. You might need some practice to get it right, so I will keep an eye on how you get on with your brother while we are practising. [The message is – I believe in you, I am here for you, change is possible.]

You could also try:

> I can see things are feeling really tricky. Remember, I am here to help you.
>
> It must be difficult being in a new family. Don't worry, I am here to help, and we will keep practising.
>
> I am sorry. This must be so hard for you.

Have a phrase connected with unconditional love and use it often. For example: 'I love you – no matter what' and 'I love you, to the moon and back!'

Step 5: build a support system

Think about your friends and family, and how they can help. Who can pop over for a chat and a coffee, or go out for a beer? Who might be able to babysit so that you can get a break? Do you have post-adoption support in place? Are you a member of an adoption or fostering group? It is essential to know how you will manage emotionally and to have this in place.

Unfortunately, many adopters have the experience that their expectations of support do not match the reality. To help avoid this situation, involve family and friends in appropriate information sharing about the issues facing parents of children with developmental trauma and the importance of therapeutic parenting, encourage them to attend preparation courses or other training, and provide them with relevant books or articles.

Step 6: application of main strategy

It will be easier for you and for the child if you maintain the attitude of PACE from the outset. Therapeutic and empathic parenting is necessary for the traumatized child, but also works for every other child!

Remember, PACE means creating an environment that is:

- playful
- accepting
- curious
- empathic.

For a more comprehensive explanation, see Chapter 2.

Step 7: create a transition plan

Use the template below to think about how you would create your own transition plan either for yourself or on behalf of a child or family.

Child's name and age					
Favourite things (e.g. snuggle toy, meal, smell)	Toys	Clothes	Sensory	Activities	Foods
Daily schedule (e.g. breakfast, medication, school, activity, rest, lunch, snack, tea)	Time	Activity			
History (e.g. hospitalization, abuse, reason for entering care)					
Chronology (date entered care, other significant dates such as date of care order, dates any further moves occurred)					

Significant dates (birthday, anniversary, parents or siblings' birthdays)	
Important people	
Contact arrangements	
Transition planning	
Information booklet given to child	
Transition point	Planned activity
Meeting no. 1 (date, time, place)	
Meeting no. 2 (date, time, place)	
Visit to family no. 1	
Visit to family no. 2	
Overnight visit no. 1	
Overnight visit no. 2	
Move	
First contact	

You should consider adding to this plan – for example, additional visits or overnight stays as seem appropriate for the individual child. You might also consider including a meeting with the previous family without the child present, follow-up appointments, contacts with extended family, etc. You need to be able to negotiate for a transition plan that will work for you, any family members (such as birth children) and the child or children that you are receiving into your home.

In the case of sibling groups, consider whether it is better to have a staged transition process or how you can meet their independent transition needs if they are all moving in at the same time. We will consider the specific difficulties of parenting sibling groups in Chapter 8.

Finally, below are some brief explanations of the three most commonly cited annoying behaviours and how to deal with them. For more specific advice and strategies, see Naish (2018).

Behaviour	Why?	What to do?
Nonsense chatter This survival technique ensures that the child is always visible to the parent. The fact that this is annoying is not important – it is essential for the child to keep the attention of the adult at all times.	There may be several underlying causes: • Fear that they may be forgotten or ignored – this is a direct survival risk from their earliest days as a result of neglect. Perhaps they were often left alone. • Secondly, nonsense chatter is a developmental stage, usually associated with acquisition of language, so appropriate to a child between ages around two and four years. It is vital for the child to feel heard and to explore language, and they are trying to expand their ideas, so they will ask many nonsensical questions or just have a constant babble. They will also be very easily upset by a disruption to their flow, especially from a sibling. Your child may still be showing these behaviours at a much older age as a result of developmental delay – where they did not have the benefit of appropriate learning and developmental opportunities, they seek to fill these gaps no matter what their chronological age is.	• This is mainly about patience and being able to accept that the child needs to do it; however, you can also use a playful technique giving nonsense answers, or you can acknowledge their need by saying, 'You have a lot of questions today! I think you have forgotten that I always care about you. Would you like a hug?' or 'I think you really need some Mummy/Daddy time. What would you like to do?' • Responding to the underlying need in this way enables the child's system to calm down. Invariably, you will have a better result sooner if you make time to allow for this one to one to take place rather than expect the child to manage to leave you alone and play independently. A few minutes of appropriate response is much more likely to earn you the five minutes break that you need! Remember Bryan Post's affection prescription – 10 minutes of focused attention in the morning, 20 minutes in the afternoon, 10 minutes before bed.

Lying Parents often get exasperated by the pointless and obvious lies told by their children – denying something that they have done even if they are caught in the act, or making up tall stories.	• There may be more than one reason for lying. First of all, the child who has low (or non-existent) self-esteem, and may furthermore have faced punishment out of all proportion to any misdeeds, will lie no matter how ridiculous the lie is. This is as a result of pervasive shame – not just being ashamed of this one thing, but feeling shame and worthlessness about every aspect of themselves. These children have never been able to separate what they do from who they are. The action proves their worthlessness. • Secondly, it is a developmental stage to try out ideas by stating them as truths – hence a little boy might aver that they are in fact Superboy, and go out to catch villains at night, or may indulge in fantasy about their birth family. The truth is too hard to manage.	• There are a few ways of dealing with this but *not* by engaging in a fruitless argument, insisting the child tells you the truth. The angrier and more frustrated you get, the more powerful and in charge they will feel. • State the reality without arguing the point. Do not respond to the fearful responses. Let them know you can see this is hard for them. 'I see you have eaten all the biscuits! You must have felt very hungry' (statement followed by naming the need). 'I see you have eaten all the biscuits I bought for tea time. That's a shame, because there will not be any more until I do next week's shopping' (statement followed by natural consequence). Or when they protest their innocence, 'I can see that this is very difficult for you. Remember that I will always help you to manage when things feel tricky, and I will just be in the kitchen if you want to talk' (empathy and reminder of support). • If you are dealing with a fantastic story, just acknowledge it as such – 'Wow, that is a great story. I wonder what it would have felt like if that had really happened?'

Stealing Many parents report children stealing, and this can be food, items belonging to other people or money. It may be from the parent, or from shops, or from school, or visitors, or family. Stealing causes huge distress to parents who are at a loss to manage and understand the behaviour.	• Stealing can come from many underlying issues of unmet needs; it is very complex. • Children may steal due to a developmental issue – not having had proper socialization or emotional support. They may (whatever their age) be at the operational age of a toddler, whose development naturally leads them to take any and all things in their exploration. This normally leads to being gently guided to understand the difference between what is theirs and what belongs to others, but this is not fully in place until around age four. In the example of the child here, it is a simple case of 'I want it, I will take it'. • Sometimes children may steal to fulfil an unmet need – or a need which they perceive is unmet. Hence they may steal sweets or food, or may steal money to buy items such as sweets and food, because many children have a sugar addiction, which is because they have learned to replace adult comfort and regulation which was unavailable with food or (as they get older) other addictive items such as tobacco, alcohol or drugs. They may steal money to buy friendships due to not having age-appropriate social skills. • Lastly, children may steal to gain a solid reminder of someone – taking an ornament from a friend's house. This will invariably be something that the person attaches importance to. It may be because of a desire to emulate.	• Dealing with this is tricky because parents believe they should be able to trust their children. A fair point, if that child had been born to you! However, for children who have suffered trauma and have developmental gaps, a big part of supporting them while they are learning is to remove the temptation. Keep money locked away. Do not leave change or purses lying about. You may even need to invest in a safe – just for now. Once your child has attained the developmental skills and trust in the relationship and understanding of their own needs, this will not be necessary any more. In the meantime, it is pointless to set them up to fail by expecting them to have impulse control and to know that what they are doing is wrong. In the moment, that knowledge will be secondary to the immediate gratification of their whim. • You may also need to warn friends to keep their bags with them, or even leave them in the car. You may need to provide everyone in the house with a lock for their door. It feels wrong, and as though it should not be necessary, but for children with trauma we have to take a different approach while we attend to their developmental and support needs.

5

Next Steps in Therapeutic Parenting

Addressing the Needs of Children with Exceptionally Challenging Behaviour

In this chapter we start to look at the additional skills, knowledge and strategies required for children with exceptionally challenging behaviours. These may include behaviours that we have already talked about.

The most challenging children are more relentless in their expression of their trauma: they can display perplexing and inappropriate behaviours that are in fact responses to their early-life experiences as a result of the way that these have affected their internal working model. To help children move past their trauma (which is the only way to resolve the behaviours), parents need to have incredible reserves of patience and be able to develop awareness of the many different factors which contribute to the additional challenges faced by both children and parents. We will be exploring the behaviours exhibited, the impact on the parents, and the strategies, models and interventions that can be employed to help, including why they are effective.

IN MY EXPERIENCE...

Having faced many challenges during my own re-parenting experience with my daughter, I am very well aware that one of the hardest things facing parents is the extraordinary resilience required to keep finding positivity and to re-frame experiences. To do this, parents need to be able to reflect and learn, adopt new ways of managing challenging situations, develop strategies that become a way of life, and maintain a consistent, reliable and predictable response. My knowledge of my own immediate family and other families that I have contact with is that giving parents a little bit of hope – some validation, empathy and celebration of small steps – is vital to the process. I would say to parents facing a day-to-day struggle that may be causing them to doubt their abilities to parent, feel as though they are worthless and that the struggle is meaningless – remember to reach out for help and support from people who understand and will not judge you.

It is clear that children have very individual responses to the trauma that they have suffered and that this is for a variety of reasons which have to do with genetic factors, in utero trauma, traumatic experience post birth, individual response, resilience and so forth. However, there are some issues that re-occur many times, such as developmental challenges. Many of our children display behaviours from a much younger age range, including some of the commonly experienced issues discussed in previous chapters such as crazy lying, arguing and stealing. Dan Siegel has this to say about the earliest human experiences:

> We begin life with just the experience of being an inseparable part of an undivided world in the womb. All of our bodily needs are met and 'just being' is a natural way. But once we're born we find life different, and hard. We are now little doings, not just beings. We need others, we rely on them for comfort, for our very survival...

> Attunement is not a luxury, it is a requirement of the individual to survive and to thrive. (Siegel 2007)

Siegel states that an interpersonal, attuned relationship enables us to feel 'grounded in the world' – our knowledge and understanding of adults, families, the community and ultimately the world plus our ability to have confidence in our approach to this environment depends on the earliest experiences which hardwire our brain to survive in the environment into which we are born. The disruption to self which occurs as a result of developmental trauma is extreme, begging the question: how can we rise to the task of therapeutically parenting these children?

Behavioural issues

What?	Why?
Destructive behaviours	• Child does not feel they deserve nice things • Child is trying not to hurt you so destroys things instead • Extreme anger (arising from fear) • Frustration • Inability to contain overwhelmingly large feelings and adrenalin surge
Violence	• Their early life experiences taught them that the bigger, stronger person wins • They are scared you cannot control them • They are scared of their feelings • They are overwhelmed and out of control: fight–flight response • Inability to understand or control feelings • Their earliest models included domestic violence
Self-harm	• Temporary relief • Control/safety • Peer pressure • 'Feels better' • Self-punishment • Low self-esteem • Poor self-image

Stealing	• 'I want it – I will take it' – no impulse control (like a small child) • Takes transitional object to remind them of the person • Had to steal to survive • Taught to steal • Peer pressure • Buying friends (sweets, alcohol) • Poor self-image
Lying	• Fear • Shame • Lying to protect (self or other) • Low developmental age • Poor self-esteem • Insecurity • Failing to believe relationship can withstand rupture

Advances in knowledge about neurological development enable us to understand better these behaviours and why they exist and persist. Therapeutic parenting can have a positive impact on challenging behaviours by addressing the causes, and we will now explore some of the models which can be helpful.

Empathic behaviour management

In her book *Why Can't My Child Behave?* Amber Elliott looks at behaviour management that is based on empathy – understanding the experiences that lead to the behaviours and the underlying feelings of the children, enabling them to feel that they are truly understood, perhaps for the first time. This enables us to find ways to increase self- knowledge and emotional literacy in the child by joining them in an empathic sense in their emotional experiences. Dr Elliott examines the reasons why behavioural strategies such as reward charts are unsuitable for children who do not have a secure foundation to manage their internal emotional state. She describes ways to manage this using an 'emotional commentary' and gives examples of narratives which help the child to make sense of their feelings and contain them. The carer is encouraged to use their knowledge and understanding of the child's history to enable them to create a different meaning for these events which is supportive and acknowledging of the child's pain. The adult is encouraged to re-frame some of the most common challenging behaviours and see these as 'attachment seeking' or 'attention needing' rather than 'attention seeking'.

Providing a narrative

We believe that this is a way to underline the re-framing messages we send to our children and help them to benefit. The narratives mimic the way that we give information to and interact with babies and small children, especially when they are pre-verbal.

Whilst children are still in their first stages of life, we intuitively know that they are operating at a physical and sensory level, so we automatically fill in the gaps for them by providing a constant narrative, whether it is discussing with a baby whether they need feeding and reassuring them about each step you take, or teaching a child about appropriate clothes by reminding them to get their wellies on because it is raining. Given at the appropriate time and in the appropriate way, this is assimilated easily in the context of a loving and stable relationship.

Because our children may well have missed some (or all) of this educational narrative, we believe that we give our children useful psychological information about their emotional and other states if we give them a narrative. To put the cherry on top, if we then let them know that we have observed this in them, we also underline our parental presence and give implicit information that we care for them and are observant of their needs. This is powerful stuff, indeed! Sometimes this is also referred to as 'shining a light' on the child. It is important also to include the extra message that you have 'seen' your child – they are important and visible to you, you think about them, you 'hold them in mind' when they are not with you. You are mindful of their emotional states.

So instead of 'Dinner time!' you might say, 'I can see you are hungry now. Good thing that dinner is nearly ready!' 'You look to me as though you could do with a hug! Is everything all right?' 'I am really happy to see you looking so happy!' The implicit message is:

- I can 'see' you.
- You are important to me.
- I understand your feelings.
- I accept you whatever mood you are in.

The crucial elements of a narrative are:

- Think toddler. Most parents report their children as having a lower developmental than chronological age and that this is exacerbated when the child is upset and anxious – often perceived as anger and fury.
- Give clear messages in which the child is not expected to manage on their own – it is clear that you will be helping them; for example, one of Sarah's is: 'I want to help you with those big feelings.'
- Be clear about safety – 'I think everything feels very difficult today. Don't worry, I will always keep you safe.'
- Give information about feelings – 'You must be hungry after all that playing! Let's get a snack.' 'I think it makes you very worried when you feel hungry. Don't worry – remember, we always have snacks as well as meals!'
- Avoid being pulled into anxiety-based dialogues, such as the following very common example. The child was scared of going to bed, so the parent always checked under the bed. The child immediately developed a second fear – was there something in the cupboard? So the parent checked this too, every evening. The child developed another issue and eventually the parent had a checklist of things to reassure the child about. But the child still did not feel safe because the underlying issue had not been addressed (which was probably fear of night times and what might happen if you fell asleep). The best thing to do would have been to throw away the checklist and meet every issue with the same narrative: 'I know it's

> hard for you and scary to go to bed and go to sleep. Don't worry, because I will always keep you safe.' No matter what the child then throws at you, the response is: 'Remember, I am your mum/dad, and I will always keep you safe.'

It is useful to reflect with children after events. Here are some examples Sarah finds useful, which all show the willingness of the parent to stand with the child, support them, and be on their side:

> I know it's difficult for you to sort out these mixed-up feelings and I'm here to help. It's my job to help you sort your muddles out, so let's give it a go.
>
> If you're not in control then you feel really bad. That makes sense. You've had to be in control for such a long time.
>
> I think you don't like it when I ask you to do something because you feel bad if you don't have control. I expect it feels as if I'm just being mean, but I promise it is because I care about you.
>
> No wonder you want to take charge...back when you were at home you had to be to make sure you were safe. I am so sorry that me making decisions for you feels so horrible. I think it's because grown-ups didn't make kind decisions for you in the past, but we are going to stick to what I have said. I'm sorry.

Support and advice

This is essential to maintaining the stability of families facing challenging behaviours from their children, as otherwise parents can become burned out and unable to continue (see Chapter 6). Families should look for supportive organizations such as the example below.

The NAoTP (National Association of Therapeutic Parents) enables all families to access support and training to be able to make change and stabilize families. The NAoTP is different because:

- we include all families

- we recognize that each situation and child is unique
- we provide webinars, resources and counselling to enable parents to better understand the children and change their strategies
- we work with the whole family
- we provide different levels of support to prevent isolation and to enable parents to share experiences and strategies
- we can provide low-cost training through our partnership with Inspire Group.

(Jane Mitchell, July 2020)

Transitions and changes

Transitions of any kind can induce extreme anxiety in children, especially if they involve moving from one environment to another, and if there are changes to be accommodated to the usual routine such as happen during school holidays, if we make trips away from home, or if there are visits from social workers. When a child is really anxious, even asking them to stop an activity due to a planned event can be hard, requiring time to process and accommodate. If your child is experiencing difficulties, try the following.

Draw up a timetable of your child's activities through the week, including outings, school, clubs, visits, etc. Then reflect on the following:

- How many transitions is your child coping with per week – home/school, school/home, school/club, etc.?
- Have you noticed any issues? Not wanting to get out of bed/into the car? Meltdowns shortly after coming out of school?
- Are there specific areas of your child's history that may make even small transitions very hard?
- Can you think of ways to notice the difficulties your child is experiencing? For example, 'I know it is very hard to stop doing

something that you are enjoying. You need to try and finish up now so that we can get ready to... I will remind you again in a moment.'

- Can you think of ways to help your child manage their transitions? For example, use a visual timetable, have a timer to let them know when an activity needs to finish, give them reminders? It is important to be sure the child can hear you by gently drawing their attention to you, perhaps by sitting down with them and placing a hand gently on their arm?

Remember that for a brain to accommodate learning, there needs to be co-regulation, stimulation, responsiveness, communication and time to process. Children who are trying to process new information need repetition, support to reflect, and support to manage quiet restful times to enable the new neurological pathways to establish.

Developmental awareness – a key concept to bear in mind

One of the things we encounter time and again when delivering training, whether to parents or professionals, is the importance of emphasizing the necessity of meeting the child at their stage of development, whatever their chronological age. Although this has been proposed as the best approach to individual assessment and planning, and the concept of the 'unique child' was central to the development of the Early Years Foundation Stage (an English pedagogy which sets out developmental stages and 'next steps' for education in the early years), this still seems to present a challenge. In addition, the approach is complicated by the fact that a child can be at a different developmental stage in each of three main developmental areas – physical, cognitive and social/emotional.

Developmental milestones

Arnold Gesell (1880–1961) developed his theory of biological maturation in the 1940s. According to Gesell, human development in all areas

– physical, cognitive and emotional/social – is predetermined by the genetic blueprint which is the result of the combined genetic background of the parents. Gesell believed in 'maturation patterns' which occur in predictable sequences. This being the case, it was possible to construct a timeline for human development. These guides could then be used as a benchmark against which to assess the development of any individual. For the first time there was a benchmark which allowed any developmental issues to be identified and followed up, and appropriate support given.

Factors which influence development

It comes as no surprise that there are many factors which influence how children develop. If we break this down, then we can look more closely at the reasons for the variations we see in individual children.

Environment

We are better placed than ever to begin to understand the impact of the environment on the developing child, as our understanding of and research into neurodevelopment grows and develops, posing new questions even as original queries are answered.

Maslow's hierarchy of needs suggests that a child's environment needs to be able to provide for physiological, safety and belonging needs (these levels of the hierarchy are also known as deficiency needs) in order for the individual to achieve their individual potential. Observations tell us it is not enough for needs to be met, they must be perceived and understood as being met by the individual for progress to be made. In other words, moving a child from a harmful home and placing them in a safe and secure home where their needs will be met means that as adults we know those deficiency needs are met, improving outcomes for the child. However, for the traumatized child, it is likely to take time, patience and repeated experience before they are able to move on from their sense of danger – their development may be delayed or arrested. Their initial reaction to the move may be fear and anger, which may be heightened by the strangeness of their surroundings, and overwhelming feelings of isolation, rejection and shame.

In 1979 Urie Bronfenbrenner published *The Ecology of Human Development*, whereby the development of an individual is placed at the centre of external influences, from family and friends to community and school, country and global influences. We now know that environmental influences can literally change the way our genes are expressed, with clear implications for health and medical issues, including mental health. For instance, children whose mothers were exposed to chronic and severe stress during their pregnancy have been shown to have a higher incidence of psychological and behavioural disorders. This is linked to the toxic effect of stress hormones, and it has been proven that these children are likely to have higher than average levels of stress hormones produced as well as higher than average numbers of stress hormone receptors. The result is a child who is easily stressed and fearful of change or transitions.

Neurological development

Richard Bowlby states that 'neuroscientists are discovering that they cannot explain the rapid neurological developments in the brain of a child without reference to the interaction between the baby and his/her environment'.

When a child feels safe, secure and loved (deficiency needs met according to Maslow), then their exploration systems are switched on and they are eager for new experiences and stimuli, which give them further information to support their cognitive development.

Where there has been a positive attachment experience, needs are perceived as being met by the individual (for an infant, this is a sensory state of comfort or discomfort), they are confident in the provision of physiological and safety needs and they have been able to engage in a loving reciprocal relationship that has enabled them to build an expectation based on the primary emotion of love. They have a core knowledge that their needs will be met, enabling them to be resilient and tolerant if they are occasionally hungry, cold, upset, have an argument, etc. They are able to manage social interactions and make connections readily. Their experience of the world as accommodating means that they can take risks, are able to bear the disappointment of being wrong and can explore different experiences with confidence. They will be able to better manage impulsivity as a result of their needs being appropriately met, and the secure unchanging nature and routine of their life gives a grounding for well-developed executive function. These individuals will be able to embrace a challenge whether this is academic, physical or emotional.

Where there has been an insufficient, absent or disengaged attachment or other developmental trauma, the individual will be focused on getting survival needs met. This focus is driven by the primary emotion of fear. The stress created by this existence will also disrupt the healthy development of the brain. This individual may filter most of their experience via fear of being able to survive in this hostile environment. It may be hard to connect and engage with others. The individual may well have issues with their self-esteem as well as finding it hard to trust or maintain a positive outlook. In this case the executive function (higher brain activity controlling impulsivity, enabling analytical thought, mediating responses, enabling capacity to be organized and to plan) is largely shut down, or dependent on information that will feed into adaptive responses based on fear and presenting possibly as anger or withdrawal that will reinforce the fearful outlook of the individual. Resilience, trust and hope may well be alien emotions. This individual is likely to be resistant to and fearful of change.

Cognitive development

There are many learning theories, but it was Jean Piaget (1896–1980) who proposed a timeline of developing cognitive function:

- *Sensorimotor* (birth–2 years): The child differentiates self from objects; achieves object permanence: realizes that things continue to exist even when no longer present to the senses.
- *Pre-operational* (2–7 years): Learns to use language and to represent objects by images and words.
- *Concrete operational* (7–11 years): Can think logically about objects and events.

- *Formal operational* (11 years and up): Can think logically about abstract propositions and test hypotheses systematically.

The problem with this theory is that these learning milestones do not necessarily occur at the age indicated as the 'norm' but depend on the pattern of the child's developmental process from conception to birth and through early experiences. Trauma, whether this is a result of early attachment history, illness, maternal substance abuse, a genetic condition or medication, affects this process with results that are entirely individual.

Furthermore, our sense of how mature an individual is, and therefore our expectations of them, is determined by size and level of physical development, not by observation of behaviour. Therefore a mature individual with a severe learning difficulty can appear to be very threatening and scary if they are trailing after their parents in a supermarket, yelling and calling for them because they are bored and want to go home, behaving like a three-year-old (level of cognitive development) even though they may be a fully grown adult (level of physical development). For this reason it is useful to consider the stages without the relevant ages:

- *Sensorimotor*: This is the stage when attachment occurs in the presence of a relationship with an attuned primary carer. Learning is sensory, as the infant has no language to express ideas, thoughts or feelings and expresses their needs or mood by the limited means available to them. Attachment is a sensory process, and at the same time the infant is developing a cognitive blueprint to understand and adapt to the environment that they are born into. In addition, the positive attachment process provides a mirror for the child to understand themselves by the responses of the primary carer and gives building blocks of consistency, pattern, trust and resilience. The negative attachment process gives a distorted view for the child to understand themselves, their importance and their impact on the world. At this time, the building blocks of psychological, physical, emotional and cognitive development are constructed based on the immediacy of the infant's needs and whether they are responded to, which in turn depends on their environment and caregivers.

- *Pre-operational*: At this stage children's learning is still a highly visual process – they believe what they can see. They have difficulty holding ideas in mind and cannot visualize something they have not seen. Imaginary play and role play will be based on observed events or TV characters. Children at this stage will still place themselves at the centre of any action – they are egocentric, and only relate to their own feelings. Their sense of their impact on the world is such that they believe everyone will share their feelings and opinions, and because they are emotionally and cognitively immature, they may assume that they are responsible for any trauma which occurs.

  Children at this stage will often tell the most incredible stories and this is a normal developmental stage for a four-year-old. As a general rule the pre-cognitive child is still also operating from a mainly emotional (limbic brain system) base, so if they are caught out in unwanted behaviour, they will in their panic tell a crazy lie. This is not naughty or manipulative, it is just panic – fear of consequences, fear of rejection. Very many adoptive parents complain of exactly these two issues – crazy lies and incredible stories. One of the problems is that when an older child is doing this, because they are at the wrong developmental stage, adults think they must be telling the truth (or if it is an obvious story, that they are being manipulative).

  Fact and fiction can be very blurred for children at this stage. Pre-cognitive learning is a visual and practical process, and you believe what you see in a very literal sense. This can have repercussions. For example, having watched her favourite Disney film, my daughter said to me how she likes Labrador puppies because they can talk! I agreed with her before gently saying to her that she did know that they cannot really talk, didn't she? 'Oh yes,' she said. Then she added: 'But those ones can!' Now we have dogs, walk dogs and frequently come into contact with dogs; however, because the Labrador puppies 'talked' on film, she believed that as truth. Her logical thinking function had not yet developed at nine years old, and she had no concept of the mechanisms of filming and camera tricks.

- *Concrete operations*: This occurs when the individual is able to keep ideas 'in mind' and has good use of symbology (numerals and language – both spoken and written), requiring less practical learning. The individual has had more extensive experiences which have further developed and extended their cognitive ability, and made basic logic achievable – at this stage individuals might be expected to predict outcomes and design ways to test their ideas. Logic will be applied to objects and events within the scope of their experience. This stage of cognitive development is governed by the 'rationalizing' prefrontal cortex.
- *Formal operations*: The individual is able to use their experiences and manipulate information in an analytical and hypothetical way. This is the final stage. However, we continue to be able to live and learn, take on new experiences and new ideas and fit them into our existing perceptions. We are able to change our minds and to see from others' perspectives.

In order for us to develop cognition, the correct developmental tasks need to be accomplished. As in the hierarchy of needs, the foundation must be secure before we can move on to the next stage, and not all individuals will reach the same levels in the same sequence. In addition, development may exceed the norm in some areas, giving rise to specialist skills and vocations. You cannot build a wall from the top down; likewise, the strength of our developmental walls depend upon their foundation and construction. In some cases there may be fundamental damage due to illness, medicines such as Thalidomide, toxicity in utero or genetic malfunction. In others developmental trauma may occur as a result of early abuse and neglect.

We can think of cognitive development as a wall, where each course builds upon the previous one. In this model, the bottom course of bricks can be viewed as the elements of the secure base proposed by Bowlby – the foundation of the child's development in all areas. If some of the foundation is removed, we get a different picture, and the resulting structure is not able to develop – there are too many gaps.

From our observation and experiences of working with children and from conversations with many parents, children seek to rebuild their walls – they may actively seek the activity that they need in order to progress, and this may not be age appropriate. Similarly, children may display behaviours which are confusing – again it may be useful to look again at the behaviour in order to get an idea of the developmental stage of the child.

A very useful tool when considering different aspects of child development for children exhibiting younger behaviour patterns is the Early Years Foundation Stage.

If we want to help our children progress, we first need to establish what stage they are at emotionally, socially and cognitively or whichever of these areas takes priority. When teaching a child new skills it is useful to remember that, with very young children, we always give simple, clear instructions, we demonstrate, we encourage, we praise, we let the child find their own pace. With older children we expect them to have the experience to understand an instruction and get on with it. Try taking a step back to build practical skills and confidence in learning.

Active modelling

Parents know instinctively that their children learn from their everyday activities – that is why we have play areas for make believe and to practise those observed skills: mechanics tool benches, small-scale kitchens, baby dolls and prams, etc. Today we know that we have brain cells called 'mirror neurones'. Perry (2008) states that mirror neurones are 'a special class of brain cells that fire not only when an individual performs an action, but also when the individual observes someone else make the same movement'. In other words, watching an action allows our bodies to understand the mechanics of that action so that we can imitate. This is an important learning tool. We assimilate and learn behaviours appropriate to our environment by observation. This can be further embedded by giving a simple language narrative to explain – 'I am cold, so I think I will put my coat on.' 'I feel thirsty, do you? Shall we have a drink?' In this way, you give a name to the feeling and a strategy for managing that feeling. At the same time, your mirror neurones and your child's are engaging, allowing the child's body to experience and understand the feeling and the action.

Key points

There are key points that we need to have in mind when therapeutically parenting children who have suffered from developmental trauma:

- Development follows consistent sequences. We can use the analogy of building a house: foundation first (secure base), then walls from ground up (simple concepts need to be in place before complex ideas can develop) and finally the roof goes on (complex, hypothetical, analytical and abstract thought processes of an adult). You would not try to put a roof on a building without walls; likewise key stages may need to be revisited, especially in emotional and social areas. In this respect, it is necessary to be able to respond to the developmental and not the chronological age of the child, and provide structured support which scaffolds learning to fill the developmental gap.
- Early attuned relationships and a 'good enough' environment are key developmental issues. Your routines, structures and boundaries will help to develop a sense of the world that is secure and predictable, as your consistent responses will build security in your relationship. However, this will take time and patience – the

child has developed a very different architecture in their brain, and it is hard to develop and strengthen the new ideas. Exactly how long is of course dependent on independent factors such as individual capacity and resilience as well as the degree of trauma experienced – but the good news is that over time you definitely do see the changes.

- Although developmental milestones have been established, developmental trauma may delay or arrest development in key areas. The result will be a young person who does not respond in an age-appropriate manner but in a developmentally appropriate one. Very often we need to think toddler – or at least observe the young person and respond to the age that they are acting rather than the age they have achieved.
- Neurological development follows a sensory–emotional–reasoning pattern which mimics the three areas of the triune brain. It is important to place therapeutic interventions appropriately within the attachment cycle. In the attachment cycle, as we have seen, there is first an uncomfortable feeling, responded to with regulation, then a narrative and meeting the need. In other words, the child expresses a need (probably in an inappropriate way). The adult notices, calms the child, names the need, offers support and comfort and regulation, then fulfils the need. The child processes this experience. Over time this new sequence is repeated very many times and becomes dominant.
- Cognitive development also depends on early experience – literacy builds on communications, numeracy builds on structure and predictability. There are also developmental tasks such as object permanence, which is when a child first realizes that an object that is hidden or in a different place still exists. We usually help accommodate this learning (without even knowing it!) by simple games of peek-a-boo and hide and seek. Some of our children

need help to play developmental games and go back to the basics of education.

- Early experience of trauma can affect the individual perception of the here and now – for some of our children, memory is held in the body and is both immediate and sensory. When a sensation triggers an implicit memory, it is exactly as though the child is having an identical experience, and the same fear will result. After the event (which may well be an aggressive one) they may not remember at all what has just happened.
- The human brain is an astonishing thing: it really is never too late to learn, it may just take more time, effort, practice and support. In some cases, developmental trauma restricts the ability of the child, but each and every one of them should be appropriately challenged to achieve their individual potential.

The table below illustrates the very low developmental stage of some of the most traumatized children – I have added a final column suggesting reasons why this may or may not be achieved. It is important to note the age range at which these skills are acquired within an attuned relationship, and then think about how our looked after children compare:

Managing feelings and behaviour

AGE	Expected behaviour – secure attachment (DfE 2013, pp.16–17)	Possible result of lack of early attuned relationship (Jane Mitchell 2017)
Birth to 11 months	• Is comforted by touch and people's faces and voices • Seeks physical and emotional comfort by snuggling into trusted adults • Calms from being upset when held, rocked, spoken or sung to with soothing voice • Shows a range of emotions such as pleasure, fear and excitement • Reacts emotionally to other people's emotions, e.g. smiles when smiled at and becomes distressed if hears another child crying	• Scared of touch • Unable to gain comfort from adults due to trauma • Lack of attuned relationship prevents effective soothing • Reduced emotional range • May misread other people's emotions
8 to 20 months	• Uses familiar adult to share feelings such as excitement or pleasure, and for 'emotional refuelling' when feeling tired, stressed or frustrated • Growing ability to soothe themselves, and may like to use a comfort object • Cooperates with caregiving experiences, e.g. dressing • Beginning to understand 'yes', 'no' and some boundaries	• Does not expect to be 'met' and understood in their feelings • May not understand own emotional state • Seeks physical discharge of emotions that are too big • Survival patterns of behaviour persist • May refuse care – controlling • May be oppositional

6 to 26 months	• Is aware of others' feelings, e.g. looks concerned if hears crying or looks excited if hears a familiar happy voice • Growing sense of will and determination may result in feelings of anger and frustration which are difficult to handle, e.g. may have tantrums • Responds to a few appropriate boundaries, with encouragement and support • Begins to learn that some things are theirs, some things are shared, and some things belong to other people	• Unaware of others' feelings • Anger and frustration results in tantrums which persist into later years • Boundaries can represent safety • Understanding of possession of objects only in so far as everything is 'mine' or 'I want' with no impulse control, i.e. younger developmental stage
22 to 36 months	• Seeks comfort from familiar adults when needed • Can express their own feelings such as sad, happy, cross, scared, worried • Responds to the feelings and wishes of others • Aware that some actions can hurt or harm others • Tries to help or give comfort when others are distressed • Shows understanding and cooperates with some boundaries and routines • Can inhibit own actions/behaviours, e.g. stop themselves from doing something they shouldn't do. • Growing ability to distract self when upset, e.g. by engaging in a new play activity	• Adults are a source of fear, not comfort • Unable to name own feelings • Unable to recognize feelings of others, or misinterprets • Still lashes out without thinking • May not have developed empathic skills • May find distress extremely threatening and frightening – may be a retraumatizing trigger • Finds safety and security in boundaries and routines. May, however, refuse to follow instructions • Poor or absent impulse control • Unable to distract self without considerable support and understanding

30 to 50 months	• Aware of own feelings and knows that some actions and words can hurt others' feelings • Begins to accept the needs of others and can take turns and share resources, sometimes with support from others • Can usually tolerate delay when needs are not immediately met and understands wishes may not always be met • Can usually adapt behaviour to different events, social situations and changes in routine	• Has difficulty or unable to name feelings • Finds needs of others difficult – strongly egocentric. Can share and take turns with support • Can find changes to routine and delay extremely hard. Needs are immediate and experienced in a very physical way • Difficulty or inability to respond appropriately to different social situations • Transitions and last-minute changes present extreme challenges
40 to 60+ months	• Understands that own actions affect other people, e.g. becomes upset or tries to comfort another child when they realize they have upset them • Aware of the boundaries set, and of behavioural expectations in the setting • Beginning to be able to negotiate and solve problems without aggression, e.g. when someone has taken their toy	• May apologize but cause and effect are difficult concepts. Expects everyone to be able to move on and forget • Difficulties in generalizing from the particular and managing social change • Frustration and overwhelm will often lead to aggression and violence

Columns one and two in the table above are reproduced from DfE (2013) Early Years Outcomes: A Non-Statutory Guide for Practitioners and Inspectors to Help Inform Understanding of Child Development through the Early Years. London: DfE under the Open Government Licence v2.0 (www.nationalarchives.gov.uk/doc/open-government-licence/version/2)

Interventions

To complete this chapter, here are some ideas about additional therapeutic tools which may be useful. Whether you are a therapeutic parent yourself, or a professional working alongside a family, it is useful to have knowledge of as many therapeutic tools as possible in order to manage the changing needs and abilities of children with developmental trauma. These are some of the best-known approaches.

Brain-based parenting

This model, espoused by Dan Hughes and Dan Siegel among others, is based on a mindful model which can transform the experience of parenting, enabling parents to gain deeper understanding of themselves and to engage in conscious rather than emotional parenting. This model has been shown in therapeutic situations to help resolve issues of compassion fatigue and enable the carer to move back to a fulfilling relationship with their child or children. This is achieved through reflection, empathy and support.

In *Brain-Based Parenting* (2012) Hughes and Baylin explain first what is meant by good parenting from the perspective of facilitating the development of the child's brain:

- Being sensitive and emotionally responsive
- Providing effective comfort when the child is distressed
- Being a good first companion and role model
- Facilitating appropriate risk-taking and challenge
- Practising self-regulation.

This reminds us of the cycle of healthy attachment, which we can then expand (see Figure 5.1).

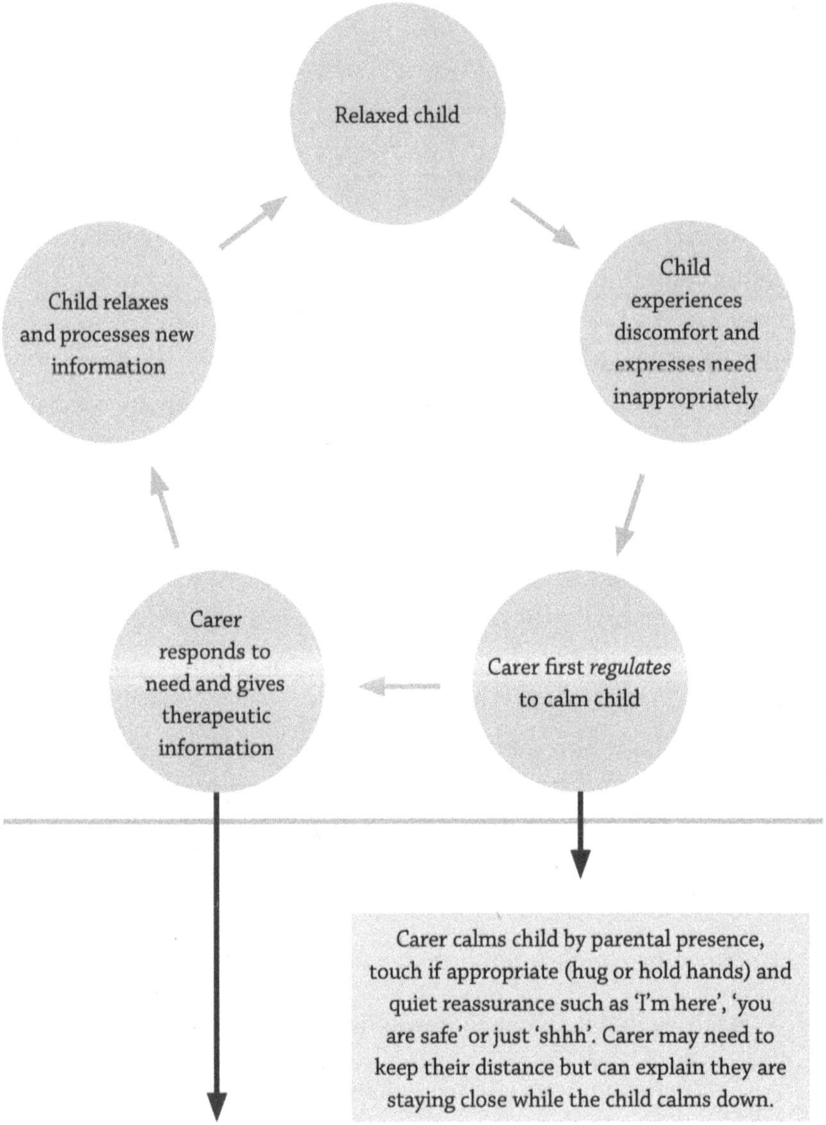

Figure 5.1 Expanded cycle of attachment

Therapeutic information (as appropriate)

Therapeutic information allows the child to reflect on and make sense of their own feelings, making links to their history and enabling them to seek appropriate support from a trusted adult as a result of the good parenting ideals given above:

Name to tame: give the child information about how you think they are feeling.

- *Curiosity*: wonder out loud why the child feels the particular emotion, such as 'I wonder if you feel scared to be alone at night because...[you were left on your own as a baby]'
- *Reassure*: 'I am here to help you with your big feelings and...[I will never leave you alone]'
- *Be available*: ask the child if they want to talk, and let them know you will be available when they are ready
- *Be empathic*: reflect back to the child how you understand the difficulty of the feeling they are having. For instance, 'I can see you are really struggling with this' or 'I can see you are feeling very wobbly at the moment'. This helps the child to feel understood in the moment.

Strike while the iron is cold: when the child is reconnected, they will be able to reflect and consider events, including what they could have done differently with the carer. Over time, the ability to put a pause between an event and their action will increase, if this is supported and validated by the carer.

TRUE – Therapeutic Re-parenting Underpinned by Empathy/experience

Sarah developed and implemented this model as manager of a fostering agency.

TRUE stands for:

- *T*herapeutic
- *R*e-parenting
- *U*nderpinned by
- *E*mpathy/experience.

Key principles

The family needs to have easy access to a supporter who fully understands their task. This could be:

- *Attachment worker/therapeutic lead*: a specialist in attachment with direct personal experience of living with children who have attachment difficulties as well as knowledge and understanding of therapeutic parenting. This person must be able to recognize and manage the family if parents are showing signs of compassion fatigue. This supporter should also have access to supervision.
- *Child support worker*: should have a long-standing relationship with the child and commit to regular meetings with the child. This relationship would be able to endure disruptions and remain consistent. This person should have an excellent working knowledge of therapeutic parenting techniques, developmental effects of early trauma and alternative models such as PACE (see Chapter 2).
- *Supervising social worker*: responsible for statutory tasks and obligations being met and with additional areas of expertise to enable them to understand and empathize with the specific challenges which are likely to occur when therapeutically re-parenting a child who has suffered developmental trauma.
- *Empathic listener*: a safe place for the parent or parents to explore their issues, successes, failures or frustrations with no fear of judgement. The empathic listener may also have a role to explore underlying causes of behaviour and assist in developing strategies.

The TRUE model relies on excellent communication between all parties. It seeks to engage professionals and align them with the parents. It implements joined-up therapeutic parenting support for the child and is compatible with other therapeutic parenting strategies such as PACE.

The Great Behavior Breakdown

This is a trust- and relationship-based intervention developed by Bryan

Post, author of two books which describe a way of managing extreme behaviours in a non-judgemental and non-blaming way – *Beyond Consequences, Logic and Control* (Forbes and Post 2014) and *The Great Behavior Breakdown* (Post 2009). Bryan puts his beliefs into practice every day within his own family and by taking extremely challenged young people into his programme. He proposes this challenge:

> This is the Great Behavior Breakdown Challenge. If you implement the information you read in this book for just two weeks, I guarantee a 50% dramatic reduction, if not elimination of your child's behavior. If you implement the information for 30 days or more, the results will be dramatic.

Key concepts

'Take on a new perspective' (Forbes and Post 2006)

Bryan and Heather ask us to review our position from one where the child has full responsibility for the change that the parents desire and instead examine our own responses and why we are finding parenting to be so hard. Throughout the book, they describe both the 'Traditional View' and the 'New View' inviting us to look again at situations through the lens of our knowledge of trauma.

'The Stress Model – the four principles' (pp.2–26)

1. All adverse behaviours arise from a stress reaction which is based on fear. It is by addressing the fear that we achieve changes in behaviour.

2. 'The two primary emotions are love and fear.' (p.9)

   This can come as a surprise to those who believe that anger is a base emotion – however trauma and stress leads to the fight flight response, leads to a presentation of anger, or rage.

3. 'There is both Positive and Negative Repetitious Conditioning' (p.18)

   This means that each of us, child or parent, has preconditioned responses and behavioural patterns. In order to help the child to trust and believe we also need to look at the root causes of our own responses and make the necessary changes.

4. 'Negative and positive neurophysiologic feedback loops exit beyond our conscious awareness. They occur at an unconscious physiologic level and we have the ability to change or add to these feedback loops.' (p.20)

   Forbes and Post explain this as how we can feel that we need to control and this can lead us to be directive and confrontational, escalating the situation. By choosing a different way of managing the situation we can affect the outcome.

Four levels of memory

Forbes and Post (p.5) discuss the four levels of memory:

Mental – cognitive, autobiographical, accessible to recall – facts, dates, names, etc.

Emotional – the feelings associated with a situation or person or place. Easily triggered by sensory stimuli – the smell of your mother's perfume, the sound and sight of a familiar place, are evocative of both the times you have experienced the same smell or view; and also the associated emotion whether this is fearful or joyous in character. Emotional memory is much more strongly linked to very significant events such as your wedding day, or the day you first walked into your own house.

Motor – like muscle memory – largely unconscious. You do not think about walking, you just do it. You only need to put effort in to learn the new skill, then it is quickly reactivated at need. For example, the first time you undertake a journey you may need a map or GPS. After a time or two it is familiar, after a few times you have recall.

State – intimately linked with your mammalian and reptilian brain, this will process stimuli and immediately initiate a fight flight response if a survival threat is detected. For children who have had trauma, this may be a simple as feeling hungry, cold or alone.

Many parents and professionals have difficulty with an intervention which is not directly punitive, thinking that children are 'getting away with' unacceptable behaviours. This intervention, however, prevents overwhelm, encourages reflection and allows the child to make a different choice – encouraging responsibility for our own actions instead of shame and blame. The question we need to ask ourselves is, do we want our children to do the acceptable thing because they are terrified, or because they know it to be a right and good choice? And how are we going to scaffold the learning process to enable the child to build a brain that is able to do this? The ability to manage this is at the heart of effective therapeutic parenting.

Parental presence

This is one of the most important tools we have, allowing for many different levels of healing to take place alongside a whole host of implicit messages which help to develop strong foundations as our children assimilate new ideas from simple, consistent interactions.

Aspect 1: 'being there'

It is really easy to underestimate the power of our calm, empathic, physical presence. No words are required as children assimilate knowledge on a sensory level – sometimes words get in the way. Simple physical presence can convey a world of meaning to a child who does not have trust in adults. If a child is overwhelmed, your calm presence can calm them down. If a child is unhappy, your empathic presence (including appropriate physical contact, if the child will accept it) will reassure them. If a child feels worthless, then spending time with them lets them know you are important to them. As a therapeutic parent, we can use our body language, facial expressions and proximity to convey emotional messages of acceptance, love, empathy, calm and reassurance. This is the essence of co-regulation – words should be kept to a minimum. During the attachment cycle, when a baby has a need the first job of the adult is to regulate the baby's emotional state, and this is what we still need to do for our challenging children. This allows movement into meeting the need and the child begins to experience:

- being important to the adult
- that adults can help
- themselves as worthy
- themselves as cared for
- developing trust
- containment
- acceptance.

Don't forget – repetition builds brains. This is a healing strategy for the long haul! Remember also that you must be in a calm and receptive state to be able to use this approach, otherwise the result may be an experience of escalation and further experience of shame.

Aspect 2: keeping the child 'in mind'

Many of our children have issues with separation and show behaviour generally exhibited by younger children: clinging, shadowing their carer, standing and yelling for their carer repetitively, following you into the toilet, stealing personal items from significant people – to name just a few. We always need to bear in mind that these children have experienced inappropriate care and therefore may not have had the developmental building blocks that allow them to separate. We need to remind them all the time that we are there for them, even if we are physically somewhere else. For this purpose we can use sensory transitional objects – spray an item of clothing with your favourite perfume. Better still, take something like a handkerchief and wear it next to your skin to absorb the essence of you, then give it to the child. Have keyrings with a family photo in them; keep many visual reminders of family around the home – lots of happy family photos. And remember to give them reminders for when they are at school or out – leave messages in their lunch box (short and simple is good – 'Love you!' or 'Hope you are having a good day'), and if they are able to manage a mobile phone send texts, emoticons, reminders (especially if they are out!). One parent we know keeps a happy memories album, and when her child is feeling shamed and rejecting, she just leaves it for him to look at in his room. It gives him a less intense way to remember and reconnect. You can also use a narrative to let them know you have been thinking about them in their absence – for example, 'I was in the shop, and noticed this [small treat or item], and I know how much you love them, so I have bought one for after tea.' The subtext here is:

- I think about you even when you are not here.
- I pay attention to your likes and dislikes – because you are important to me.
- I think you deserve treats (unconditional expressions of love and approval).
- You are good.

And if the child is older and you are texting reminders:

- I care about you.
- I want you to stay safe.
- I want you to come home where you belong.

As always, try to keep your patience. If we think about how babies and small children assimilate learning by repeating the same small tasks or games endlessly, then maybe we can get an insight into why it takes so long for a child who has missed the brain building that a secure attachment gives you to learn things. They are re-framing their world, one step at a time, with your help and love.

Aspect 3: providing a narrative

This is a way to underline all the re-framing messages that we send to our children and help them to benefit, just as we give information to and interact with babies and small children, especially when they are pre-verbal.

As discussed previously, this is a way to meet the unmet needs of the child, whatever their age, by providing the reassurance that they are 'seen' by their parent/s and that they are loved and cared for despite any arguments or misunderstanding that may arise. Their behaviour has consequences, but it is clear that it is the behaviour that is unacceptable, not the child.

Aspect 4: acceptance

This aspect of parental presence offers the fabulous gift of accepting the child and loving them unconditionally. This does not mean no boundaries and allowing a child free range, which would only increase a child's insecurity and anxiety, but it does mean understanding the child, helping them to understand themselves and encountering adverse behaviours in ways that help the child to move on from previously held survival strategies. So this is clearly a big ask!

- *Bear the child's history in mind*: Use your own reflective capability to help you to understand or have curiosity about the behaviours they are demonstrating. Here again an appropriate narrative helps the process and enables you to work with the underlying anxiety – 'I wonder if you do not feel safe in your bed because you were left alone by your birth mum. That must have been so hard for you. Remember I will always keep you safe.' Or in the case of crazy lies, Sarah's approach – 'I know that you took the [biscuits, money, personal item], but I can see that you are finding this very difficult. I will be ready to talk with you whenever you are ready.'

- *Keep developmental cues in mind and accept your child at the age they are showing, whatever their physical age*: It is perfectly possible for our children to be teenage and still exhibit much younger behaviour in social/emotional/cognitive areas. This may be shown by, for example:

  - needing baby comforts by making baby noises or needing a bottle or even by suddenly showing very young toileting – wetting or soiling
  - displaying the reactions to frustration of a two- or three-year-old – temper tantrums, throwing things around, biting, spitting
  - behaving like a three- or four-year-old – incessant chatter, tall stories, getting overexcited and overwhelmed, unable to calm down without help.

  Try to give them emotional information to help them, using your narrative and 'I can see...' skills and containing them in a strong structure while they are working it out. You would not leave an 18-month-old to play alone, so if your ten-year-old is showing 18-month-old behaviours (jealousy, striking out at siblings) then keep them near and tell them, 'I can see you are finding things difficult just now. I am going to keep you near to keep you safe.'

- *Pick your battles*: Your adopted/fostered child did not grow up with your values and rules – it will take time to learn. In the meantime, decide which behaviours you can 'let go of' just for now. This will reduce stress all round.
- *Repair the relationship after a rupture*: This is more important than the rupture itself, as it teaches that disagreements and arguments do not inevitably lead to abandonment and rejection, that relationships based on acceptance are resilient and strong. For us as parents it is so useful to remember that our lapses from the ideal are actually as necessary for resilience and modelling as all the times we get it right! This gives the child acceptance in the face of all their behaviours.

Aspect 5: connection and repair

Sadly, in the face of overwhelming situations this can be very hard for therapeutic parents, because sometimes we are in a state of compassion fatigue, where our ability to empathize with and care for our children has been compromised by our need to protect ourselves.

First, therefore, we need to take time for ourselves, and reconnect with our own emotions. This means asking for help, and then using those little spaces of time we carve out to do something that makes us feel good. I am talking about the simple things here – talk to a friend; go for a swim, a run or a walk; read your favourite book; give yourself a treat. Take a deep breath. Reflect on your feelings about your child, and try to remember when you last had fun. If that seems impossible, then try to remove some of the stress from your life by 'letting go' of some behaviours – just for now. Make a choice to focus on only two or three behaviours and make sure those are worth the stress. You are not giving in, you are recognizing the overwhelming nature of re-parenting for your child as well as for yourself, and making a valid choice to enable you to reconnect and reduce tension and opportunities for arguments, which creates more space for closeness.

Now remember when you last laughed together. Laughter is such a healing and connecting thing to do – how can you recreate that? Think of this as a shortcut to establishing the caring core of your relationship, consolidating all that you have achieved and encouraging the child to feel valued and therefore building their self-esteem. Once this is established, trust develops and shame is reduced, because you show repeatedly that your love is unconditional and accepting. Ruptures are followed by repair. Mistakes happen and are forgiven. Apologies can be accepted and reconciliation can take place. Gradually over time and with many repetitions, the child comes to believe in their family and to trust their place within the family unit.

What can you do?

- Join your child in their games – ask to join in and enjoy being part of their world.
- Give an unconditional gesture of regard – a swift hug, or a smile. If asked, have an answer as to why you are smiling – 'It makes me smile when I see you.'

- Notice their favourite things and just occasionally surprise them with a treat.
- If they like games or jigsaws, start one off and ask for their help.
- If they ask you to come and sit with them, say yes, even if it does mean turning the dinner off for five minutes, or stopping the housework. This is more important. If you need to, just say, 'I really love sitting with you, but I know you are hungry, so I can only stay for five minutes, then I must cook your dinner!', or whatever.
- Have a bedtime 'meeting' to talk about your day. Make sure to notice three things you have loved about your child that day – or at least one!

The models we have talked about in this chapter focus on changing the perspective of the adult and managing their expectations of the child's ability to process and utilize the new experiences and choices they have. The primary focus is the relationship, and the main barrier to carers is often compassion fatigue, where as a result of the parent not receiving positive feedback from the child or any joy in the relationship, their need to protect themselves from the exhaustion and fatigue that results means that they effectively withdraw from the relationship, only ensuring that basic needs are met.

6

Compassion Fatigue and Self-Care

> In this chapter we explore the immense physical and emotional stress that can occur when re-parenting a child or young person who has developmental trauma. If there is insufficient support, research shows that the result can be compassion fatigue on the part of the parent or significant carer, and this has been shown to cause disruptions and breakdowns to placements in both adoption and fostering (Ottaway and Selwyn 2016).

This chapter is for all parents who are at risk of or are suffering from compassion fatigue as a result of the extreme and complex needs and challenging behaviours of the children or young people in their care. It's also for the professionals who are in a position to provide the support necessary to maintain placements and secure a successful outcome for children, young people and their families. To give an idea of the extent of the problem, the Centre of Excellence in Child Trauma carried out a survey which had 1250 responses from foster carers and adoptive parents to gauge the issues faced. Sixty-three per cent felt that key information had been withheld by social services, 89 per cent felt that supporting professionals did not understand the impact of child trauma or the need for therapeutic parenting, and over 90 per cent had experienced compassion fatigue.

IN MY EXPERIENCE...

I have delivered training to literally hundreds of families, and I have also experienced compassion fatigue myself – the feeling that nothing you can do will ever be enough, that nobody understands you, you are on your own. Even close friends and family are unable to understand and support you. Forced into isolation, it is easy to shut out everyone and to feel that you carry the whole burden of responsibility on your own. When families break down, every single person involved feels broken, worthless and as though they have failed. This was of course the very reason that Sarah set up the Therapeutic Parents Facebook Page – to give every parent a safe place to explore and vent their frustrations, and get advice, sympathy and validation from others who 'get it'.

More about compassion fatigue

As discussed in Chapter 3, compassion fatigue is the term used to describe the situation that occurs when the parent, unable to manage extreme stress states associated with parenting, finds it impossible to maintain the intense nurture and empathy required to maintain a commitment to the child. In these cases, the adult is not able to maintain their own regulation and self-care in the face of the overwhelming emotional needs of the child, who may also be extremely dysregulated, displaying very challenging behaviour and perhaps violent behaviours directed at carers and/or siblings. The carers become scared – terrified even – at the level of chaos and disruption that they are living with. Feeling out of control, they withdraw from the child emotionally, losing essential connection with the child who then operates from their own fearful state, increasing the attention seeking, controlling, oppositional or violent behaviours that have caused their parent to shut down. This produces a toxic cycle which further disintegrates the relationship (see Figure 6.1).

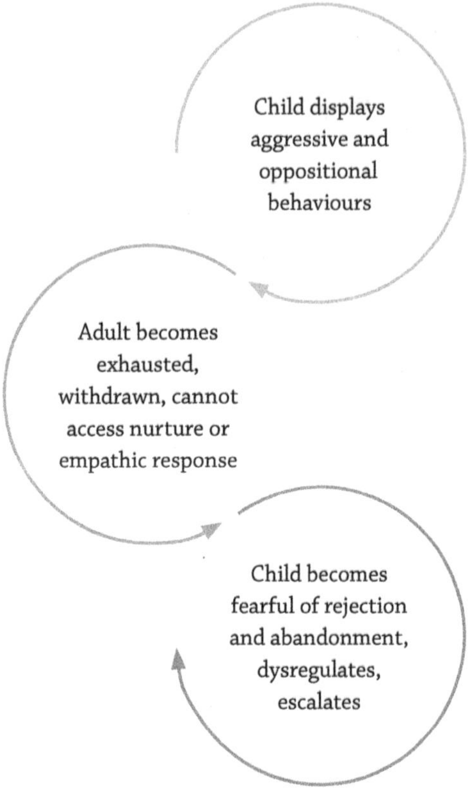
Child displays aggressive and oppositional behaviours
Adult becomes exhausted, withdrawn, cannot access nurture or empathic response
Child becomes fearful of rejection and abandonment, dysregulates, escalates

Figure 6.1 Compassion fatigue

Sarah Naish talks about her experiences and why she funded groundbreaking research:

I identified this as a growing issue from my own experience of running a fostering agency and delivering training to fostering and adoptive families.

In 2016, I worked with Dr Heather Ottaway of the University of Bristol's Hadley Centre for Adoption and Foster Care Studies to produce the first national study of compassion fatigue in foster carers in England, *No-One Told Us It Was Going to Be Like This* (Ottaway and Selwyn 2016).

Compassion fatigue is described in this study as 'a physical and emotional response to the stress of caring for those who have experienced trauma'. The research clearly links provision of appropriate support to increased ability to parent in a compassionate and therapeutic manner, and an increased ability to maintain the mindful stance towards the child that enables an empathic and nurturing response. This is particularly important in view of the national study of adoption breakdowns, *Beyond the Adoption Order* (Selwyn, Wijedasa and Meakings 2014), which outlines an increase in child-to-parent violence, leading to breakdowns in family relationships and often permanent disruption to the placement. Anger and aggression, especially during adolescence, present a major challenge to therapeutic parents, with violence towards carers and siblings being the reason young people had to leave the family home in 80 per cent of cases.

Ottaway and Selwyn's (2016) research found that parents reported feelings of isolation, becoming detached emotionally 'just to get through each day', and an inability to manage more than the child's most basic needs. It was also reported that social workers had little or no understanding of the reality of the challenges faced on a day-to-day basis, and that blaming and judgemental stances adopted by professionals were further damaging the confidence of therapeutic parents and their ability to maintain compassion for their child or children.

Summarizing and defining compassion fatigue, the report states that:

> Compassion fatigue is a physical and emotional response to the stresses of working with traumatized people. It has long been recognized as a condition affecting the performance of police and fire officers, hospital staff, mental health professionals and social workers, but it has received little attention in respect of foster carers.
>
> Compassion fatigue involves a decrease in empathy and feelings of pleasure and an increase in stress, anxiety, fear, sleeplessness and negativity. It can affect our ability to work sensitively and effectively with those who are traumatized. Compassion fatigue can occur in foster

> carers because of the demands of being a therapeutic parent to children who have experienced trauma, and it prevents the foster carer staying close and connected to the child. A foster carer's home is also their place of work, so having some 'time out' from caring, which is seen as essential to decrease symptoms of compassion fatigue in other stressful helping professions, is difficult to achieve. (p.5)

The symptoms of compassion fatigue are listed below:

- Exhaustion
- Fear of child – 'sinking feeling' in pit of stomach at thought of child returning home from school, or weekend approaching
- Lack of interest in child/lack of joyful experience of child
- Only able to fulfil basic needs of child
- Undermined
- Depression
- Blaming child for situation
- Isolation
- Misunderstood.

Parents suffering from these feelings may start to 'focus on behaviour from a critical, judgemental stance' (Hughes and Baylin 2012, p.133). Parents may turn back to standard parenting techniques such as planned ignoring or sanctions which are not a natural consequence. This increases the child's sense of disconnect and escalates the behaviour. Dan Hughes states that 'stressed out parenting stresses the child and tends to promote a runaway feedback loop that ramps up mutual defensiveness between the two' (Hughes and Baylin 2012, p.96). Unfortunately, one direct effect of stress on the brain is that under the influence of cortisol the brain makes rapid, simplistic assessments. There is limited ability to access higher functions and reflective thought patterns that enable a more considered and therapeutically effective response. Again, it is Dan Hughes who explains that a stressed carer is in survival mode with reduced rationality:

> Survival is all about rapid assessment and quick action, requiring the reduction of complexity and the narrowing of options. This is not a job for those higher, uniquely human parts of the prefrontal cortex that would only gum up the works with subtlety and complexity. (Hughes and Baylin 2012, p.97)

The Parent's Perspective
The parent experiences what is happening as highly PERSONAL, it is happening to THEM, it is about THEM. This is why it is so difficult for carers to deal with rejection from the child, it feels personal. The parent might say: 'What's the point?', 'This is endless', 'The child doesn't care about me.'

The Child's Perspective
When the child experiences the emotional withdrawal of their parent, it is likely that this triggers stress-based reactions (anger, aggression) due to their previous experiences and expectation of rejection. This is because their very sensitive amygdala will interpret the flattened response and lack of emotional connection as being a survival issue – probably there will have been similar sensory input as has happened previously: a blank withdrawn expression, angry face, a refusal to engage. This will activate implicit memories for the child, making them respond to a perceived danger. Their view due to their internal working model may include confirmation of SELF-LOATHING, WORTHLESSNESS, and terror of the repeated cycle of REJECTION and ABANDONMENT. This may be further reinforced by a behavioural approach which is critical and judging. The effect of these overwhelming feelings which are compounded of past and present experience trigger the child to fall into their trauma room where their fears and therefore their responses are massively amplified.

Contributory risk factors

Ottaway and Selwyn's (2016) report clearly showed that there are factors which increase the risk of developing compassion fatigue to such an extent that placements may break down.

Isolation

The parent feels that there is no one they can talk to who will simply listen and understand in a non-judgemental manner. Parents felt that informal peer support would be invaluable, and the benefits were clearly stated by those foster parents who had access to this kind of facility:

> It's like having a sounding board...and we sit and cry sometimes because we've had really bad weeks. We all understand each other and we've all been there... I could not pick up the phone to my supervising social worker because I would feel judged, or I would feel like a failure. (Ottaway and Selwyn 2016, p.36)

This 'sounding board' phenomenon is common when delivering training if sufficient time is given to allow parents to talk about their stories within the safe and non-judgemental environment of the training room. This is because all the families participating in training have experiences, fears, and (hopefully) small pleasures on the same spectrum – to put it simply, they speak each other's language. Responses are spontaneous and compassionate, and families finally feel heard and validated. This allows their brain to re-engage creatively and find new meaning for behaviours and to try new strategies. Dan Siegel explains that by achieving this connection on an emotional level first, you enable the brain to then redirect, explore the context and find a solution (www.youtube.com/watch?v=ZcDLzppD4Jc).

Unfortunately, those parents who live in isolation – and many report loss of friendships and withdrawal of family members, as well as disapproval or judgement from professionals – do not have this extremely valuable space to 'offload'.

Lack of support

This is a crucial factor, and closely related to isolation. Some families report having had no preparation for the challenges that they may have to face, whilst some talk about lack of peer support or lack of professional support, with social workers being specifically mentioned in the report:

> The total lack of understanding of the most basic rudiments of attachment theory displayed by my supervising social worker...has completely put me off attempting to access [support]. (Ottaway and Selwyn 2016, p.25)

> The social workers and their lack of understanding/training cause me far more problems than the children I care for. (Ottaway and Selwyn 2016, p.25)

Reasons for this perceived lack of support are seen to be lack of time, training and resources. There is also an underlying issue of blame, where the parent is made to feel that their skills are deficient, or that they are making a fuss about nothing ('all children do that') or there is inadequate structure and boundaries, and that appropriate strategies and sanctions are not being employed. Very often, it is recommended that parents use standard punitive techniques such as time out, or a 'naughty step' or reward charts, which at best are ineffective for children who do not have a secure attachment, and at worst activate fear-based responses that make the situation worse.

Lack of time

In most stressful jobs, you can achieve a brief respite by going home. For parents of children with developmental trauma there is no 'going home'. Their home is their place of work, and in the worst situations the home – which is supposed to be a place of safety and rest – can become the focus of fear and aggression. Under these circumstances it is not surprising that parents begin to feel unable to continue with the task of re-parenting the child – they have had no space to relax, to process and to gain some perspective. Respite is not always offered, and need for respite can be seen as a sign of failure.

> There were also many instances of respite being seen as the carers not coping (often from LA carers), and they felt judged and blamed for this. Behind this, the carers felt that there was a fundamental lack of understanding about the realities of fostering traumatised children,

> which meant that either the need for respite was not supported, or a flexible understanding of respite was not present. (Ottaway and Selwyn 2016, p.41)

Lack of knowledge of therapeutic parenting strategies

This applies to both families (lack of preparation and support) and social workers, who have often studied attachment but may not understand the practicalities of how this affects the ongoing development of the traumatized child even when placed in a safe environment. This leads to feelings of being judged and blamed:

> Some foster carers felt judged and blamed by social workers for the difficulties they experienced in caring for traumatised children. Feeling judged led to a reluctance to ask for help and concerns from carers that if they were honest about the way they were feeling they might get de-registered. Lack of support is likely to have contributed to the moderate to high levels of burnout and secondary traumatic stress, and moderate to low levels of compassion satisfaction which many foster carers reported. (Ottaway and Selwyn 2016, p.38)

> Lack of knowledge or understanding on the part of social workers was also seen as a contributory factor in not being able to access adequate support. Most foster carers felt that the social work professionals supporting them did not generally have the appropriate knowledge and understanding of issues of attachment and trauma, its effects on children and the challenges of caring. As a result, the support provided did not meet their need.

The cycle of blame

Blame is a negative response to situations which make the recipient of the blame feel uncomfortable, stressed or in pain. It is also the product of stress in itself. The cycle of blame is illustrated in Figure 6.2.

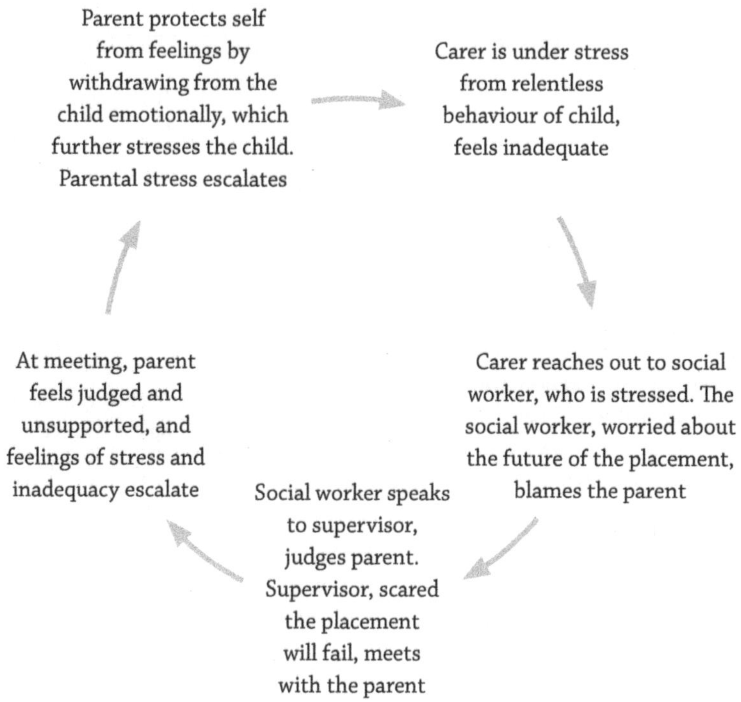

Parent protects self from feelings by withdrawing from the child emotionally, which further stresses the child. Parental stress escalates
Carer is under stress from relentless behaviour of child, feels inadequate
Carer reaches out to social worker, who is stressed. The social worker, worried about the future of the placement, blames the parent
Social worker speaks to supervisor, judges parent. Supervisor, scared the placement will fail, meets with the parent
At meeting, parent feels judged and unsupported, and feelings of stress and inadequacy escalate

Figure 6.2 Cycle of blame

In this too familiar cycle, we can see that at every step along the way anger, stress and pain are discharged by blaming an external factor. The social worker blames the parent, the manager blames the parent, inadequate support is given, the parent becomes more stressed and blames the child, and the child in their stress blames the parent for their emotional pain, which escalates the situation. Here we have a situation where there is no accountability, just passing the buck. This damages all the relationships involved in the cycle, leading to lack of trust, lack of confidence in the other person, increased stress and shaming, and unhelpful responses. This in turn leads to isolation and withdrawal, particularly on the part of the parent, who may stop asking for help and give up, and withdraw from the child. At no point do we see validation of experience or strategies which support the carer first, allowing them to re-engage in their parenting role. In a worst case scenario, the child is moved on, which is likely to result in the cycle repeating itself. It is easy to see that there have been opportunities for an empathic response which were missed on all parts. If we remove blame, and add in empathy, then we can visualize a very different picture (see Figure 6.3).

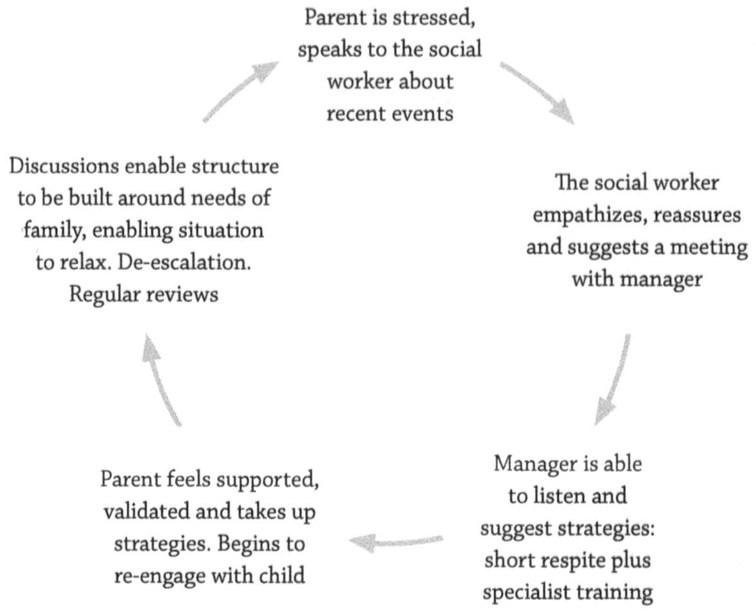

Figure 6.3 Cycle of empathy

In this model, based on empathy, we can see that the team are using effective strategies to support the parent and increase the level of skill starting from a secure knowledge of the parent's current level of knowledge and experience. This is TRUE (Therapeutic Re-parenting Underpinned by Empathy/experience; see Chapter 5), and it uses the following direct working strategies:

- *Empathy, exploration and application*: Time is taken to listen to the experience of the carer, and understand and share in their perspective. The themes which are developing through the behaviour of the child are explored in a supportive way, perhaps exploring the child's history to enable connections to be made which may inform future strategies. These strategies are applied with support and additional professional input where necessary. Regular meetings and supervision help to maintain the situation.

- *Affective and cognitive empathy*: The two branches of empathy are essential to the TRUE model. Affective empathy is a subjective state driven by 'emotional contagion' – the ability of the limbic (emotional) parts of our brain to 'feel' the emotional state of another individual on a very personal level. (This, incidentally, is the basis of co-regulation and gives some understanding of how it is that parents can 'catch' the emotional – chaotic, fearful – states of their traumatized children.) On the other hand, cognitive empathy is the ability to intuit how another person may be feeling by joining them in their perspective on events. This skill enables us to recognize how someone might be feeling and to understand this. It is a wholly non-judgemental stance that is centred around the other person. Integrating these two branches of empathy will enable conversations where the carer feels safe, contained and supported in their emotional state.
- *Knowledge and understanding of compassion fatigue*: It is essential that professionals understand compassion fatigue, both causes and effects, and that there is sufficient awareness of the symptoms for early indicators to be acted on – for example, fatigue, stress or difficulty in connecting with a child. This needs to be a subject which is openly talked about as a consequence of parenting a traumatized child, which is very understandable and a normal reaction to the parenting challenges faced. In this way, parents feel validated, supported and able to continue.
- *Knowledge and understanding of developmental trauma*: It is essential that professionals have knowledge and understanding of developmental trauma and developmental awareness (developmental versus chronological age) in order for them to be able to move the parent into understanding, reconnecting and willingness to try

appropriate strategies. It is also essential to offer parents access to such training to develop their skill set – to educate parents about compassion fatigue before it happens.

- *Team problem solving and information sharing*: Once the empathic and knowledgeable environment has been established, all professionals involved and parents (who should *always* be included) can work together to find the most effective strategies for the family's needs, but starting always from a basis of understanding and support with the priority being on education in developmental trauma. Team working or professionals' meetings should enable the child to be assessed holistically and aim for achievable goals to be set, in small steps, which should be developmentally appropriate.
- *Brain-based parenting*: Professionals and parents need to have training in and understanding of parenting strategies which promote the forging of new neurological pathways in order to override the child's early experiences. This work focuses on the relationship and follows the steps of the healthy attachment cycle (see Chapter 1). In addition, the parent has to have empathy for the child who has never learned the give and take of relationships. They cannot give you emotional rewards as they have never experienced them from others. Emotional support and care needs to be modelled so that the child experiences this multiple times. This is very hard to do when no positive response is forthcoming – even harder when the only response forthcoming is fear based – and therefore rejecting and dismissive, even cruel. Because our children are unable to give us the small rewards that help us to carry on when it feels like we are banging our head repeatedly against a brick wall, it is necessary to have emotional support and validation from people around you, whether they are partners, family, friends or professionals.
- *Avoid damaging interventions and language*: The professional should be aware of interventions and assumptions which disempower

the parent, forcing them into isolation and reduced confidence in their ability to care for the child therapeutically. These include:

- minimizing – 'It's normal for his age'
- misplaced sympathy – 'All children do that; my son does just the same'
- blaming language – 'Have you tried a parenting course?' The implication is that the parent's parenting approach is causing the issues
- reliance on standard parenting methods – reward charts, withdrawal of toys/privileges, 'unnatural' consequences
- exclusion – the parent is excluded from planning, meetings and decision making.

Overcoming compassion fatigue

When effective interventions are put in place, including regular structured brain breaks (useful for both parents and child); emotional support – preferably allocating an empathic listener to the family; mentoring, peer support and education of family members as well as professionals, the following benefits are likely to be seen:

- Reduced incidence of placement disruption
- Ability for child and parent to repair relationship
- Facilitating the formation of secure attachment patterns by minimizing placement moves
- Inclusion of parent in planning and other meetings, meaning that the ability of the child to 'split' or 'triangulate' is reduced, giving the child more security as there is a more cohesive team approach.

Self-care is not selfish

Many parents feel that they cannot manage self-care. They do not have the time; they do not want to leave the children and re-traumatize them; and so on. However, self-care is not selfish. It is an essential part of therapeutic parenting and models to the child that this is important, and that you place a value on yourself. Here are some suggestions:

Simple self-care: When your child is at school, make the most of the time to fill up your own resources. Do things that help you to decompress and give your brain a mini-break. For instance:

- Get your partner (if applicable) to take a day off work and have a date day to rekindle your relationship.
- Go for a walk.
- Take a gym or aerobics class – concentrating on what you need to be doing will stop you thinking about your children and give your brain a break! (I used to go to a dance class – it was great!)
- Take up a hobby.
- Meet a friend.
- Bake!

Whatever you do, do it mindfully, even in the shortest moments. Give yourself small treats – your favourite brand of tea or coffee, your favourite bath or shower products. Take the time to enjoy them whatever the sensory element!

If you find it hard to switch off your brain, try this mindful exercise: Stop whatever you are doing with your brain cycling round what is happening with your child or children. Notice your surroundings, pay attention to them. Then make a mental note of three things you can see, three things you can feel, three things you can hear. Now, think of another two things you can see, two things you can feel, two things you can hear. Finally, find one thing you can see, one thing you can feel, one thing you can hear. You will find this helps to bring you into the here and now and switches your brain to the moment you are in. Enjoy that moment! In truth, these small breaks are more useful in the long run than anything else, giving you an opportunity to take a pause in your busy life and encouraging you to find new ways to take care of yourself and relax.

Extended self-care: Take yourself out one night every week. This will not harm the child or children. Make it a routine, the same night every week, and make sure you go every week. The pattern soon becomes part of their expected routine (although it may take a few weeks to establish!). This is an important way for the children to learn that you will come back, and an opportunity for you to reinforce it with a narrative: 'I promised you I would come back and here I am!' If you are able to have brain breaks provided (brain breaks are sometimes called respite; however, this is a term which is derogatory to the children concerned and therefore avoided here), maybe by your agency or by a kind friend or family member, then make sure the children are invited – it is a treat for them. This gives you an opportunity to model the underlying resilience of the family by saying that you will miss them, but you know they will come back to you, and you hope they have a lovely time.

7

Adolescence and the Teenage Brain

In this chapter we discuss the challenges faced by young people and their parents during puberty and adolescence, and examine the neurological changes which drive this process.

Adolescence is a critical time in the development of a young person, which allows them to achieve the transition into adulthood. During this period, which lasts from onset of puberty until around age 24 (longer than most people believe), all of the developmental domains are affected – physical (including neurological), cognitive, social and emotional. This chapter explores the different areas of development with the reader to give an understanding of the biological background to this developmental stage. We will then explore advanced therapeutic strategies to enable parents to support young people with developmental trauma through adolescence.

IN MY EXPERIENCE...

I have parented three biological children through adolescence, and at the time of writing I am still parenting my adopted daughter through the process, albeit at a distance. My daughter lives in fully supported adult accommodation due to her vulnerability and disabilities, and this transition to adult care, which has happened in the last few months, has had a massive impact on her and caused some distress to both of us. Part of what we will address in this chapter are the difficuties encountered by our most vulnerable young people when they are transferred to adult care and how the way that they are approached and supported changes fundamentally as their chronology tips over into post 18. In the UK an 18-year-old is deemed to have capacity and ability to take responsibility for themselves despite their diagnoses or developmental age. There is a framework for assessing capacity but the bar is set unrealistically low. The main challenges this presents for the parent is to be able to work alongside professionals to ensure that there is a way to maintain safety for their daughter or son. But really, it felt to me (and to my daughter judging by the consequences) as though she was pushed off a cliff, and then everyone waited to see if she bounced or not in order to establish her care needs (which were fully documented at the time of transfer).

THINK ABOUT IT...

When I am delivering training about adolescents, one of the first things that I do is to ask the parents to take a few minutes to remember and discuss with each other in groups their own experience of their teenage years: how they felt, how they behaved, how life changed for them. It is useful to do this in a very honest way. By remembering our teenage selves and having empathy and compassion for the young people we were, it is easier to achieve understanding, empathy and compassion for the young people in our families. Before you read any further, I would like you to take a few moments to reflect on your own experiences as an adolescent.

- Were you confident? Or wracked with anxiety?
- Did you experiment in risky behaviours such as sex, alcohol or recreational drugs?
- Were you led by a need to emulate your peers, or did you find your own way?
- Were you lonely or popular?
- What were the things that were important to you?
- How did you feel about your parents and the way they responded to you?

When we talk about the issues facing adolescents, and therefore the difficulties that their parents encounter, it is useful to bear three things in mind:

1. The young person's history and current developmental status
2. The physical changes that are happening in the body
3. The neurological changes that are happening as the brain enters a second phase of development.

These three factors will inform our understanding, expectations and therefore our ability to support the young person.

The physical and neurological changes that start around 11 with the onset of puberty continue until around age 24, with changes also occurring in the biological drives of the young person during this time as their bodily systems and their emotional, cognitive and social maturity develop, leading to independence and development of adult relationships, responsibilities and preparation for parenthood. Puberty as a process can start as early as eight (females) or nine (males).

Hormones and physical development

Males and females alike develop secondary sexual characteristics. These changes are triggered by a hormonal 'pulse' which originates in the hypothalamus. The hormone is called 'gonadotropin releasing hormone' (GnRH). GnRH stimulates the pituitary gland to release follicle stimulating hormone (FSH) and luteinizing hormone (LH). These activate the development of the gonads – ovaries in girls and testes in boys.

Girls

One of the first signs of puberty in girls is a growth spurt; however, after onset of menarche (menstruation or periods), girls rarely grow more than an additional 6cm.

Ovaries secrete two hormones, oestrogen and progesterone, which govern the menstrual cycle during which the female body prepares the reproductive system for production of ova (ovulation) and pregnancy (proliferation of the lining of the womb, which is shed if no pregnancy occurs). In addition, oestrogen causes changes in body shape by causing fat to be laid down, especially in the hips and bust.

Other changes include the following:

- Mood swings as a result of hormonal surges. These may form a regular cycle before there is any evidence of menstrual bleeding
- Maturation of genital area
- Growth of pubic hair around genitals and in the armpits
- Skeletal growth – height, changes to pelvis, facial structure matures
- Skin changes that may lead to spots or acne
- Increased sweating that may lead to body odour.

Boys

Unlike girls, boys continue childhood growth until later in puberty, and then have a late growth spurt when they will grow up to 20cm in a year.

Testicles produce testosterone. As the testes mature, they start to produce sperm. Testosterone triggers growth of muscle and increases haemoglobin and therefore oxygen flow to those muscles in order for them to be exercised and develop fully.

Changes in boys include the following:

- Physical growth
- Increased strength
- Changes to voice
- Erections (may be involuntary)
- Ejaculation (may be involuntary 'wet dreams')
- Maturation of genital area
- Growth of pubic hair around genitals and in armpits
- Skin changes that may lead to spots or acne
- Increased sweating that may lead to body odour.

Secondary physical development is part of a physiological biological process which is not dependent on the ability of the child to manage what is happening to them cognitively or emotionally. My own daughter was horrified by the emergence of puberty, which happened early in her case – at age nine she showed signs of an emotional cycle, and had her periods at age ten.

Secondary neurological development

We now know that there are three main processes happening in the brain of the adolescent:

1. *Proliferation*: a rapid growth in brain matter. At age six the brain has achieved 95 per cent of its final size. Girls achieve their maximum brain size at age 11.5 years, boys around 14.5 years.

2. *Myelination*: specialist cells facilitate formation of the myelin sheath. **Myelin** is a fatty substance which increases the speed of transmission of impulses along the axons (long nerve cells) of the central nervous system throughout the body. This means that sensory information and the way this is processed, analysed and acted on according to our previous experiences and expectations happens many times more quickly – the myelin sheath enables impulses to travel at 70–120 metres per second, equivalent to the speed of a racing car. Imagine or try to remember how this feels. All of a sudden your brain is flooded with data which is arriving much more quickly – it's quite overwhelming! At the same time, the brain is maturing and reconfiguring to enable the individual to take up their adult independent status. As this is a physiological process, it happens in a chronologically determined way, not due to appropriate cognitive/emotional/social development having occurred.

3. *Pruning*: neurones or pathways which are used least frequently are destroyed. This happens in a general way throughout life (hence 'use it or lose it'). In the teenage brain, however, this is much more pronounced as it is part of the preparation for adulthood. The pruning process starts at the rear of the brain and works forwards, so the parts which develop maturity first are physical activity, emotion and motivation, but the part of the brain that develops last is the prefrontal cortex – near the front of the brain and controlling reasoning, impulses and organization. This is not fully mature until age 25. Whilst all of this is happening, there is impairment of usual function. I think of it in technical terms – like a laptop that needs to have a defragmentation program run so that it can function more efficiently; however, while the program is in progress, the laptop is effectively shut down and unable to function.

To recap – these three processes are designed to improve the effectiveness and integration of the brain. However, whilst this is still a 'work in progress', the initial impact can be that some functions of the brain are impaired (such as communication), whilst some functions are heightened (e.g. emotional responses) and at the same time, due to the myelination process, sensory data is overwhelming the brain, which will not finish its job of integration and reach full maturity until around age 24 and continues to adapt and integrate new information throughout life.

But that's not all. Whilst all this is happening, it appears that adolescents operate more from the limbic area of the brain and therefore have heightened emotional states – it's not just raging hormones. Increased activity of reward centres in the brain predispose teens to high-risk and exciting behaviours. At the same time, the need to establish themselves as individuals who are separate from their parents leads to their seeking approval from their peers, giving rise to impulsive and sometimes dangerous situations. During adolescence we are far more vulnerable to addictions of any sort. Addictive substances all involve release of dopamine (a feel-good hormone) and firing of the reward centres of the brain. We make a connection between feeling great and the addictive substance and seek to recreate the experience. Addictions to alcohol, recreational drugs or highly processed foods and sugars all create the same dopamine surge.

In his book *Brainstorm* (2014), Dan Siegel explores the essential features of adolescence, creating the acronym 'ESSENCE'.

- *ES – Emotional Spark*: the intense emotional experience of adolescence which Dan suggests creates meaning and vitality throughout our lives
- *SE – Social Engagement*: important connections with others
- *N – Novelty*: seeking out new experiences that are exciting, challenging or fascinating
- *CE – Creative Explorations*: new ways of thinking that drive new ideas and new ways of viewing the world.

Learning to embrace a new concept of adolescence which celebrates these elements can help us to develop new empathy with our young people and give us greater understanding of the importance of this phase of life. By being open to our young people's views, ideas and perspectives we are more likely to be able to maintain good communication which is essential to helping them make good decisions.

Challenging changes

During our adolescence, the many developmental tasks that happen in our bodies and brains make it hard for us to stay centred and reasonable. This difficulty is exacerbated by the effects of developmental trauma, which is likely to have affected cognitive and/or social and emotional development to a greater or lesser extent. We will examine social, emotional and cognitive issues which are likely to emerge or intensify during adolescence. However, we first need to consider the expectations likely to be faced by our children as they enter puberty.

Age 11 sees a transition to a different way of educating with different expectations of the young person. At 11, the young person is expected to be able to work in a more symbolic, analytical way, as education from the age of 11 tends to be more formal than it is at primary school. They are expected to be able to manage their time, take responsibility for following rules, retain information from one day to the next in different subject areas and be organized and ready to work – in other words, to have executive function skills. In addition, there is a sense of the need to promote independence and to move the young person towards meaningful employment and leaving home. This is part of a 'normal' biological separation process which, however, is not developmentally appropriate for young people who are challenged socially, emotionally or cognitively.

At the other end of the adolescent period, other important transitions may take place – transitions into jobs, leading to greater independence, responsibility and also a need to manage finances and budgets; and separation from family – this is sometimes achieved by means of an annexe or separate space within the family home. These transitions can be very beneficial, producing a sense of growth and self-esteem, and allowing the new adult relationship with parents to be explored.

Coping Skills for Kids (copingskills4kids.net) suggests that hormones acting on the brain result in challenges for adolescents as they struggle to cope with additional sensitivity to stress and emotional pain. This can cloud their ability to focus and to learn, leading to confusion and mistakes. The following table gives some key brain and behaviour changes, and then the additional issues faced for a young person with a background of developmental trauma.

Adolescent brain and behaviour changes (Coping Skills for Kids)	**Additional stressors as a result of early childhood experience (Jane Mitchell)**
Young person has age - appropriate development across social, emotional, cognitive and physical domains. They are able to manage and accommodate the changes happening to them with support of family and friends	The young person is likely to have reduced functioning in social, emotional and cognitive domains, and be operating at a significantly younger developmental level. This greatly reduces the young person's ability to cope with the changes that are happening. The challenges of managing their social needs may result in dangerous behaviours which are adopted to help fit in to the peer group of their choice. The young person is easily manipulated or encouraged into risky behaviours such as stealing, drinking, drug misuse or sexual behaviour
'I'm not a child, and not yet an adult, so who am I?' This is a core identity task which is scary and can be observed as the young person oscillates between dependence and independence	The essential tension in this crisis of adolescence is made much more difficult if you do not have a solid sense of yourself as part of a family. Young people who have suffered trauma are not likely to be operating from knowledge of a family going back generations with links to appearance and skills. (Kinship carers or special guardians may be an exception – however, the enhanced knowledge may bring its own set of difficulties.) Key aspects of how they view themselves and their core identity are unknown or damaging

Turning away from parents and towards peers	Attempts to engage with peers can be difficult as social skills may not be developed. Younger behaviour patterns may frustrate and sabotage friendships. Misunderstanding of social cues and facial expression add to difficulties. The young person is vulnerable to bullying or exploitation to gain entry to a social circle
Being more critical of myself and others	Existing poor self-esteem and self-loathing can escalate into self-harm. Doubts about birth parents feed in to this, as does doubt about whether parents really care or are just doing their job because they have to. Disparagement of parents fuelled by stress and fear can lead to escalations and frequently voiced rejection of the parent, which in turn lead to a dispirited parent who has a sense of failure
Increased self-consciousness and sensitivity to stress	If the young person's system is already on cortisol overload, the sensitivity to stress will be heightened. The young person's capacity to self-regulate (which is unlikely to be well developed) or accept regulation will be massively reduced, resulting in heightened emotional states and therefore more arguments
Intense need to belong and be accepted by others	Poor social and emotional functioning leads to extreme vulnerability. This may be further exacerbated by poor self-esteem, self-loathing and feelings of being unworthy of being included or loved. Even if the young person identifies themselves as part of a peer group, they may well lose their confidence in this bond when they are not with their friends. In addition, relationships can be further compromised by social media, which enables comments to be made and responded to instantly and provides a new area for bullying and victimization
Having mixed feelings of liking and disliking the same person	These feelings of trust versus mistrust are at the heart of many families of young people with developmental trauma. Fear of rejection or abandonment can lead to rejecting or violent behaviour

Society, stereotypes and expectations

Social expectations and teenage stereotypes can contribute to the already poor sense of self and identity faced by some of our young people. Expectations of teenage behaviour can be very poor, and attitudes can reflect this (e.g. notices in shop windows allowing no more than three schoolchildren in at a time). For a child who has poor self-esteem, and a model of themselves as being worthless, unimportant and unlovable, this is validation of their worst fears. Social awkwardness in adolescence is exacerbated by difficulty in 'reading' social situations and finding it difficult to communicate and form an appropriate response when talking to adults.

Adults and peers are likely to have an age-appropriate rather than a developmentally appropriate expectation of understanding and behaviour, and adults can also fall back on negative teenage stereotypes. Given that teenagers typically are caught between their need for nurture and support and a secure base and their biological drive to separate and achieve independence, and taking into account their increased size, weight and strength, this causes issues when expectations are met with fear and frustration and typical toddler/young child expression of anxiety, such as lashing out, shouting (often equals swearing in teen terms) and rejecting language or behaviour. For the young person who has experienced severe neglect or other abuse, fear and distrust of adults can re-emerge or intensify, causing additional issues at home and at school due to reduced ability to manage the internal emotional roller coaster experienced as a result of physical and neurological development. There is also a tendency for us to have expectations of a young person to behave in a way that corresponds with their developmental size. Hence we see someone occupying a (nearly) adult-sized space and we expect adult behaviours. Parents of very tall children get used to this when their children are still very little, when they look a year or so older than they are, and of course act according to their actual age, not their physical age. Our children with a history of trauma have a different problem, which is that their development does not match their chronology; however, their brains and bodies are still following a pre-programmed itinerary. This makes it very hard for us, and them, to negotiate the challenges of adolescence.

Cognitive function – being able to self-regulate, organize self, control impulsivity, follow rules, recognize different rules in different settings

– all these abilities are compromised by hormones and developmental activity of the brain. This causes frustration and friction in many households. Typically parents complain of rudeness, lack of respect, swearing and lying. However, we need to remember that our developmentally challenged children need to have behaviour and strategies modelled and repeated again and again to enable these skills to be formed and strengthened (neurones that fire together, wire together – Dan Siegel). Practical strategies, visual aids, gentle reminders and modelling will all be invaluable, as will having a support system that enables you to withstand the rejection which your child or children may offer you.

Relationships and identity

Identity and belonging issues cause difficulties for the young person who has suffered developmental trauma and has little sense of their place in the world as secured by a sense of family and belonging. Multiple placements could cause more confusion. Think about it – what are the things that help you know who you are?

- Family features – facial, physical similarities, colour of hair and eyes
- Skills – reminiscent of other older members of your family
- Knowledge of your place within a family as a son or daughter, sibling, cousin, nephew or niece, grandchild – you can visualize this extending into the future as a mum, dad, aunt, uncle...
- Feedback from those close to you
- Cultural roots
- Religious beliefs
- Family rituals and traditions
- House rules and values
- Education

- Job
- Social circle
- Interests.

And this is not an exhaustive list. Now imagine the difficulty for the child who is trying to make sense of all this information from several different sources – birth family, foster family, adoptive family. In the event that there have been multiple placements, it gets much harder – I was told of a child who had had 17 placements by their early teens; in that case, there is no consistency or stability except for the expectation that this family, like all the others, will reject you in the end. In the event of abuse and neglect, it is harder still because of the action of all of the above on an already poor internal working model, which serves only to intensify whatever negative belief you already hold.

Identity issues

Quite apart from the issues discussed above, we also have the problem of our vulnerable young people seeking information about themselves by finding out about their birth family – via Facebook and other social media sites. During adolescence the young person is likely to experience feelings of isolation and self-doubt. This may be worse if birth parents have had more children and have managed to build a family. The risk of further rejection or abandonment by the birth family, along with misinformation and idealization by the looked after child, can cause huge problems with managing stressful circumstances such as contact. Also, the birth family are of course not likely to agree with the history the young person knows, protesting how the child was taken from them against their will and how they have always loved the child and thought about them every day. The young person will really wish to believe this, and further upset is experienced.

Adolescents frequently have a poor sense of self – both from their experiences and from a heightened and stressed emotional state. Adolescents typically display low self-esteem and feelings of worthlessness from time to time as their emotional state see-saws. This is likely to be much more intense in the case of a looked after or adopted young person, and may result in harmful adaptive behaviours such as promiscuity, alcohol or substance abuse, self-harm or bullying. The young person is therefore more vulnerable to consequences such as sexually transmitted diseases, pregnancy, addiction or conviction.

During adolescence young people turn to their peers for support and validation of their experiences. This is part of a biological process set in motion to aid separation and individuation. Unfortunately, this can lead to vulnerability to peer pressure and exploitation in order to fit in and be able to identify as part of a group. Bullying as a victim or a perpetrator can be an issue, and the heightened emotional state due to the hormonal activity can lead to increased risk of self-harm and also of suicide. This whole picture is currently underlined by the use of social media as a means to take bullying into the home, and also as a way of grooming vulnerable children or expose them to inappropriate violence or sexual images.

Self-harm

Unfortunately, this is a very common issue, and one which is mediated by social media, where whole sites are devoted to self-harm challenges, with lots of ways to increase the risk. The methods employed may be cutting (easy to get a blade out of a pencil sharpener or razor), ligatures (for self-strangulation) or embedding foreign objects such as staples under the skin to cause infection. As stated elsewhere in this book, self-harm is a way to manage psychological pain. In fact, the endorphins produced in the process do literally dull both physical and psychological pain, but this is temporary. Sometimes for a young person, however, the psychological pain of their life is too much and they do wish for death and attempt suicide.

Mental health

Many adolescents struggle with their mental health and their inability to express themselves, and feel completely at the mercy of their mental health with issues such as anxiety, depression and poor self-esteem becoming very prevalent, partly because of the increased reliance on the limbic brain which reduces the ability of the adolescent to rationalize, have impulse control and make sense of their situations, but partly because of the social anxiety that is part and parcel of adolescence. It is beyond the scope of this book to go into detail about mental health; however, I have been given permission to include the following – written by a looked after child and expressing how having poor mental health affects her:

Living with mental health Anon
Mental health affects me from being confident because I can become very anxious which prevents me from being able to be confident.

My whole head feels like it has so much information that it literally feels like my head is going to explode. I find it hard to explain how I feel sometimes. I feel anxious at the moment and overwhelmed. I feel anxious when I am around a big group of people. When I'm at home in the dining room. When I'm sat in the classroom. At my low points I get to the point of feeling like I can't stop myself from feeling that I want to end my life. I don't want to feel this way and I try to stop myself from feeling this way but it makes me feel so low within myself that I hate myself altogether. This makes me feel like I'm such a bad person. I can only see the negatives and never think about the positives. Even when people compliment me I can't believe it. Simple compliments I can take but never fully. Because I don't like myself I can never see myself as what other people tell me I am.

I wake up anxious about what the day ahead is going to be like. Will I be happy? Will I be sad? Do I have to carry on with everything? When I am feeling down I can be surrounded by staff and people in college but I still feel lonely. I become obsessive. Obsessed with using lots of toilet roll. Obsessed with washing my hands to the point they can turn red. Obsessed with situations. It can be explained to me over and over again but it still doesn't stop me from obsessing with overthinking but people don't understand that this is me.

Sexuality

Sexuality may be complicated by emerging memories of sexual abuse. Looked after and adopted young people are also extremely vulnerable to grooming, especially via social media. Additionally, lower developmental age or past experiences may lead young people to attempt sexual activities with younger children or siblings or exhibit sexualized behaviour towards carers or other adults. A good website to look at for yourself or direct your child to is Thinkuknow (www.thinkuknow.co.uk), which has information for parents, professionals and children and has a focus on staying safe.

Safeguarding

Many adolescent activities can give rise to concerns about safeguarding when there is a vulnerable young person involved. Many have been mentioned, but are reproduced here for the sake of clarity:

- Sexual activity
- Promiscuity
- Sexually transmitted diseases
- Vulnerability to grooming
- Risk taking
- Self-harm
- Suicide
- Alcohol or substance abuse/addiction/overdose
- Young person is vulnerable to bullying
- Young person becomes a bully.

Strategies

Keep connection

I believe that this is the most important strategy of all for keeping our adolescents safe, and to be able to predict a better outcome in our future relationships. Like toddlers, teenagers should ideally be learning to explore the world from a secure base – of course their horizons are much wider this time! Like toddlers, the rate of development is extraordinary and change takes place very quickly – as parents it is difficult for us to keep up with our teenagers' changing needs.

IN MY EXPERIENCE...

Very often, as my oldest children were going through this stage, I would find my head spinning as I tried and often failed to keep up with them. What helped me in the end was realizing that very often I said no to them just because I had not had time to adjust to the new ideas they were introducing – so I sat them both down and explained to them that if they wanted to do something new – stay out later, make their own way home, go to a late night disco, whatever – to pick their timing – i.e. not when I was busy, on the phone, or two hours before they wanted to go as my default reaction was likely to be a 'no'. I suggested instead they ask in good time, and have their arguments ready as to why whatever they were suggesting was OK. This definitely helped, and I then applied the same to my third child.

I would also point out that there is still a need for that secure base, even if it seems that it is only to have a wall to kick against. Teenagers need to have consistency and know that your boundaries are still secure in the essentials, also to know that you can allow them their independence, try and help them to make good choices, and still be there to mop up the fallout after their mistakes – so easy to say and so hard to do. This closely aligns with the Bryan Post approach described earlier: maintenance of boundaries and structure whilst being very clear that your concern is for the young person's safety, and encouraging the young person to make good choices for themselves. What this means in practice is swallowing a lot of fear-driven rejection from your child – alongside swearing, opposition and defiance – and continuing to offer support and time.

IN MY EXPERIENCE...

I remember so well a client of mine being at her wits' end with her oldest child – she would invite her daughter to family 'meetings', where she and her husband would meet with their daughter and discuss how to meet in the middle, and somehow keep moving forward. She was very motivated at the time not to have lasting arguments with her, because at age 16 two young girls that her daughter knew were killed in a car being driven by one of their boyfriends, and I remember my client saying that it made her feel so upset thinking that they might have been like her own daughter, who might have slammed out of the door in the middle of an argument and left no opportunity to make amends, so my client was very motivated to be understanding and conciliatory.

Allowing your child's views to be heard and understood and being responsive to this is crucial, and can make the difference between a young person who will in the end trust in the relationship and a young person who digs themselves into a hole that they cannot get out of. I am not suggesting that parents should be doormats for their child – there needs to be rules and consequences – but there also needs to be understanding and unconditional repair. Children have to grow, they have to make mistakes. We can understand the reasons for this without condoning their actions, and we can try and maintain a safe space for them.

IN MY EXPERIENCE...

This can be an important way to safeguard children, demonstrated by the case of a young person of age 19 I was involved with. This young adult was very vulnerable, and as a result of her own anxiety she became prey to a man who was able to groom her and then manipulate and coerce her. The main aim in this situation was for her mother to align herself with her daughter's wishes and views as far as she could, as otherwise she could have been pushed into a point of no return. So the mother and professionals concerned had meetings with the young person, accepted her views and her wishes, but pointed out that everyone needed to be able to keep her safe, and that therefore it was necessary to come to an agreement about how to manage and support her. The end result was that the young man involved lost interest, partly because it was all brought into the open as an agreed 'relationship'. When the young person then disclosed additional information, her mother was able to support her and in fact strengthen their relationship. This was far from easy, but the potential risk of being directly oppositional to her was far greater than simply listening to her and being able to impose some structure.

A word about communication – this is very hard for adolescents. Don't talk a lot to them, keep messages short and simple, send emojis to remind them that you care about them and are thinking of them. If they are out send text reminders about getting home, etc., or remind them to call you if their plans change. Their lack of impulse control and the effects of peer pressure will make it less important to them to stick to agreements (and they may not remember them once they get involved with other things), so reminders will help them. Secondly, if they do suddenly want to talk to you – and it is likely to be at an inconvenient time: my son always seemed to want to have important conversations at 11pm when I was ready for bed! – please do make time for these conversations. For some reason at that point in time their communication centre is up and running – if you ask them to wait until tomorrow, you will miss the opportunity, and they will be less likely to give you the option in future.

Boundaries and structure

- Simple (and few) house rules.
- Routine and structure around timing of meals, relaxation, activities, screen time and rest time. Be prepared to negotiate, as your adolescent's abilities and needs will change rapidly – think toddler.
- Rupture and repair – there will be arguments. Be prepared to repair the relationship.

Appearance and adolescent self-expression

One of the jobs of adolescence is to redefine your identity – a deliberate separation from the family identity, which is also a declaration of independence. This may mean a whole load of superficial changes to body (piercings, tattoos), different hairstyles and colours, new ideas about clothing, etc. It is only superficial – so try not to worry about it too much. Certainly being judgemental is not likely to achieve anything. Hair colour and style can be an issue at school, so encourage any dramatic experiment to happen in the long holidays!

Natural consequences

- Breaking equipment means they will not have it to use.
- Too much alcohol means feeling ill.
- If you spend all your money, you may not be able to do the things you want to with your friends.

Where teaching new skills, ensure that they are supported and scaffolded and repeated to allow new neural connections to be made. Think developmentally.

MODEL appropriate behaviour, and give a narrative

Show your children the behaviour you expect, the attitude you expect and the language you expect. Remember that there is brain building in progress and be patient.

Increased parental presence is a cornerstone of the approach recommended by Peter Jakob in his model non-violent resistance (NVR) (discussed in detail in Chapter 9), and emphasizes the need for the parent to be alongside the child and keep them in mind, demonstrating that the child is important to them. This is harder as children get older, but can be accomplished by:

- waiting to collect your child
- sending caring text messages
- leaving notes (e.g. sticky notes)
- making spontaneous gestures – buying a treat, offering a shopping trip
- being a taxi service (so you know more or less where they are)
- allowing their friends round
- taking opportunities to spend time enjoying the young person – at their convenience!

Praise

Praise is hard for young people to accept when it does not match their self-image. Praise should be:

- appropriate to their developmental ability, especially if praise is for behaviour, e.g. an incident of self-regulation or helpfulness
- specific – e.g. 'You got 9/10! That is great work, and I know you worked hard to achieve that. Well done! I am so proud of you.' If the child finds direct praise too tough, talk to someone else in front of them about why you are proud – again be specific.

PACE

Use the Dan Hughes approach to create an attitude of safety and acceptance by use of playful interactions, loving attitude, acceptance, curiosity and empathy (see Chapter 2).

- *Be aware* of the young person's level of development and respond accordingly to their needs.
- *Pre-plan* any event, outing or celebration with your child in mind. Use visual aids to help them and to build executive function. Don't be sidetracked by what other people (e.g. grandparents), however well meaning, think would be fun. Use your own knowledge of your young person's current state of mind to plan events which they can succeed at enjoying.
- *Be responsive* to the young person when they need to talk, especially about tricky subjects. Use developmentally appropriate resources. Be responsive to their methods of communication: talking, texting, writing notes, keeping a diary.
- *Step back*, mentally or physically if it helps, before responding to your young person. Use empathy for their state of mind. Reflect back what they say to you and use your curiosity to wonder why that is. Have they 'flipped their lid'? Then de-escalate.
- *Strike while the iron is cold* – another technique from NVR. This reminds us not to try to engage a young person in a discussion or logic while they are in overwhelm, feeling scared, threatened and angry. We can defer our response, and ensure that this is an appropriate and natural consequence.
- *Self-care* – build time for yourself into your routine. If necessary, take time off while the young person is at college. Find small ways to reward yourself that you can easily do to take a break – walk the dog, have a cup of tea, chat with a friend, take a bath, go to the gym, take turns taking time out with your partner (if you have one) – but build it into the routine so that young people expect it

to happen. Practise self-calming, breathing or mindful techniques that help you to de-compress after stressful incidents.

- *Be kind to yourself* – especially if you feel you have made a mistake. Model appropriate reconciliation and give the child the valuable opportunity to see that mistakes happen – that is how we learn and develop.

Becoming 18 – adulthood

If your young person is unable to function at their expected chronological age at 17.5 years, it is clearly unreasonable to expect this to happen at age 18, but this is what happens, and foster parents often find that children are moved on to semi-independence or independence whether they are ready or not. Much of the support falls away, and they are left to sink or swim. The options are limited: the '**Staying put**' arrangement allows young people to remain in their provision for longer – up to age 21, or 21 plus if the young person is undergoing extended education such as a degree and wishes to remain in the foster home during vacations. There are financial implications for the family and the young person concerned. If the young person has a high level of disability and vulnerability, then they may be eligible to move into an adult provision or to a provision with a degree of support.

Supporting teenage parents

Very young parents need a great deal of support to manage the emotional, physical and cognitive skills needed to parent a baby. Some young parents come in to specialist placements where they are supported in developing the nurturing and structure needed by a newborn and developing baby, and a robust attachment between parent and baby. This is much more difficult if the young parent has not had experience of a safe and attuned relationship themselves in their early years.

Re-parenting the parents

One of the most effective ways to support development of these skills is for the foster carer as role model to parent the parent. This may mean:

- providing a safe and secure home, warmth and shelter
- agreeing house rules to provide structure and boundaries
- structuring healthy mealtimes and involving the new parent in planning and budgeting for healthy meals, shopping and cooking
- establishing routines to support parent and baby
- ensuring a clean and hygienic environment, modelling cleaning routines and establishing chores and routines for laundry, bed linen and bathing
- engaging in a relationship with the parent, creating an environment based around PACE, which may include Playfulness (teasing, shared jokes, fun times with baby), Acceptance (that the parent is doing the best they can, accepting their circumstances and taking a non-judgemental approach), Curiosity (engaging the parent's thought processes by asking them questions) and Empathy (non-judgemental acceptance of their experience, and empathy with their struggles and their achievements).

By engaging in this process, the foster carer will scaffold the development of 'good enough' parental responses and be able to support the parent to find joy in their relationship with their child by providing a secure base for the young parent. Practical skills are learned by observation and practice, difficulties are accepted and empathized with, and solutions are explored in a nurturing way.

8

Impact on Siblings

This chapter explores the complex issues which arise when a sibling group is adopted or fostered, or where a child is adopted into an existing birth family, or where a new sibling joins the family. In this chapter I am indebted to Sarah for understanding the challenges facing families who adopt or foster sibling groups and for her insights and strategies.

IN MY EXPERIENCE...

In this context, my experience is of bringing an adopted child into a family where there were already birth children. Of course, I did not really expect any major issues, although I did recognize the challenges that I was taking on! As far as I was concerned a few months should do the trick, with all the knowledge that I had from years of working with children – but I had never worked with a child who had suffered extreme neglect, and soon found out my ignorance!

My experience as the oldest of a sibling group of five tells me that relationships within the group are complex and that each child will have a different role within the group; my age has given me the additional experience that these roles can change over time. However, for me it is absolutely true that my four full siblings are the most important people in my life other than my own children and grandchildren. Our knowledge of each other is unique because of the shared experience, and whatever our differences I believe that we all know that if one of us needs the others we will be there for each other. They are part of a structure that helps me to know myself.

Adopting and fostering sibling groups – the benefits

In looking at the benefits of fostering or adopting a sibling group, there are two points of view which need to be taken into account: the children themselves and the therapeutic parents.

Benefits to children

There are many reasons why it may be beneficial to keep siblings together, primarily because of an expectation that the relationship will provide them with a source of warmth and affection. It gives them some security and continuity – the familiarity of the relationship can be a source of stability and safety for the children. Living with your siblings also gives some sense of family and identity which can be explored and re-examined as children get older and develop new knowledge and perspectives. Saunders and Selwyn (2011) explain that sibling relationships are likely to play a significant role in their lives and form an important part of an individual's sense of self and their identity. Keeping a sibling group together can therefore mean that there is a reduced sense of bereavement and abandonment, and that grief is reduced for the children. Sibling groups have a great understanding of each other as a result of their common experiences, and this is the basis for early socialization as well as exploration, imagination and play. Especially strong bonds can occur when children are expected to help out and be responsible for each other. It is even likely that one of the children will have taken on a responsible 'parenting' role. In any event, the children retain primary attachment figures. Taken together, the elements of retaining a sense of companionship, love, protection and understanding can indicate a positive outcome for the children as they grow and mature.

THINK ABOUT IT...

Take a moment to think about your own siblings, if you have them, or a sibling group that you are aware of.

- What is the relationship between you and your siblings? Or the siblings you are thinking of?
- Why is that – and is it influenced by any of the following:
  - shared experience
  - sticking together
  - 'being there' for each other
  - knowledge of early history – painful or happy?
- Whether you enjoyed a close relationship or not, would you have wanted to be separated from the others?
- How might you have felt if you had been a child who was sent away while others were kept?

Benefits to therapeutic parents

There are many reasons for parents to wish to adopt sibling groups – for instance, always having wanted to have a large family, or more simply seeing a sibling group and absolutely knowing that these were the children they had wanted. There are also many cases where parents started fostering or adopted one or two children, and then were given the opportunity to bring a further sibling into the family if the birth mother had another child which was taken into care.

Saunders and Selwyn (2011) explain that for many parents it is important to know that they have kept a family intact and provided a loving home. In addition, it is pointed out that it may be that being retained in a sibling group reduces the possibility of the placement breaking down. Another reason Saunders and Selwyn give is that by adopting the whole sibling group, adopters reduce the risk of their children being contacted in later years by siblings who may have established unhealthy or dangerous lifestyles, therefore making their children vulnerable to exposure to adverse lifestyle choices. Yet another group of potential parents identified that they felt that it would be easier to have a sibling group who might then be more self-sufficient, with ready-made playmates.

Adopting and fostering sibling groups: the challenges

Parenting challenges

Throughout this book, we have explored the challenges which are inherent in therapeutically parenting a child who has suffered developmental trauma, and so for the purposes of this chapter we will concentrate on the additional issues that can occur when parenting more than one child.

The first obvious issue is the task of managing the diverse needs of several children at the same time. Each child may show a different response to their early trauma, but the underlying issues are likely to be present in all of the children and will include many of the trauma-related responses that we have talked about, so that fear of adults and survival responses provoke responses such as absconding, withdrawal, aggression, violence, defiance, anger, destruction, stealing, lying or nonsense chatter (to name the most commonly quoted). Children may also be more or less demanding of time and attention, have different levels of need to be catered for at school and have suffered or witnessed different levels of trauma. These diverse needs will need to be identified and then met in very specific ways.

When thinking about having to manage the diverse parenting needs that each child may have, we soon realize that an intense emotional, physical and energetic burden is placed on the parents, especially when these children may not be able to show signs of genuine affection or be able to manage fun or playful interactions for some time. If there is no reciprocity in the relationship, the parent is likely to become exhausted – drained by the effort of continually pouring emotional resources into children who have difficulty in trusting and being open to the relationship. This may lead to compassion fatigue, where the parent or parents become unable to meet more than the basic needs of their children. This is even more likely to occur where the therapeutic parents do not have a robust support system. In a worst-case scenario, compassion fatigue can lead to family breakdown, resulting in increased trauma for the child, the rest of the sibling group and the parent.

Stress on parental relationships may also present a challenge, especially if partners have different ideas about parenting and start to blame or judge each other. The time necessarily taken up by the needs of the children can also mean that there is no time to maintain the closeness necessary for the adults' relationship (if they are in a partnership). It is essential for parents to be able to carve out time for themselves as a couple as well as individual time. This may be through a break provided by the agency or family and friends, or by taking time off when children are at school and by having date days. When built into the routine of the week as a standard event, this can usually become acceptable and teaches the children the valuable lesson that parents can leave and return, developing a new understanding for them.

Finally, parents can be faced with two challenges. First, and especially where siblings have been split into several foster homes, the children will have experienced a range of different ideas about what parents mean to them, and what is appropriate behaviour at home, as each home will have had different rules and routines. Secondly, there may be 'parentification' of older children who may have assumed a parental role for their younger siblings, looking out for them and keeping them safe. This can be a response to the conditions that they are living in, or it can simply be the cultural norm. Although this can be something which increases the sibling bond, it is also necessary for children to acquire new ideas about having parents who are able to meet their needs, and for them to develop new relationships with their siblings based on shared experience and fun, as well as competition and arguments, allowing growth of capacity for relationship repair, different perspectives but an overall sense of belonging.

Re-traumatization

In some cases, when sibling groups are placed within a single family, re-traumatization can occur. Siblings who have lived together in their birth home will have shared memories and learned behaviours, and are likely to have had similar experiences shaping their neurological development. There are instances (e.g. such as Dave Pelzer describes in *A Child Called It*) where one child in a family is severely scapegoated and abused. In this case, siblings are still witness to trauma and abuse, and removal of the child who is the focus for abuse can then mean that the focus shifts to another child. Sibling responses to each other will be hardwired, and they may be a trigger for bringing past experiences to the fore. Parents may see re-enactment of abuse, or inappropriate responses to anger, or arguments between siblings who recreate their early experiences. There may be, for example, recreation of emotional abuse by bullying or belittling, or physical bullying and threats towards siblings or parents. Some children on the other hand may act in sexualized ways in order to gain attention or affection.

Unfortunately, some siblings will recreate past trauma in a way which constitutes a threat to their siblings – recreating original abuses which have been suffered or witnessed as old family dynamics play out. One way in which this can emerge is in attempted or actual intercourse or sexual activity with a sibling. Another way can be extreme violence and aggression towards family members. In these cases, the options can be very limited due to safeguarding concerns as in the fictionalized case studies below.

CASE STUDY 8.1 – INAPPROPRIATE SEXUAL BEHAVIOUR

Bill had seen and possibly been subjected to sexual abuse within the birth family. His adoptive parents had split up, and he lived with his adoptive birth mother, his female sibling Susan and a birth daughter called Angela who was born after the adoption. Bill has multiple issues as a result of his early trauma, including some cognitive disability, and his developmental age is considerably younger than his actual age. There had also been difficulties with his aggression. After Susan disclosed that Bill had attempted to rape her, Bill had to move out of his family home, and he went to live with his father, who enlisted family and friends to help care for Bill. As a result of this arrangement Mum is able to remain involved and provide consistency and support. There is no likelihood of him being returned to his mum's home, as the girls are not able to manage contact with him at all.

This is the best outcome for this family as Bill remains identified as part of the family and retains his relationship with Mum and important family members whilst interventions are put in place to help him and his father.

CASE STUDY 8.2 – EXTREME VIOLENCE AND AGGRESSION

Dan, part of a sibling group of three adopted by two professionals, found more and more difficult ways to express his feelings, until the family were at breaking point, children and parents alike. Dan was placed in a foster home for three months and was then re-integrated into the adoptive home with additional support for the parents in the form of training and a support group.

This was a good outcome for Dan, but Dan and his family will need to be supported in case of a further crisis, especially as Dan enters his teenage years.

Sibling rivalry

In all sibling groups you will find an element of sibling rivalry – bickering, fighting, falling out and vying for parental favour and attention. However, if we are talking about sibling groups who have been traumatized through the early part of their lives, there are additional issues which intensify 'normal' sibling rivalry, and for some children these experiences (which have their roots in fear and terror) feel like a challenge to their ability to survive.

For sibling groups, as with other traumatized children, knowledge of their history is vital to providing clues to reasons for their behaviours – for example, the child who has observed parental or other domestic violence may have integrated this behaviour into their own survival pattern; the child who has been subject to sexual abuse may seek to visit this on siblings or use sexualized overtures to gain the favour or attention of adults; the child who sought to protect and care for younger siblings may find it extremely hard to relinquish this role and trust in an adult, and the siblings of such a child may still seek parenting from this sibling. For each child in a sibling group there will have been an individual experience, perception of and response to these events. It is easy to see how this presents an incredible challenge in parenting terms.

Behaviours	**Possible reasons**
Children compete to 'be the best' (including being the best at being bad...); each has to be the 'winner'	• Fight for survival • Fear of invisibility – especially if other children are getting attention for positive *or* negative behaviours • Needing to feel powerful and in control
Children literally fight for parental attention	• Recreating a familiar environment • Needing to feel powerful and in control • Child recreating parental role (taking charge, being 'bossy')
Children fight for seats and space in car, at table, etc.	• Recreating a familiar environment • Seeking proximity to parent (and therefore being first in line for attention) • Rewards children with a reaction, such as parent acting as referee, which gives scope to maintain argument... • Rewards children with a reaction as parent is triggered into emotional response
Children take each other's possessions	• Recreating a familiar environment • Fight for survival, especially where there was abuse or neglect
Children argue almost constantly	• Rewards children with a reaction from parent, possibly triggering an emotional response from parent • Children need to be in control • Recreating familiar environment/observed behaviour

Children hurt each other, sometimes seriously	• Recreating familiar environment/observed behaviour • One child feels need to protect the parent from the needs of the other children • Expression of stress and overwhelm. Children are re-traumatized by each other's behaviour and responses • Children need to feel powerful and in control
Child perceives that they get less than other children, parent is 'unfair'	• Engages parent as referee • Triggers parent's emotional response • Expression of child's fears and anxiety

Meeting the challenges

Be kind to yourself!

- Establish a support system – friends and family – and join a support group or organization such as the National Association of Therapeutic Parents (NAoTP) to keep in touch with others in similar circumstances. This will give you a safe place to vent, celebrate or seek supportive advice in a practical and non-judgemental way.
- Get as much information about the history of the children as possible.
- Ensure robust transition planning – have a staged removal so that younger siblings are integrated into the family and become accustomed to being parented by adults, with boundaries and trust being established before the older siblings join the family.
- Practise pausing, patience and stepping back from an emotional response.
- Remember where they have come from.
- Be consistent.
- Follow routines and timetables strictly to establish safety, consistency and predictability. Include time for yourself in this timetable.

- Make time to have fun!

Strategies

As always, the focus is on providing a predictable, reliable and consistent environment to provide a structure that will both contain the children and enable them to develop new behaviours. Once again, a key element is the self-care that will enable the parent to meet the challenges 24/7. Lastly, do remember that being able to play together may not have been part of these children's experience. They are very likely to need the same amount of support as any single child from a traumatic background to re-visit developmental stages and learn to play together.

Strategies	How to put in place and why the strategy works
Rules and boundaries	Firm boundaries increase security and lower anxiety. Use visual reminders, especially during early days. Visual reminders should be pictorial as well as having words. Images speak to the brain quicker than words do!
Routines	Keep routines simple and rigid, making use of a visual timetable which can be referred to. Keep to mealtimes and have regular activities clearly identified, including screen time, bath time, story time, bedtime. With repetition, this increases the child's sense of safety, reduces anxiety and decreases escalation Remember to timetable in your own time to recharge – this will soon be accepted as the norm and can also underline that if you go out (without them) you will always come back
Keep it simple	Identify key areas and use your structure and rules to address them, but prioritize! One thing at a time. Trying to keep control of too many things at once is exhausting and stressful for the whole family
Protected spaces	Assign places at the table, in the sitting room, in the car. Do not allow this to vary! Enable children to protect their individual possessions and spaces (e.g. their own bedrooms). This allows the children to feel that they have a place (literally) in the family home or car, that their rights will be protected, and therefore that they themselves are important

Turn taking	From talking at table to chores to special time with adults, ensure that these are clearly identified. Use a visual timetable so that this is kept clear. This strategy ensures that each child is given equal importance and is 'seen' and 'heard' and that each individual is able to explore their ideas and interests on a 1:1 basis
Minimize barriers to supervision	For example – going open plan in the house so that you can keep children in your field of view. This prevents escalations and arguments the minute your back is turned (designed to re-capture your attention)
Avoid comparisons	Keep praise specific, focused and individual. This enables each child to feel valued and minimizes the risk of competition, escalation and argument due to perceived favouritism
Reflect after the event, whether it's a positive or negative event (when everyone has calmed down if it's negative)	Allows children to identify for themselves the areas that have gone well and why. Encourages them to reflect on their adverse behaviours and how they have affected them and other members of the family. An ideal opportunity to use PACE (see Chapter 2)
Take a deep breath...	Before responding – pause. Take a step back (literally, if necessary). This allows time for your brain to re-engage in a conscious way so that you can identify what is happening for you as well as them and avoid escalation
Be kind to yourself – and your partner if applicable	No one ever learned anything by getting things right all the time, and ensure you have enough time to recharge your own batteries

The impact of adoption or fostering on existing children and the therapeutic parent

We will examine both positive and negative effects.

First, the effect will depend to an extent on the age of the birth child, and clearly there is a difference between a placement where there are already birth children and situations where a child is born subsequent to placement. To an extent, where there are already children in a family, they may have been part of a process and their views on the placement may have been taken into account. However, the harsh reality is that the impact 24/7 of a child who has suffered great trauma through neglect or other forms of abuse or as a result of in utero damage is greater than can easily be imagined. The following issues may easily arise:

- Children (especially younger children) may feel neglected due to the extreme and complex needs of the adopted or foster child, which always seems to mean that they get priority when it comes to parental attention and availability, and indeed this may be the case. Such a child may have a feeling of displacement – a cuckoo has landed in their nest and taken it over.
- Children may be subject to frequent verbal abuse from the looked after child.
- Children may be subject to physical abuse from the looked after child.
- Children may feel displaced by the newcomer – rather than gaining a sibling they have lost their place and even their importance in the family. Family dynamics may shift suddenly and severely to cope with the demands of the looked after child, which may threaten the stability of the other children.
- Children may lose their sense of the home as a safe place and a sanctuary as they may be physically attacked, their room may be entered without their permission, and their possessions may be lost, stolen or destroyed during traumatic incidents.
- Children may develop primary trauma as a result of being attacked by the looked after child or they may develop secondary trauma as a result of the adaptive behaviours of the looked after child.

CASE STUDY 8.3 – BIRTH SON'S ACCOUNT OF THE EFFECT OF ADOPTION

Beth, aged three, was adopted into a family where there were three existing birth children aged 11, 16 and 17 at the time of placement.

Mum ran a childminding business that included working with vulnerable families, and this is how she met her fourth child. Mum and Dad made the decision to adopt her if possible when this became an option. She was then two years old and had been known to the family for over six months. The adoption was finalized when she was three. All the birth children had been consulted prior to adoption.

Beth showed challenging and aggressive behaviours from the outset, as well as having delayed growth and speech due to neglect. She was extremely needy and attention seeking, and required a great deal of one-to-one time with her mum. At the same time her mum was the target for her most challenging behaviours.

After 11 years, following the breakdown of the marriage and the other siblings moving out due to natural progression, Beth was accommodated under section 20 of the Children Act 1989 due to the extreme violence Mum had been subjected to. Mum and Dad retained parental rights and contact. Her behaviours included verbal and physical abuse and attacks with weapons. There had been intense involvement of professionals, including the police and CAMHS (child and adolescent mental health services). The birth son, Dave, had also been threatened with a knife, and his own son as a baby had been the object of nasty comments and jealousy. Dave discussed his feelings with his mum 14 years after the adoption:

> When she came she took all your time. You didn't have any time any more for any of us. We missed out on some special time with you. Lauren and I missed out, but we were older, we could understand it a bit and deal with it, but Molly (youngest birth sibling) didn't get any of your time and she was neglected and ignored because Beth took all your time and energy. I do love her, she is my sister, and I remember her being so cute, I can't bear to think of her wanting to kill herself...
>
> I was scared, she came after me with a knife, and she was nasty to Mason (his son) and I remember her being so jealous. She is the reason you could not spend time with Mason when he was a baby. He missed out on that special time with you...
>
> It worries me that she still knows where we live.

While accommodated under section 20, Beth had weekend contact with one or other parent every weekend. Her sisters remained in contact with her by phone and visited when possible. They still care about, protect and help their sister as much as they can. After Beth had to leave, the older children all spent time at home, thus regaining some of the ground they had lost. Mum continues to advocate for Beth, as does Dad. Dave is now considering whether he feels able to manage a phone call or a visit himself. All birth children display considerable emotional maturity and literacy, compassion and empathy.

As we can see, the impact on Dave has been enduring, and he remains very conflicted.

There are positive aspects of bringing a foster or adopted child into an established family: children can welcome and accept their new sibling and offer unconditional love. In Case study 8.3, the two female birth siblings are still able to offer unconditional love to their adoptive sister and remain very much part of her life, despite being the focus of destructive and aggressive behaviours, especially the youngest birth sibling.

From the perspective of the fostered or looked after child entering into a 'ready-made' family, there are many positives: inclusion in a family structure and the possibility of forming new bonds, giving eventually a sense of belonging and knowledge that there are significant people in their life who are reliable, predictable and consistent in their love and care. The child will (as with any looked after child) be introduced to new experiences and new models of behaviour as shown by their new family. This may add to their confusion and sense of loss initially, but over time new understanding and behaviours can emerge. On the other hand, for a child who has been neglected and has had to fight for their very survival, there will still be an expectation of needing to keep the attention focused on them by whatever means, with jealousy leading to attention-seeking behaviour if their new siblings receive attention from their parents. Their expectations will be based on their previous experience. If their experience has been neglect, rejection and cruelty, then their experience will lead them to expect more of the same. If their peers were a danger to them, then they will be fearful of their new siblings. They may also have a sense of loss if they have been removed from their birth siblings.

As with all the children we have talked about, there is often an overriding need to control. This is a survival strategy and is based on the fear and the unpredictability of their early life.

Impact of contact with separated siblings on the child and the therapeutic parent

Thinking first about the child, Saunders and Selwyn (2011) report from their research that very often contact with siblings can be child led – parents were much more likely to accommodate contact if they could see this was what the children wanted. For these children, parents reported that contact was enjoyable for their children, enabling them to have continuity of relationships and to reconnect. This is described by one mother as a 'warm and natural' relationship, and another talks about contact as promoting an open and honest conversation about birth siblings. Clearly, as the child matures and their perspective and view of the world change, access to siblings will give them context for their history, adding to their autobiographical knowledge and understanding over time. Many parents spoke positively about the effects of contact, even where there were some emotional reactions from the children: 'I think for all of them it evokes painful feelings, but they love seeing them, and I think overall the relationships are healthy' (Saunders and Selwyn 2011).

On the other hand, there can be negative outcomes – a sense of loss and grieving for siblings, and poor self-esteem reinforced by knowing that some birth children remained in the family, are two issues. However, it could be said (as quoted above) that such feelings are natural, and gaining understanding and knowledge will enable these to be worked through to the benefit of the child.

Some children suffer re-traumatization as a result of contact, perhaps because contact fails (letter box contact not sent, contact appointments not kept), which increases the child's sense of themselves as a 'bad' child. It can also be confusing if the birth parents always seem lovely, kind and attentive, bearing gifts and seeming to be fully engaged, as it will conflict with the information that they have and their knowledge and memories of their birth parents.

From the foster parent's perspective, contact can trigger very painful memories and lead to re-traumatization and escalation which can last for some days, possibly with regression to much earlier patterns of behaviour. This response is often reported by parents in support groups and training sessions. Foster parents find that they need to manage the environment and have clear boundaries, which helps – for example, 'It works now we have somewhere neutral, where there is something to do, and we keep it fairly short. We had a couple of contacts that were very difficult. We try to avoid Christmas and birthdays' (Saunders and Selwyn 2011).

The child's confusion may lead to rejection and unacceptable behaviour post contact which the foster parent needs to try to help the child to manage as they struggle with incompatible ideas about their birth mum who was unable to care for them, who has been lovely in contact.

The more positive outcomes for the foster parents can be that contact presents an opportunity to gather information about the child's history and wider birth family, which may be useful for life story work and giving them a greater depth of understanding. These insights will help in their planning and strategies. In addition, the foster parent is able to maintain the model of the predictable, consistent and stable parent who is able to provide and maintain a secure base for the child.

Abusive contact

Many foster parents sadly report that contact with birth families, especially parents, is simply an opportunity for continued abuse, either directly or through covert threats to the child and which terrify them. Whilst this is a debate that is gathering force in the media, the balance is still weighted towards protecting the rights of the adult, not the rights of the child. All that parents can do is to advocate for their own child.

9

Living in Fear

Managing Aggression and Violence

This chapter discusses one of the most difficult situations faced by many parents who are living with a child who has suffered trauma.

In 2019, the Centre of Excellence in Child Trauma developed a survey to establish key issues faced by parents, which was responded to by 1125 people (www.coect.co.uk/2019/09/30/child-victims-of-trauma-forced-to-visit-parents-that-abused-them-this-should-be-illegal). The results showed that the majority of parents who care for children who have experienced trauma face violence in the home (79% of respondents) and suffer poor mental health. The violence and aggression may take many forms: vile and abusive language, threats, using body weight to control a parent, punching and kicking, all the way through the spectrum of violence, to using weapons which may range from fallen branches if you are out and about to picking up knives and either threatening or actually cutting the parent. The parent is trapped; often violence happens in secret – the parent will protect the child and not be clear about the extent of the abuse they are suffering, and when they attempt to disclose, they find themselves being judged and blamed for their poor parenting skills and lack of ability to control the child. Parents using restraint techniques are told that they may be investigated for abuse of the child if they do this, but are not given effective techniques to try. Violence and aggression are among the main reasons that families break down, and families cite lack of professional support and training as well as blaming and judging attitudes from social workers as being major contributing factors.

The outcomes are often catastrophic. Families break down, parents split up, children have increased trauma, and parents suffer from mental health issues such as depression, secondary post-traumatic stress disorder (when you are severely affected by your knowledge of your child's history and how it has affected them) and post-traumatic stress disorder as a result of repeated assaults and injuries that have been received.

Developmental trauma and impact on the child

Conception to birth

We have discussed the causes of developmental trauma, and identified different routes by which a baby or very young child can suffer developmental trauma with subsequent effects (see Chapter 1). The extent to which this happens is governed by individual resilience as well as the quality of care that the baby or young child receives subsequently, but in some conditions, such as foetal alcohol syndrome disorder (FASD), there may be permanent damage which may limit the developmental ability of the baby or young child as they mature. Many families and professionals find it hard to accept that newborn babies can suffer developmental trauma if they have entered a stable and nurturing environment immediately after birth, but experience shows this to be untrue, and there are many reasons for this:

- *In utero trauma*: Genetic factors may influence some traits of mental illness. Maternal stress leads to cortisol toxicity for the embryo and consequent damage to neurological development. Toxicity from drug or alcohol misuse, or even medical mistakes (as in a generation of children affected by Thalidomide prescribed for morning sickness), can cause trauma to physical development, including development of the neurological system.

- *Early separation and loss*: We are beginning to understand that as well as physical trauma, an unborn baby can suffer psychological trauma, which can easily be sufficient to cause issues of separation and loss and consequent issues of unrelieved emotional pain and feelings of worthlessness and confusion even if the child has been handed straight into the arms of their new parents or carers.

Nancy Verrier explored this subject in her book *The Primal Wound* (1993) as a result of her intuitions about her own adopted daughter. These are some of her ideas:

> Many doctors and psychologists now understand that bonding doesn't begin at birth, but is a continuum of physiological, psychological and spiritual events which begin in utero and continue throughout the postnatal bonding period. (p.1)

> In his book, *Babies Remember Birth*, Dr Chamberlain goes on to say 'Babies know more than they are supposed to know. Minutes after birth, a baby can pick out his mother's face – which he has never seen – from a gallery of photos.' (p.5)

We would add that it is also a well-established fact that a baby can identify breast milk from their own mother by smell and will turn towards this in preference to the milk of other mothers.

> It has been noted by some clinicians in working with adoptees that they all have essentially the same issues whether they were adopted at birth or as teenagers. These issues centre around separation and loss, trust, rejection, guilt and shame, intimacy, loyalty and mastery or power and control. (p.7)

> All this rhetoric ignores one simple but critical fact: The adoptee was there. The child actually experienced being left alone by the biological mother and being handed over to strangers. That he may have been only a few days old or a few minutes old makes no difference. He shared a 40 week experience...with a person to whom he is biologically, genetically connected. (p.10)

Antenatal stress and trauma

After birth, the work of the baby's whole system becomes that of adapting to the environment that they have been born into. The primitive structures of the brain – the reptilian structures governing our unconscious bodily functions (such as breathing, digestion, blood pressure, heartbeat, temperature control and survival instincts – fight or flight) and the limbic system (primarily responsible for emotional states and interactions) – are in place.

There are two other important structures we will mention briefly. The amygdala is the 'filter' for all sensory information coming into the body, and also information from within the body itself. Hughes and Baylin (2012) explain that the amygdala has a specialist action in threat detection and activation of the fight–flight stress response.

The hippocampus works alongside the amygdala and has a role in creating our narrative – our autobiographical memories. This enables perceived threats to be put in context and the stress response system to be regulated (Hughes and Baylin 2012).

The amygdala and hippocampus form (with other structures) the subcortical region or 'downstairs' brain. The cortex or 'upstairs' brain (supporting voluntary actions, communication, planning, organization and reasoning/cognitive skills) has a structure, but is not 'on line'. The neural connections required to develop this part of the brain are formed by sensory stimulation and experiences. This is part of our ability as humans to be adaptable and allows us to develop within a cultural and environmental context but also ensures our best chances of survival. This is essential to the understanding of the behaviour patterns that children will adopt in response to their situation.

In her book *The Selfish Society* (2010) Sue Gerhardt explores the importance of the interactions between the baby and the parent that is attuned to the baby's needs: 'the baby's early experience of dependence determines his unconscious attitudes to the world' (p.108). As soon as we are born, we have a survival drive. Babies soon learn how to get their survival needs met, and the way that they do this will depend upon their experiences of their developing relationship. Therefore, as Sue Gerhardt states: 'A baby who finds himself in a stressful home with unpredictable or punitive caregivers will develop differently from a baby who finds himself in a kind and supportive environment' (p.106).

Children who learn from their earliest days that families are based on kindness, consideration for others, the need to protect those members of the family that are weaker and that relationships are resilient will naturally have an open and trusting interaction with society. However, children who have to fight for even their most basic needs, or come from unpredictable, scary or chaotic homes where individual members are not valued, or maybe are abused, neglected or ignored, will not develop a sense of empathy or learn how to have a positive interaction – they cannot know what they have not experienced.

...some maltreated children behave in a rather shocking way to other children who are in distress; instead of comforting them they react with anger or fear. The more negative the mother-child relationship, the less able the child is to respond to others with concern. (Gerhardt 2010, p.180)

We can therefore see that our child's perception of themselves, adults and the world in general has its foundations in the baby's earliest experiences, which will create neural connections, forming the first 'blueprint' of how to approach the world in order to survive. For a baby, born completely dependent with the option only to make their distress and discomfort known, this is a crucial time.

We speculate on the impact of parenting styles in a very simple way in the table below.

Parenting pattern	**Child's developing sense of**		
	Adults	**Self**	**Environment**
Attuned to child Nurturing Predictable/consistent 'Good enough' parenting	Safe Dependable Comforting Loving Trustworthy	Lovable Safe Important Interesting Secure	Safe Welcoming Nurturing Interesting

Not attuned to child Neglecting Unpredictable/ inconsistent	Unsafe Scary Untrustworthy	Unlovable Worthless Insecure Under threat Unimportant Helpless	Unsafe Hostile Unhelpful Pain filled World does not make sense Chaos
Other abuse – physical, sexual	Unsafe Scary Will hurt you	Unlovable Worthless Insecure Under threat Unimportant Hurting Helpless	Unsafe Hostile Unhelpful Pain filled No one can help

These early ideas (schemas) lay down the blueprint for the expectations the child has of adults and the world, and their view of themselves, the internal working model, which we have already discussed. Like all of us, the baby and young child is forced to adopt behaviours that will ensure their survival, and these responses are hardwired because the only context that they have established in their hippocampus and sensory memory is that the world is hostile and adults bring emotional or physical pain. This results in behaviour patterns driven by fear that ensure that their survival needs are met.

The behaviours and attitudes that we see as a result are predictable.

Behaviours:

- Aggression
- Controlling behaviour
- Manipulation
- Splitting
- Violence
- 'Jekyll and Hyde' mood changes (due to stressors)
- Opposition and defiance
- Hypervigilance.

Attitudes:

- Adults are not trustworthy.
- Adults are dangerous.
- The world is dangerous.
- Take what you can while you can get it.
- The world is unpredictable.
- I am in danger a lot of the time.
- If I am not in control, I will die.

These are as a result of early experience, and are 'hardwired' and resistant to change (Hughes and Baylin 2012).

Stressors and triggers

In the context of developmental trauma, a stressor is anything which raises the anxiety of the child producing a stress response. This can be any transition (change of teacher, stopping play, going out) or any sensory input which triggers a strong memory from their trauma such as feeling hungry (internal state) or a particular smell. For instance, I know of an adult adoptee who is stressed by flies, because of the domestic environment she was raised in.

We know that stressors increase output of cortisol and that this has a direct effect on our ability to make considered decisions and contextualize our experience, as this requires integration of the brain: 'The stressed out brain, needing to keep things simple, has no time for ambiguity, complexity or uncertainty. Survival is all about rapid assessment and quick action, requiring the reduction of complexity and narrowing of options' (Hughes and Baylin 2012, p.97). If we relate this to the experience of the child, then the stressors in the child's life may be considered to include:

- fear of abandonment or rejection
- very poor self-image

- fear of pain, both emotional and physical
- busy overwhelming environments (e.g. school, college, theme park)
- fear of adults.

These stressors mean that the child's stress levels may be much higher than is the norm (see Figure 9.1).

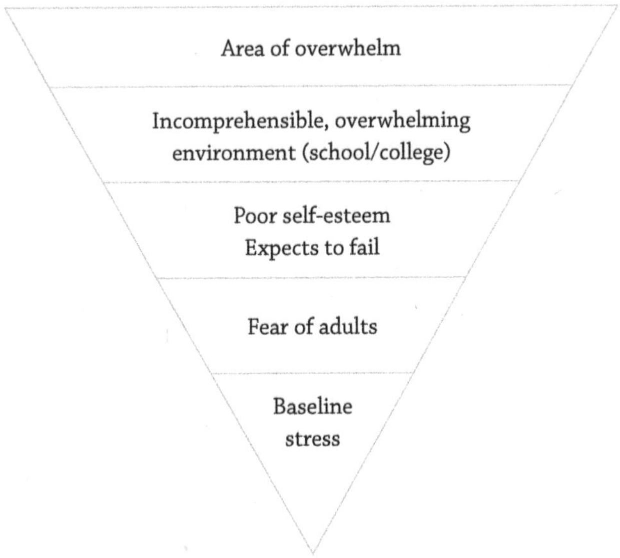

Figure 9.1 Stressors

We can see that this level of stress is hard to manage, but the child may just be able to maintain control until there is a further incident or trigger.

In the context of developmental trauma, a trigger is a specific and known factor that will cause the child to escalate into dysfunctional behaviours such as violence or aggressive language. A trigger is a strong connection to a traumatic event. For example, a child might always become dysregulated around certain dates (Christmas, anniversaries of moves, birthdays) or because they see a strong visual reminder. The effect is like a flashback, where the child feels the trauma as happening in the here and now.

A trigger can happen in a heartbeat, and for a child whose norm is so close to overwhelm, this is likely to erupt in disproportionate ways which are very sudden and unpredictable – for example, the parent says 'No' or 'Just a minute', triggering memories of being ignored and needs not being met, and sending the child into overwhelm.

Given that triggers are not obvious to us all the time, we need to try to identify what the stressors are in the child's life and try to change these. Reduced stress increases rationality and the ability to reflect and take on new ideas.

CASE STUDY 9.1 – EFFECTS OF STRESS IN EDUCATIONAL SETTING

Jemma is a 16-year-old girl living in a residential unit. Her diagnoses include attachment disorder, autism and generalized anxiety disorder. She is unable to live with her family due to her inability to manage the emotional dynamic. However, they are very much still a part of her life. She lives in a specialist unit with very caring professionals. Jemma has low self-esteem and an absolute belief that she will be abandoned and rejected, and that this is because she is 'bad'. This has not been helped by an adoption breakdown and two fostering placement breakdowns.

She settled well at her secondary school, a specialist school, and was very happy there. However, big problems started after her transition to college with high expectations of her cognitive levels and ability to manage the academic level, and she was unsupported. Within a few weeks of starting, Jemma reverted to extremely dangerous behaviour, putting both herself and her carers at risk. This continued until she had an admission to a psychiatric unit and a break when she calmed down. Subsequent attempts to return her to college resulted in disruption, further attempts to self-harm and leaving class. This proved to be a very negative cycle, leading to negative impressions of herself and others being confirmed.

However, during the holidays she calmed down and was able to relax, repair relationships with staff and pursue her interests as well as take on new activities. Staff noticing this decided that to maintain Jemma's mental health she needed to pursue a different educational course, such as an apprenticeship, which is more hands on. Initially, a greatly reduced timetable was put in place, and subsequently an application was made to an alternative provision offering a land-based study course working with small animals. Jemma has been able to calm and accommodate to this in a very positive way, with visible benefits to her levels of anxiety and overwhelm.

Jemma is currently feeling much better, looking forward to her new college, and much more able to engage in her relationships in a positive way, feeding a positive cycle.

It can be seen in this example that, as illustrated in Figure 9.1, Jemma had a baseline of stress which was very high, and that the additional stress of the expectations placed on her in a busy college environment were enough to push her into overwhelm and cause real safety issues, especially if there were additional factors such as news from home.

Please review 'Room 1' (Dillon 2019, Chapter 1) for further information about this complex subject.

Non-violent resistance (NVR)

Dr Peter Jakob is a consultant clinical psychologist and the first person to use NVR in the UK. He has adapted the approach for traumatized and multi-stressed families. NVR has become widely advocated as a means to reduce child-to-parent violence, which has emerged as a significant threat to placements over recent years.

It is important to remember that pure NVR may not be appropriate in all cases, as some aspects may be found too challenging and confrontational for a traumatized child to manage, such as the announcement and the sit-in – a way of demonstrating to the child that they have behaved inappropriately. In our experience, using this type of strategy with a traumatized child can provoke an extreme shame-based and fearful reaction. There are, however, many elements of NVR that can be usefully adapted and which do offer the scope to make changes, and the principles of de-escalation, parental presence, establishing support and gestures of unconditional regard are extremely useful.

NVR seeks to rebuild relationships within families using a child-focused approach and specific strategies and interventions to support and empower parents and create a positive environment of reduced stress, acceptance and reconciliation. This is achieved by key aspects of the NVR approach (for the following information I am indebted to Dr Peter Jakob, PartnershipProjects UK Ltd, and for my 2015 training with Rachael Aylmer of PartnershipProjects UK Ltd):

- De-escalation and avoiding conflict
- Building trust in the relationship between parent/s and child/ren
- Building a team – creating a support network
- Unconditional repair – building resilience and self-esteem
- Recognizing that change takes time.

These key aspects are linked to the underlying structure of the NVR approach which Dr Peter Jakob calls the 5 cornerstones:

5 cornerstones

The 5 cornerstones which I describe below form the foundation of the NVR approach:

1. *Refuse to give in and breaking taboos*: A vital part of this approach is to enable the parent to provide a secure and unassailable safe base (refuse to give in) and to break their silence (break taboos). Often parents will not disclose the violence they are experiencing as they are scared about the repercussions for the child and the family.
2. *De-escalate*: Stepping down from battles and having the ability to take a new perspective on behaviours and household stressors often has an amazing spontaneous result in reducing the overall stress load for parent and child alike. This enables the brain to remain in a calmer, more integrated state. From this perspective, it is easier to be mindful of the child's experience and to continue to be able to access compassion and empathy.

3. *Develop support*: A secondary issue to breaking taboos, this cornerstone recognizes the need to have strong and structured support with specific roles to play in providing a safe infrastructure around the family.

4. *Raise presence*: Classic NVR seeks to raise presence through organized protest – this is generally too shaming for very traumatized children to experience, so has been amended for the purpose of this chapter. Parents of children with developmental trauma who adopt this confrontational stance will certainly be attacked. Parental presence is, however, an immensely important factor in attempting to rebuild the stable foundations of a secure base that is often missing. This is made more difficult if the child is older due to the expectations of family members, friends and professionals for them to act their age. However, if the child's developmental social and emotional age is five, that is how they will act, regardless of their chronological age.

5. *Reconcile and repair*: The magic of reconciliation and repair cannot be overestimated. This allows a child to separate actions from self, and to experience the security of a loving relationship.

Looking at these in more depth:

Refuse to give in and breaking taboos

The important thing here is that the issue is out in the open where it can be managed in a very different way. As part of the process, parents identify people who can help and are able to withhold judgement and provide support without creating additional stress by making blaming comments. They could be:

- family members
- friends
- adoption team professionals

- teachers
- youth workers.

Their roles will depend on the support they feel able to offer, such as:

- being a witness to events
- providing a 'listening' service
- emergency help
- mentoring the young person
- noticing positive events
- childminding and giving parents a brain break for a couple of hours.

The adult is then in a safer place where there are others in the process who are being supportive and helping to maintain the focus in a helpful way.

De-escalate

It is a considerable challenge for parents to take on board that by adopting a deferred response rather than a reactive response, they are not condoning or allowing the child or young person to 'get away with' behaviours. It means accepting that during periods of overwhelm and consequent adaptive behaviours, it is important for the adult to stay regulated by stepping away from control issues as a considered response, knowing that the issue will be dealt with later in a way that allows the child or young person to feel validated and motivated to change their behaviour. This is very hard work for the adult; however, this is about recognizing the roots of behaviour and choosing to step away and stay in control rather than escalate the behaviour by attempting control.

De-escalation:

- Parents and carers are given strategies and tools to enable them to take a different approach to the child's controlling (untrusting) and challenging behaviour.

- Parents and carers practise strategies to enable them to stay calm and to de-stress.
- The approach is non-judgemental and supportive.
- Parents and carers do not aim to change the child during an aggressive incident. All action aims to minimize risk and lower psycho-physiological arousal of adults and child.

Deferring the response:

- Instead of reacting to provocation, caregivers act at a time of their own choosing and in a way they themselves determine. When they do take action, later, they aim to raise their personal presence as parents, carers or teachers, not punish or change the way the child sees things.

De-escalation strategies:

- The parent or carer remains calm by ensuring the environment is safe.
- Parental presence – the parent or carer stays with the child.
- Calming strategies for parents and carers.

In attempting this, other aspects of therapeutic parenting are useful strategies, such as naming the need and using the attitude of PACE. In addition, it is essential for the parent:

- to take time to discharge their own stress in an appropriate way (e.g. by talking to a trusted friend or counsellor or member of a listening circle or support group; having a regular night off, or taking time for themselves during the day when the child/young person is at school; exercising; giving themselves small rewards and treats)

- to pick battles carefully and prioritize the behaviour they would like to change, acknowledging that this will also require change from them as well
- to ensure that any consequences are natural and do not cause the conflict to escalate
- to understand that to change their own attitudes and their child's understanding and experience takes time and repeated experience
- to take care to repair the relationship and offer reconciliation gestures which model how to do this – for example, offering a drink and a snack or leaving a loving note.

Develop support

This means taking action within an established community that understands and is prepared to continue to support to ensure that the young person experiences support and stable relationships and that the carer has additional security. Supporters should understand that this is a different approach to behavioural challenges and be able to support the changes that the family are trying to make. They should be clear that lack of a punitive base does not equate to acceptance of the behaviour, but that this will be addressed in a very different way. Case study 9.2 demonstrates how this might work.

CASE STUDY 9.2 – SINGLE ADOPTER EMMA AND 13-YEAR-OLD SON JASON

Emma had experienced violence and aggression from Jason since adoption but this had grown worse as he entered his adolescent years. Emma was terrified of approaching social services, fearing that Jason would be taken from her, so she was in a very hard place when she contacted a support service which offered child-to-parent violence (CPV) training.

First, there had to be work to support Emma to understand some of her son's behaviours to help reconnect her with his experience as she was approaching compassion fatigue. This involved revisiting some of his history and re-assessing expectations to reduce stress. Emma also developed a great support system:

- An SOS text system to a number of trusted people – 'If you get this text, respond quickly'
- A trusted relative who her son looked up to who could give appropriate praise but also talk to Jason about his behaviour using a specific format: 'Hi Jason – great to see you! I really like your new look! By the way, your mum told me that… and I want to remind you that we have agreed this behaviour has to stop. Anyway, I am looking forward to this afternoon, I hope you are too!' This was someone who could be trusted not to lecture but to maintain the relationship whilst taking a firm position that the behaviour must and will change
- Telephone CPV support and advice for an extensive period of time
- Friends to deliver hugs and provide coffee
- Neighbour to escape to if necessary
- Social worker involved
- School involved.

After a great deal of work, this relationship survived a crisis and is headed back to stability and confidence.

The effectiveness of NVR is partly due to the careful supporting structure which is put in place. Supporters can be drawn from any area of the child or adult's life and have clearly defined roles – supporting parents by providing parental presence, and supporting the child by 'witnessing' their behaviours but remaining a constant presence themselves. They may be available for parents to call on to help them to calm down; be a witness to both the child's adverse behaviours (demonstrating that they find an act unacceptable but are still there for them) and the child's successes, giving messages of encouragement.

The NVR 'sandwich' is a way of giving behavioural information to the child. In a sandwich, the top layer is positive: 'I really enjoyed spending time with you at the weekend!' The middle layer gives the child the message about an incident, showing that the behaviour is known about. However, this is delivered in a factual, non-accusatory way: 'Your mum told me you hit her again yesterday. You know this behaviour is not acceptable.' The last layer returns to the positive, giving the child a vision of a better future: 'I am looking forward to another great visit this weekend!' The process is repeated multiple times.

Raise presence

This factor assumes that traumatized children need to know that their parent is there for them and cares about them no matter what. This is, very importantly, not confrontational. It might be about time in (sitting with your child) but it might be about other things that let your child know you are present in all aspects of their life – collecting them from friends, phoning friends' parents, texting to be sure they are OK, leaving notes in their bags or under their door. This is also about letting the child know that you can 'see' what they need and that you keep them 'in mind'.

One of the ways in which we can raise parental presence is by meeting the unmet needs of the child. This relies on having a knowledge of your child's history, developing the observational skills to assess what age your child is showing in their behaviour and then supporting them at their developmental rather than their chronological age. This may also involve the use of narrative as discussed previously in the book. For instance: your 11-year-old adoptive daughter still wishes to play predominantly with dolls, prams and pushchairs. Because you are aware of the trauma she suffered through her first three years, you reflect that this is a stage of play that she still needs in order to process her feelings about being a baby, and to revisit that younger stage of life. You might get full-size prams and pushchairs (second hand!) that allow her to do this. You might then engage her in talking about her doll as though she was a three- or four-year-old if this seems appropriate. Or maybe your 13-year-old foster son still wants to play guns and action heroes – just join in with him and allow him to experience the joy of having an adult join him in his play.

Reconcile and repair

Ruptures are followed by repair. Mistakes happen and are forgiven.

Apologies can be accepted and reconciliation can take place. Gradually, over time and with many repetitions, the child comes to believe in their family and to trust their place within the family unit.

Sadly, in the face of overwhelming situations, this can be very hard for therapeutic parents, because sometimes they are in a state of compassion fatigue, where our ability to empathize with and care for our children has been compromised by our need to protect ourselves.

First, therefore, carers need to take time for themselves and reconnect with their own emotions. This means asking for help, and then using those little spaces of time they carve out to do something that makes them feel good – we are talking about the simple things here: talk to a friend; go for a swim, a run or a walk; read your favourite book; give yourself a treat. Take a deep breath. When you feel able, try one of the following:

- Give an unconditional gesture of regard – a swift hug, or a smile. If asked, have an answer as to why you are smiling – 'It makes me smile when I see you.'
- Notice their favourite things and just occasionally surprise them with a treat.
- If they ask you to come and sit with them, say yes, even if it does mean turning the dinner off for five minutes or stopping the housework. This is more important. If you need to keep it brief just say, 'I really love sitting with you, but I know you are hungry, so I can only stay for five minutes, then I must cook your dinner!'
- Leave an affectionate or fun note.
- Offer a drink and biscuits.

The announcement

Once the work of establishing a structure which focuses on the needs of the child whilst supporting the adult has been established, with a support system and a clear idea about exactly which behaviours need to be addressed, the family may decide to create an announcement, which informs the child about the steps that are going to be taken to create a change for the family.

The announcement is a written communication which explains to the child that their parents have noticed their behaviour and care enough to take steps to help them to manage and for the whole family to make changes for the better. The announcement gives the child notice of the steps that will be taken and reassures the child that the parents are looking forward to a brighter future as a happy family.

Structure of the announcement

- *Problems – be specific, concrete, neutral*: 'Jim, for a long time, you have been violent by hitting Mum and breaking things in the house, and you've been saying abusive things to everyone in the family.'
- *Concerns*: 'We are concerned for your mother's safety, and for the fact that this violence is hurting her emotionally. We are concerned for you, because you are on the wrong track, and your relationships are being damaged.'
- *Pledges*:
    - To resist – 'This violence must stop. From now on, we will do everything in our power to resist this violence. This is our responsibility as your parents.'
    - To use support – 'We will need to involve other adults to support us in resisting your violent behaviour. We will not keep it a secret any longer.'
    - To be non-violent (can include accepting responsibility for their own past aggression): 'We will not humiliate or hurt you. In the past, we have shouted at you. We have said things we regret. We are sorry for this and will not repeat this behaviour.'

- Preferred future: 'We are looking forward to the day when we can go on holiday again as a family and be happy together. We love you.' Mum and Dad

Managing violent behaviour – Inspire Training

In recognition of the serious issues facing many families, and the huge levels of disruption as a direct result of violence and aggression (Adams 2017), the Inspire Training Group together with Dynamis – providers of bespoke training in conflict management, breakaway training and physical interventions (see www.dynamis.training/mvbresources) – created the only course available in the UK which demonstrates physical intervention as well as de-escalation techniques. This is in recognition that first there have been media cases clearly showing the necessity for formal training, and secondly that there is a basis in law for this to happen, and that failure to recognize the risks and provide clear information and training with regard to potential violence in the home constitutes a failure in the duty of care of the local authority.

The two-day course looks at the Kaplan-Wheeler Violent Crisis Behaviour model showing the profile of an aggressive incident. Using this profile, the course identifies areas where de-escalation may be effective, the 'point of no return' where a violent escalation is inevitable, and points of resolution and reconciliation. For up-to-date information on this course as well as other courses on behaviour management and de-escalation, please visit www.inspiregroup.com/face-to-face.

Stepping down from stress

Many parents get extremely stressed as a result of trying to modify multiple behaviours and becoming in the process involved in a battle for control. Making a conscious effort to step away from this process and re-evaluate your priorities does not imply that you relinquish control, just that you have made a different choice in the face of the information you have.

Bearing this in mind, try this:

- What are the behaviours that stress you most? Why is that? Make a list of all the behaviours, and prioritize three that you are going to try and change – but these should be based on safety for you, the child and your relationship.
- What can you let go of – just for now?
- Which behaviours can you let go of completely?
- In reflecting on this, consider your child's history, levels of cognitive, social and emotional development and whether you have appropriate expectations with this in mind.

De-escalation

De-escalation involves having empathy for the child and mindsight – understanding how the situation feels for them and what the likely reasons are. In using de-escalation techniques we make a point of stepping away from conflict. When they are stressed our children will invite us to argue. They will do this very simply, by not following instructions or by being oppositional, inviting us to join in a battle for control. At this point we have a choice: we can be confident in our parenting (what Sarah calls 'the unassailable safe base') and continue what we are doing exactly as if the child was complying, or we can engage in a fruitless battle which the child will win. If we offer resistance to the child who is seeking a fight (because they are anxious), it is like giving oxygen to a fire – the resistance provides the energy for an escalation. If we refuse to engage, the child will find it very difficult to escalate further. Whilst doing this, it is wise to have 'plan b' in place so that you can stay calm. This might mean arranging appointments to give you plenty of time, or carrying spare supplies, or even making sure you have keys and money and phone with you at all times. That way, if you are running late you can let people know, if the child locks you out while you are waiting in the car you can get back in, or if they end up going to school in their pjs or slippers you have their uniform hidden in the car. There are often crisis points in the day when it is very easy for the child to hijack the day.

CASE STUDY 9.3 – MORNING SCHOOL RUN

Young Judy at five years old loved to sabotage the school run. While Mum tried to get breakfast, showered, dressed and then got Judy ready, Judy had a lovely time disrupting the entire process until Mum was worn to a frazzle. One day, Mum thought to herself – I must do something different. I think I will get up earlier so that I am completely ready, then I will not get stressed, because I know Emily will get herself ready, and I can manage Judy better.

Next day, and Mum is up, showered, dressed and having a coffee by the time Judy gets down. As usual, Judy has a lovely time refusing to get dressed, jumping on sofas, etc. For some odd reason, Mum does not seem to care (she has already put spare uniform and school shoes in the car). When it is time for school, Judy goes out in her vest and pants and a coat, feeling very pleased with herself. Emily is dropped at school first, and then Judy says, 'We need to go home now, Mum!' Mum responds, 'Why is that?' 'I have to get changed for school.' 'Oh don't worry about that. I expect you can wear your sports clothes today.' Mum is being very careful to monitor Judy's level of stress to prevent an escalation in the car. When they get to school, Mum says to Judy very calmly, 'I have your uniform in the car this time. Next time I might not.' Judy gets dressed. She never tries this again!

The reason for the success is simply the fact that Mum kept her cool because she was prepared, which is exactly our point – if you take down the 'target' and step away from the argument, it takes all the energy and 'fun' out of the situation.

During the course we talk about the different levels of indication we get that our child is escalating – normally parents become very sensitive to early signs, and the sooner the child is calmed, the less likely you are to get an escalation.

- *Stage 1*: nonsense chatter, clingy behaviour, lying, etc. Reduce the behaviour by using empathy, narrative and curiosity.

- *Stage 2*: escalation with demand avoidance, oppositional behaviour. Reduce using a useful narrative such as 'I can see you are finding something difficult. Don't forget I am here to help you.' Refuse to take the bait. Think toddler and use distraction techniques, a change of activity or a change of scenery.
- *Stage 3*: threats and threatening behaviour. Take a non-threatening, reassuring stance – 'I can see you are feeling very anxious [or upset or angry]. I am right here, it's OK' – and use calming, non-threatening body language. Avoid confrontational language such as 'Don't you dare' and try 'Put that down now. Let's just sit down. How can I help?'
- *Stage 4*: the point where an attack occurs.

Remember that a child who has experienced trauma will frequently have high-circulating cortisol, which means that their levels of stress are already very high and their trigger points are very sensitive. It may also mean that a child can present as absolutely fine at one moment but attack you the next. This is because their hypersensitive amygdala has identified a threat to survival and triggered a fight–flight response. In this state the child is in overwhelm and is not going to be responsive to words (although they may respond to a third party). At this point, therapeutic parenting is all about keeping everybody in the house safe. It most emphatically does not mean allowing the child to beat you. Keeping safe may mean leaving the room, leaving the house, even calling the police.

10

Syndromes, Disorders and Survival Behaviours

> In this chapter we try to shed some light on some of the syndromes, disorders and other behaviours which are most commonly associated with early childhood trauma.

There are so many syndromes, disorders and behaviours associated with developmental trauma, it can be completely mind boggling! To make matters more difficult, some of these are not likely to be true diagnoses but developmental issues caused by the original trauma. These developmental issues are also found in the ordinary range of childhood disorders (i.e. where there is no associated trauma). The difference usually lies in the additional difficulties the child faces due to their attachment and other issues.

The aim of this chapter is to help parents extend their knowledge and understanding of these syndromes, disorders and behaviours, enabling better management and development of strategies and giving some information about where additional information can be found. When we develop our understanding of the reasons for our child's behaviour we can more easily separate the child from the actions, which reduces shame and blame within the family (including shaming and blaming of parents from others in the circle who simply do not 'get' it).

We are seeking to understand some of the disorders which may affect our children, but this is not a diagnostic tool. Although there may be indications in the individual that you are thinking of, and some ideas for understanding and managing the condition, remember that assessment and diagnosis can only be made by a professional who is qualified in the relevant field.

These syndromes, disorders and behaviours may arise from genetic factors or from environmental factors (lack of attuned attachment figure leading to failure to develop social, emotional and cognitive skills within age-appropriate parameters).

Syndromes	• Pathological demand avoidance syndrome (PDAS) • Neonatal abstinence syndrome (NAS)
Disorders	• Disorganized attachment disorder/reactive attachment disorder (RAD) • Attention deficit hyperactivity disorder (ADHD) • Sensory processing disorder (SPD) • Oppositional defiance disorder (ODD) • Autistic spectrum disorder (ASD) • Post-traumatic stress disorder (PTSD) • Foetal alcohol spectrum disorder (FASD) • Eating disorders (e.g. anorexia nervosa, bulimia) • Dyspraxia • Narcissistic personality disorder (NPD)
Cognitive and social functioning and behaviour (ability to self-regulate and behave in a way that is socially acceptable)	The syndromes and disorders listed above give rise to issues with: • Cognitive functioning – problem solving, organizational skills, perception, judgement • Learning styles – practical, rigidity of thought, literal interpretation • Social functioning – sensitivity towards others' emotions, effective decision-making, ability to self-monitor and self-regulate, demonstrate flexibility, effective organization skills • Behaviour – acceptable, reasonable, developmentally appropriate • Isolation

Syndromes

Pathological demand avoidance syndrome (PDAS)

The Pathological Demand Avoidance Society (PDA Society, pdasociety.org.uk) identifies the following as the main features of PDAS:

- Obsessively resisting ordinary demands
- Appearing sociable on the surface but lacking depth in understanding (often recognized by parents early on)
- Excessive mood swings, often switching suddenly
- Comfortable (sometimes to an extreme extent) in role-play and pretending
- Language delay, seemingly as a result of passivity, but often with a good degree of 'catch-up'
- Obsessive behaviour, often focused on people rather than things.

PDAS is identified as being on the autistic spectrum or related to it, and the syndrome is attributed to extreme anxiety around not being in control. We know that controlling behaviour is a feature of children who have suffered developmental trauma as a result of abuse and specifically neglect. Survival depends upon management of the environment, which shows the levels of stress involved for the child.

Many families struggle when children present as controlling and refuse to cooperate with ordinary everyday requests. The behaviour is often interpreted by observers as rude and undisciplined, causing additional pressure on parents to ensure the child conforms to expected modes of behaviour. This can easily lead to a battle for control where the anxiety of the child ('I must control my environment') meets the anxiety of the adult ('I must control my child. They must acknowledge my parental authority and do as I say!'). This is reinforced by a society where we have an understanding of acceptable and unacceptable behaviours which are often underpinned by how children respond to adults. The result can be a stress-filled confrontation.

Neonatal abstinence syndrome (NAS)

This is the name given to the collection of symptoms which may occur if a child is born to an addicted mother who has taken opiates (drugs derived from the opium poppy, including heroin, morphine and opium) during pregnancy. The same can apply to a baby whose mother is taking part in a programme and using prescribed drugs to overcome her addiction under supervision. Such drugs include methadone or buprenorphine. The symptoms could be exacerbated by other substances which are toxic to the developing foetus such as tobacco, amphetamines, codeine and alcohol.

The symptoms are related to the drug ingested (which will have entered directly into the baby's circulatory system via the umbilical cord) and will be as a result of withdrawal from the substance. Symptoms are diverse and can include diarrhoea, excessive or high-pitched crying, excessive suckling, fever, poor feeding, seizures, sleep problems, sweating, tremors and vomiting.

Complications, aside from the trauma of a life which begins with unendurable pain, include birth defects, low birth weight, premature birth and problems with development and behaviour. There may be issues with developmental capabilities of the child in the future. The presentation can be further complicated by the fact that babies that have NAS have frequently also had in utero exposure to nicotine, alcohol and environmental issues such as stress from a chaotic lifestyle or domestic violence. There are long-term developmental issues associated with NAS specifically in cognitive and motor skills. A child who has this diagnosis will need intensive therapeutic parenting to enable them to meet and manage their challenges.

Disorders

Disorganized attachment disorder/ reactive attachment disorder (RAD)

Disorganized attachment disorder results from a failure of the attachment process which occurs between an attuned adult and a baby, and which is essential to provide a foundation for the development of empathy, compassion, trust and love. This child will be chaotic in their responses and easily overwhelmed due to this early developmental trauma.

The signs and symptoms are consistent with a failure of an attuned early relationship; so an infant will try to get attention by whining but not engage in eye contact, be indifferent to others, not have a smile response and will have a weak sucking response, whilst in children as they develop we see lack of conscience development, absent eye contact (except when lying), they may be superficially charming but unable to develop meaningful relationships and friendships or give or receive affection. These children may be cruel to others or to animals, and be extremely controlling. Some of the behaviours which we most frequently see are around food – stealing or hoarding food is extremely common and is unrelated to whether the child is currently receiving proper nutrition or not, this is a trauma-based response relating to earlier neglect and malnutrition. In addition, such children may talk incessantly – nonsense chatter which serves to keep your attention centred on the child, are very demanding, destructive and show no impulse control. There may be associated learning difficulties.

The theory of attachment was first proposed by John Bowlby and this work was continued by Mary Ainsworth. We now understand that attachment is one of the processes that happens as a result of the first relationships experienced by a new born and, which affects the way that the individual will approach their future relationships. This is not to say that our early relationships cast our future attachment patterns in stone – as we have already discussed the plasticity of the brain means that we can engage in new learning processes through therapy and counselling and other interventions such as mindfulness which can help us to understand our responses and choose to interact in a different way; likewise, we can support our children with help from therapeutic professionals to reframe their experiences and create new attachment connections in their brains.

- *Ambivalent*: This is the child who will approach and then run away from you, fearful of engaging but desperate for attention, this child is very difficult to connect with. Their desire and need for attention is in conflict with their fear of adult responses.

- *Anxious*: Clingy, anxious and fearful, this child will shadow your every move and show extreme anxiety at times of separation.
- *Avoidant*: This child has learned to make themselves 'invisible' – perhaps it was best to avoid being noticed by adults in their early life. They will be overly compliant and superficially engaging and helpful; however, there is no real emotional involvement.
- *Disorganized*: This child has had such a chaotic, inconsistent early experience that they do not have a clear attachment style and can behave in bizarre ways, defying understanding on the part of the parents. This child can present as violent and aggressive as they strive to survive. They have been helpless and powerless through their early experiences – I believe that they will then strive to be powerful and in control.

Treatment: Therapeutic Re-parenting using the strategies and models promoted throughout this book.

Attention deficit hyperactivity disorder (ADHD)

ADHD is characterized by the child who is unable to keep still either in mind or body. There seems to be no thought before action (impulsivity), no thought before speaking (blurting out information) and a general difficulty with maintaining focus and concentration. These children can be misunderstood, and their restlessness can cause issues at home, at school and in their social lives.

CASE STUDY 10.1 – MARCUS AND THE EFFECTS OF ADHD

Marcus, who lives in Surrey in the UK, is eight years old. He is very active, and he also has been developing his skills with video games – this also means that he can stay connected with his friends even out of school time.

Marcus is the oldest of three children, and has a very loving and secure family. Sometimes though he finds life to be very challenging: it can be hard to stay focused, even when he is doing things he likes; and he finds this intensely frustrating and will suddenly appear to fly into a rage, throwing things around and lashing out. At other times he can be quietly enjoying the television and then suddenly start fighting with his younger sister – he does not remember that he is bigger and stronger than she is – it seems that he suddenly needs to move his muscles all at once. He might also discharge this by jumping all over the furniture and racing around the family home.

He finds it very hard to be interrupted if he is in the middle of something that has held his attention, but will be very frustrated if he is being asked to focus and concentrate on subjects that he has difficulty with, which can cause battles over homework when he would rather be doing something else. He will fly into a rage and start issuing threats to his family, even though he is at heart a very loving and sensitive boy.

It can be difficult for him to manage his moods, and this can create problems with some of his social groups.

Signs and symptoms

- Overactive, impulsive
- Inattention to detail, makes careless mistakes
- Difficulty maintaining focus
- Easily distracted
- Difficulty completing tasks
- Impatient
- Restless.

Causes

A difference in brain chemistry, specifically low levels of dopamine and norepinephrine. According to Sue Gerhardt (2010), levels of dopamine can be influenced by the state of mind and therefore hormone levels of the birth mother. Dopamine has a positive effect on the developing brain.

Treatment

The treatment of ADHD is by use of stimulant medicine, Ritalin being commonly prescribed in the UK. Other management of ADHD includes exercise (physical discharge of mental stimulation), healthy diet, sleep management and behavioural therapies to help the child to learn adaptive behaviours which may help to overcome some of the issues.

Sensory processing disorder (SPD)

The Sensory Processing Disorder website (www.sensory-processing-disorder.com/sensory-integration-dysfunction-symptoms.html) explains that '[s]ensory integration is a normal, neurological, developmental process which begins in the womb and continues throughout one's life'. What this means is that our brains receive sensory input (touch, taste, hearing, taste and smell) from specialized organs (i.e. the ears, eyes, nose, mouth and sensory receptors such as those all over the surface of our bodies enabling us to recognize touch). Stimuli are received and the brain processes this information so that we can respond appropriately to the environment (e.g. to sensations of heat, cold and pain, which help us to survive and stay safe). This gives us an ability to explore because we have confidence in our ability to interact with and adapt to the environment. The process looks like Figure 10.1, and the cycle is continuous.

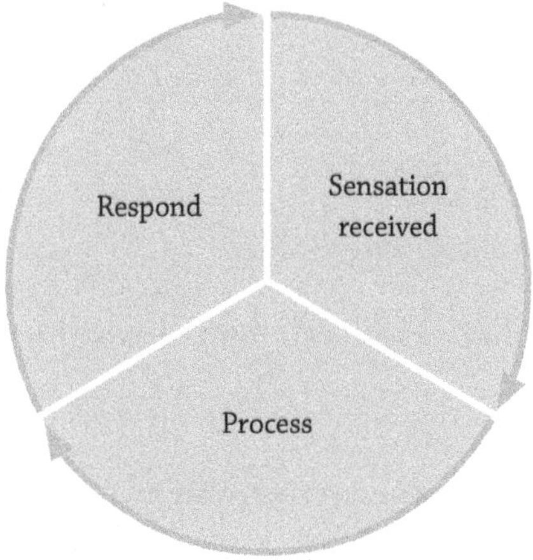

Figure 10.1 Sensory processing

This process, like so many other developmental factors, is impacted by the input from parents, i.e. it is relationally mediated. Ideally parents have a crucial role in helping the child make sense of their sensory experiences, giving names to them and helping the child to explore the sensations. Parents also give names to the internal stimuli (interoception), helping our children to understand when they are hungry, tired, cold, when they need help to balance, when they need to use the toilet. Parents also have a role in mediating and encouraging physical development of the senses, playing with our children and stimulating their senses and encouraging their attempts to gain control over their musculoskeletal system. As we have discussed already, early disruption to development, both in utero and due to post-birth factors such as neglect and abuse, has an impact on the development of the brain and therefore the neurological receptors and ability to process. The effects can include hypersensitivity to touch (think of the traumatized child who will only wear certain clothes, or hates having teeth brushed or hair brushed), taste, hearing and sense of smell; the feeling of integration of body parts – joints and muscles (proprioception); and ability to coordinate balance and movement (vestibular system).

This dysregulation affects our emotional regulation and therefore our ability to think rationally.

Signs and symptoms

- Social engagement
- Environmental engagement
- Sensory difficulties with clothes
- Sensory difficulties with activities such as brushing hair or teeth.
- Eating issues
- Difficulties in focus and concentration
- Dysregulation
- Sleeping difficulties
- Fidgeting, need to move, need to push, pull, stamp
- Lack of awareness of where body is in space.

Treatment

Children may need to have professional support from an occupational therapist and support to manage school life, but activities include:

- Fine motor skills: messy play, modelling clay, drawing circles, pens and pencils with special grips
- Gross motor skills: heavy muscle work – work in gym, monkey bars, climbing, trampoline.

Children with SPD will also often find it helpful to have weighted blankets, weighted lap pads, 'wriggle' cushions or sensory jackets providing a 'portable hug' for sensory-seeking children.

For further information about specific aspects of this disorder, check the Sensory Processing Disorder website.

Oppositional defiance disorder (ODD)

The NHS classifies ODD as a 'conduct disorder'. Conduct disorders are cited as the most common expression of mental health and behavioural problems in children and young people. Five per cent of all children between 5 and 16 years of age are diagnosed with this condition. The child may find it hard to exhibit empathy and may demonstrate increased levels of risk taking. This behaviour is rooted in anxiety, especially at times of transition – even times when a transition is very small such as a change of activity or transition from play to mealtime. The main symptom may be refusing to comply with ordinary requests, and insistence on compliance may result in a disproportionate escalation of frustration and anger on the part of the child.

Causes include

- Parental depression
- Parental drug abuse
- Environment issues such as divorce
- Feelings of failure (low achievement) on the part of the child.

Signs and symptoms

- Refusing to comply with adult requests
- Controlling behaviours
- Aggression
- Stealing
- Fighting
- Inability to regulate
- Social isolation.

Treatment

There is no treatment per se – however adopting a therapeutic parenting style using the models proposed in this book will be extremely useful in enabling the child to develop to their full potential. Developing a team around the child to support the family may be very helpful in some cases. This could involve many professionals such as health professionals, school and social workers and may involve therapeutic input where indicated by the child's history.

Autistic spectrum disorder (ASD)

> "Autism is a lifelong, developmental disability that affects how a person communicates with and relates to other people and how they experience the world around them." (National Autistic Society)

ASD is typically characterized by a failure to engage socially and there is often an underlying component of anxiety. Behaviours can cover a huge range and may include sensory issues; difficulty with transitions (even moving from home to school, or class to class); resistance to change; adherence to routines and rituals; and focus on specific areas of interest to the exclusion of others in a way that onlookers find obsessive. An autistic child may respond to a perceived challenge or change as a threat and show extremely challenging and aggressive behaviours. An autistic child may only wear one set of clothes; watch the same film obsessively; have a fixed obsession (e.g. Thomas the Tank Engine); be resistant to change; show rigid thinking patterns; be very literal in their interpretation of language; find social contact overwhelming. These children can also show signs and symptoms of pathological demand avoidance, dyslexia, dyspraxia and oppositional defiance disorder. These issues may be mild or pervasive, making the world a confusing and overwhelming place.

Children with ASD may present with any or all of the following:

- Difficulty with social interaction
- Difficulty with communication
- Restricted and repetitive patterns of behaviour
- Restricted fixed interests to the exclusion of other pursuits
- Restricted fixed activities
- Require high levels of routine – changes to timetable cause intense distress
- Anxiety and perseveration (fixed on a thought pattern, very hard to shift the individual from this)
- Rigid, literal thinking and interpretation – so that common idioms such as “it’s raining cats and dogs” (meaning that it is raining extremely heavily) will be met with confusion as the literal translation is impossible.

ASD has now become the the common diagnosis replacing terms such as "Autistic disorder"; "Asperger disorder" and "Pervasive Developmental Disorder – Not Otherwise Specified".

Three levels of ASD have been identified: requiring support, Requiring substantial support, and requiring very substantial support. This enables us to understand the extent to which the diagnosis affects the individual and gives an indication of the likely levels of support required.

Naoki Higashida, author of *The Reason I Jump* (2013), explains his experience in the preface to his book:

> When I was small, I didn't even know that I was a kid with special needs. How did I find out? By other people telling me that I was different from everyone else, and that this was a problem. True enough. It was very hard for me to act like a normal person,... I can't respond appropriately when I am told to do something, and whenever I get nervous I run off from wherever I happen to be, so even a straightforward activity like shopping can be really challenging if I am tackling it on my own. (p.15)

Naoki goes on to explain that for him it would be much easier if autism was seen differently by the general public. This ties in with the new awareness of invisible disabilities where the person with the diagnosis has no obvious physical indicators of the internal struggle that they face on a day-to-day basis. Disability is still regarded by many as a physical restriction, not an emotional or social mental health condition. Naoki expresses his concern that many autistic children lack the means of self-expression and his wish that he can help to increase awareness:

> ... So my big hope is that I can help a bit by explaining, in my own way, what's going on in the minds of people with autism. (p.16)

Causes

This is a relatively grey area, and still under investigation. However, autism seems to be caused by physical factors affecting brain development. There may be some genetic factors, but work is ongoing to identify which genes may be implicated. This seems to be partly because it is likely that there are multiple genes responsible, not a single gene.

Treatment

There is no treatment for the condition; however there may be aspects that can be alleviated by using tried and trusted interventions. Because autism is a spectrum condition it is expressed differently from person to person, and therefore support needs to be engineered to the individual as seems appropriate to their specific areas requiring support and skill set. I give some useful interventions below.

SPELL (Structure, Positive, Empathy, Low arousal, Links) approach

SPELL (Structure, Positive, Empathy, Low Arousal, Links) approach (NAS) – this Framework has been developed by the National Autistic Society and the letters are anacronym of 5 elements that have been identified as essential in supporting children with ASD to manage the demands of everyday life. It is recognised that in order to achieve this the unique nature of the individual must be taken into account in order to best meet their needs. Anyone supporting the child – whether parent, teacher, mentor, group leader or other – will need to be part of a consistent whole to maintain a supportive environment. This framework is also described as being compatible with TEACCH which is described below. (www.autism.org.uk/about/strategies/spell.aspx)

It is clear that there is some overlap here with the high structure and nurture that is required in Therapeutic Parenting – minimising high arousal and maximising structure, consistency, predictability and reliability.

TEACCH (Teaching, Expanding, Appreciating, Collaborating, Co-operating and taking a Holistic approach)

TEACCH is part of the National Autistic Society's EarlyBird parent support programme and embraces staying focused on the individual's needs. This requires that those working with autistics have an understanding the culture of autism and incorporates tools such as using visual aids in the environment and using practical hands on techniques to teach skills. TEACCH also advocates provision of broad based support at work and during leisure time. The overall concept suggests that we understand the need of the individual to be able to function within a community to whatever extent they are able to do so, and places no limits on future achievement but recognises that progress is made over time.

Whereas SPELL aims to create structure and a consistent environment around the individual, TEACCH encompasses values which are essential in creating a team around the child, empowering those working with the child by increasing their skill set, helping autistics in society by raising awareness in the community, and enabling the child, young person or adult to achieve the highest level of autonomy and independence that they are able to.

The NAS incorporates aspects of the TEACCH approach in the Earlybird parent support programme.

(www.autism.org.uk/about/strategies/teacch.aspx)

Post-traumatic stress disorder (PTSD)

Most of the research leading to a definition of PTSD was carried out on individuals who had suffered a threat to life, especially Vietnamese veterans. PTSD UK characterize PTSD as an emotional response to a deeply shocking and disturbing experience. There will be an underlying condition of intense anxiety, and fear-based reactions will give rise to adaptive behaviours which are hard to manage. Criteria for a diagnosis of PTSD include:

- The individual has had involvement in a life-threatening event involving intense fear, helplessness or horror.
- The individual has intense and immediate sensory recollections of the event, which are very scary, such as obsessive thoughts or dreams which colour their everyday perceptions.

- There is increased arousal (i.e. sensitivity to stressors) – the person is easily overwhelmed due to massive base-level stress.

Symptoms include

- Nightmares
- Perception of being unsafe
- Hyperarousal
- Intense distress at triggering stimuli – these can be sensory and not accessible to rational thought
- Feeling as though the traumatic effect is occurring in the present – sensory and somatic (physical) memories
- Disturbed sleep patterns
- Angry/aggressive/violent outbursts
- Hypervigilance.

Many children who suffer abuse at the hands of adults have PTSD and chronic long-term stress resulting in high-circulating cortisol. It is also possible for families engaging in the care of children with PTSD to have secondary PTSD as a result of the effect of living with a traumatized child, or primary PTSD if they are parenting a child who is aggressive and violent.

Treatment

The National Institute for Clinical Excellence (NICE) has published guidelines for different treatment approaches and reminds us of the individual nature of the condition whereby some individuals may recover over time with little or no help; however for others the severity of the response is such that there will be a need for psychological intervention and medication may be considered. (www.nice.org.uk)

Foetal alcohol spectrum disorder (FASD)

NHS.uk explains that FASD is caused by maternal alcohol consumption during pregnancy. Because of its structure, alcohol is able to cross the placental barrier and enters the baby's bloodstream. However, a developing embryo, foetus or baby is unable to process alcohol, which can be very toxic and damage the developing cells of their neurological system (spinal cord and brain) as well as other organs. Some babies will miscarry, but those that survive may be left with lifelong issues as a result of the damage that has been sustained in utero.

Symptoms

There are some facial indicators; but these may not always be present.

- Small head
- Small eye openings
- Folds of skin between the eyes and nose
- Flat upper part of the nose
- Smooth area between the nose and upper lip
- Short nose
- Thin upper lip
- The child may have cerebral palsy, affecting their movement and coordination.
- There may be learning difficulties.
- There may be social and communication issues similar to ASD.
- There may be issues with mood, attention and ability to focus similar to ADHD.
- There may be organ damage to liver, kidneys or heart.
- There may be sensory issues such as impaired hearing or vision.

Treatment

Although there is no specific treatment, the child will benefit from support from professionals, such as paediatrician, education professionals, social worker, etc.. Parents will need support to enable them to manage a child with this condition. Approaching the child from a developmental need point of view rather than an age-related expectation will enable the child to develop according to their abilities. (Information adapted from www.nhs.uk/conditions/foetal-alcohol-syndrome/Pages/Introduction.aspx.)

Eating Disorders

The two specific disorders I will discuss in this book are anorexia nervosa and bulimia.

Anorexia

Anorexia is an eating disorder classified as a serious mental health issue, and there are clear links to issues of control and body dysmorphia (having a distorted self-image). The affected person (who can be male as well as female, although this is predominantly a female issue) will obsessively lose weight by diet control and excessive exercise. Weight can also be controlled by vomiting, which we will consider under bulimia. As a result, the body is denied essential nutrients and serious complications can arise.

Signs of anorexia

- Missing meals
- Lying about food
- Taking weight-loss medications (e.g. fat burners, diuretics or laxatives)
- Weight loss which may be disguised by wearing looser clothing
- Headaches

- Tiredness
- Low self-esteem.

Complications of anorexia

- Poor circulation
- Absent periods
- Hair loss
- Malnutrition
- Osteoporosis
- Heart failure
- Kidney damage
- Liver damage.

Treatment

Treatment may be undertaken by a team of professionals and will involve therapy and supervised weight gain. The affected young person may need to be hospitalized. Professionals involved may include:

- GP
- Specialist counsellor
- Psychiatrist
- Specialist nurses
- Dieticians
- Paediatricians.

In addition, the whole family may need support in coming to terms with this diagnosis and in helping to put a care plan in place which will support not only the individual but also the family.

CASE STUDY 10.2 – BECCA'S STORY

Becca was a 15-year-old girl from an academic background. She had a very stable family life and was doing exceptionally well in school as she had above-average intelligence but struggled to fit in with her peer group. Becca had several friends including Judith, and there are several other girls in the same peer group with a loose friendship. As time went on, some of the girls formed 'best' friendships, and Judith was trying to maintain acceptance with two of these girls, not paying any attention to the fact that in doing so Becca was in effect being isolated.

It became apparent that Becca was losing weight and she was tearful at school, thinking that maybe her friends did not like her any more. She started to feel out of control, and wondered if she might be more acceptable to her friends if she was more slender – her friends were on the very slim side, and whereas she was not at all overweight, she was not skinny. Eventually Becca became so ill that she had to be hospitalized – back in the 1970s this was the only known treatment – and she was isolated and then rewarded with activities or given access to letters, etc. if she ate. She came back to school and found her friends just did not know how to deal with this situation, or tried to invite her to tea and tempt her with different food, even following her to the toilet in case she was vomiting.

In the end, Becca and her parents chose to change her school to a more academic environment where she thrived and was able to regain her self-esteem and develop into a healthy and well-adjusted adult.

Bulimia

Similarly to anorexia nervosa, bulimia is eating disorder classified as a mental health issue, with the focus being weight control. Bulimics will binge eat, and then purge (induce vomiting). Purging may occur when the individual gives in to their urge to eat and then feels disgust. As with anorexia, this is also linked to low self-esteem, depression, self-harm and alcohol or substance misuse. The condition has been linked to complex and intense emotional states. In this respect there is also a similarity to anorexia where controlled eating can be a response to feelings of vulnerability and being out of control. There is also an element of body dysmorphia. Bulimia affects both men and women.

Sufferers from bulimia – both men and women – can initially feel that they have found the answer to their problems – they can eat as much as they like and then purge and avoid the weight gain. However, the cycle becomes one of self-disgust, followed by gorging, followed by purging. Eating can feel like an addiction, something to be ashamed of, and then hidden – sufferers may eat at night or the whole issue of eating may become guilt ridden.

Symptoms

- Obsessive attitude to food and eating
- Unrealistic ideals about body image
- Depression
- Anxiety
- Isolation
- Bad breath
- Sore throat.

Complications

- Dental issues – erosion of enamel
- Disruption of menstrual cycle
- Poor skin and hair due to lack of nutrition
- Round-looking face (swollen glands)
- Bowel problems
- Heart arrhythmia
- Kidney damage.

Treatment

Similarly to anorexia, treatment involves therapy to insitute healthy attitudes to food and eating. Again, support and involvement of the family are essential, and therefore the whole family may need support and information. Bulimia is sometimes treated with antidepressants. It is less likely that an individual with bulimia will be referred to hospital unless they have complications requiring medical intervention (www.nhs.uk/conditions/Bulimia).

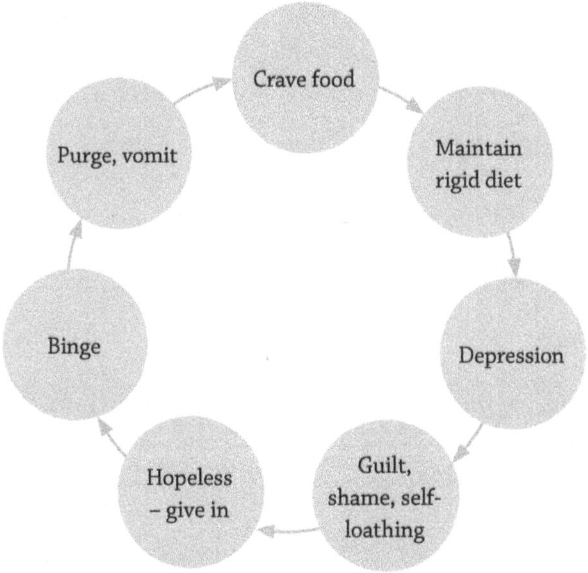

Figure 10.3 Bulimic cycle

Dyspraxia

Dyspraxia UK (www.dyspraxiauk.com) state that dyspraxia (also known as developmental co-ordination disorder) is a neurological (brain based) condition which affects co-ordination and perception (vision, hearing, and sense of yourself in space – proprioception). There may be additional developmental issues; it is also found alongside other issues such as hypermobility, dyslexia, dyscalculia and ADHD, etc. This can cause difficulties in education, work and employment, especially as the individual may present with emotional difficulties and poor organization and time management. The cause is thought to be immaturity of neuronal development rather than brain damage.

Symptoms include

- Lateness in achieving physical developmental tasks such as rolling over and sitting
- Speech and language issues
- 'Clumsy' child
- Poor coordination
- Social difficulty
- Practical learner
- Poor pencil grip
- Anxious
- Difficulty remembering and following instructions
- Avoids PE.

Treatment

The individual will need support with physical tasks and fine motor skills and may require additional support in school and throughout education. Occupational therapy exercises and support may be beneficial.

Narcissistic personality disorder (NPD)

Individuals with this disorder will come across as being self-centred and demanding. This is how it is defined in *Psychology Today*:

> Narcissistic Personality Disorder involves grandiosity, a lack of empathy for other people, and a need for admiration. People with this condition are frequently described as arrogant, self-centered, manipulative, and demanding. They may also concentrate on grandiose

> fantasies (e.g. success, beauty, brilliance) and may be convinced that they deserve special treatment. These characteristics typically begin in early adulthood and must be consistently evident in multiple contexts, such as at work and in relationships.
>
> People with narcissistic personality disorder believe they are superior or special, and often try to associate with other people they believe are unique or gifted in some way. This association enhances their self-esteem, which is typically quite fragile underneath the surface. People who have high self-esteem are often humble, whereas narcissists rarely are. Instead, they seek excessive admiration and attention in order to know that others think highly of them. Individuals with narcissistic personality disorder have difficulty tolerating criticism or defeat, and may be left feeling humiliated or empty when they experience an 'injury' in the form of criticism. (www.psychologytoday.com/conditions/narcissistic-personality-disorder)

NPD is a mental health issue and involves an inflated self-importance and need for validation. It should be noted that this disorder is often reported as emerging in early adulthood – young children are necessarily narcissistic on the road to developing their ability to separate self from other and receiving information from an attuned other person. This overconfidence is indicative of a hidden fragile self esteem. (Mayo).

Symptoms include:

- Exaggerated sense of self-importance
- Wishing for recognition of superiority
- Association with extra special people
- Sense of entitlement
- Requiring admiration
- Taking advantage of others

- Failing to recognize the needs and feelings of others (lack of empathy).

Treatment is through therapeutic input.

In this chapter I have dealt with some of the most commonly occurring syndromes and disorders associated with developmental trauma. However, I feel it is important to remember that although these diagnoses can be invaluable in accessing tools and support to enable us to be effective therapeutic parents for our children, at the same time the essential work of the therapeutic parent is in the consistent, predictable and reliable application and repetition of routines, structures and narratives so that the 'bottom up' developmental stages of the child can be reinforced.

11

Building a Team

Parents and Professionals

When adopting or fostering children with developmental trauma, there is a bewildering array of social work, education and health professionals who may become involved in the support necessary for the child and the family. In this chapter we will discuss professionals who may be involved at the outset or may become involved through various agencies, their roles and how to access necessary support. We will also discuss the importance of building up a strong supportive professional network and describe the difficulties that may arise in achieving this. *Please note: I am only able to discuss the roles and agencies I see in England in this section, however most countries have equivalent organisations.*

First, we would like to be clear that we are of the opinion that we are all professionals – experts when it comes to discussions about our own children. Foster parents are of course also fulfilling a professional role; however, for all of us, the most important role we are fulfilling is that of parent. In looking at these professionals I have examined the structure that we have in England, on the premise that there may be equivalent professionals or agencies globally.

Secondly, we want to look at the importance of establishing your own supporters, maybe from family or friends, and how they may be involved in the family.

IN MY EXPERIENCE...

As an adoptive mum, my experience was that over time as challenges grew, the support I had from family and friends reduced. Many family members were unable to manage my daughter's behaviour and her need to interrupt any interactions I had with anyone else; some undoubtedly felt that I pushed them away in favour of my daughter; many felt that my parenting stance was wrong and were prepared to argue with me about it. And for at least two important members of my family, bringing my daughter home was the worst decision I ever made.

This made it very hard for me to share any of the difficulties I was facing, as I felt I would be blamed or judged or have it pointed out to me that this was bound to happen. My circle reduced to one or two very close friends, and I stopped talking about family life with most people, having decided that on the whole people were not interested, and that I would not speak about my daughter unless I was directly asked about her. In fact, I keep to the same rule today, having also realized that most people are unable to manage the relentless nature of the troubles I faced at the time and which can still crop up to this day.

Having said this, I should also say that despite severe misgivings (because she had worked in social work) my mother-in-law supported us to the best of her ability, collected my daughter from school and spent valuable time with her one day a week (only stopping when the situation became completely untenable) and continued to visit and to try to understand until she became extremely ill herself. I also had (in an unusual twist) help and support from my ex-husband and his new wife, who would come at a moment's notice to support my second husband and me.

I had support from a friend of ours who would every few months invite my daughter for a sleepover, and from another friend of mine who would be interested, make coffee, listen and never judge. Finally, my dear aunt and uncle offered us all shelter and a place to holiday. In addition, I met Sarah and became her friend and part of her organization, which has given me an additional extended 'family' at work.

These relationships contribute massively to my ability to manage day-to-day life and the occasional massive challenges that are still thrown up as a result of parenting my daughter. This is a job that is shared by my (now ex-) second husband and my two birth daughters, who have given new meaning to the expression that my daughter is loved to the moon and back, no matter what.

The following section contains roles which are applicable in the UK or England only; however, many of the principles involved will be the same whichever country you are in.

Background to multiagency work

In 2000, Victoria Climbié died in hospital after sustained cruelty and abuse at the hands of her aunt Marie Therese Kouao and her lover Carl Manning. At the time of her death the hospital recorded 128 separate injuries and scars in a case which was described by the Home Office pathologist as the worst case of child abuse he had ever encountered. Lord Laming was requested to head an inquiry into Victoria's death, which opened in 2001. During the course of the inquiry 12 separate occasions were identified when agencies could have intervened and saved Victoria's life.

It transpired that Victoria had had contact with two housing authorities, four social services departments, two child protection agencies, a specialist centre managed by the NSPCC and two separate hospitals to which she had been admitted due to suspected deliberate harm. That this did not lead to appropriate intervention was attributed to 'sloppy and unprofessional performance' by key professionals and general bad practice.

Moving forward, Lord Laming made the point that 'effective support for children and families cannot be achieved by a single agency acting alone. It depends on a number of agencies working well together. It is a multi-disciplinary task.' He identified that 'improvements to the way information is exchanged within and between agencies are imperative if children are to be adequately safeguarded'.

Lord Laming recommended a 'fundamental change in the way that services to support children and families are organized and managed' and that there should be a national database to facilitate information sharing which would enable families to be identified even through changes of address. He also concluded that there was no justification for claiming that abuse is a cultural issue.

His ideas were published in the Green Paper *Every Child Matters* (2003) and included the five outcomes that mattered most to children and young people:

- being healthy
- staying safe
- enjoying and achieving
- making a positive contribution
- enjoying economic wellbeing.

Key professional roles

Due to the immense diversity and number of roles within the social work system, I have chosen to focus on those roles which I have found to be key in my own experience.

Social work team

There are several different social work roles associated with adoption and fostering, relating to different areas of social services (care, education and health) and having responsibility for different individuals. Hence, foster carers have a supervising social worker and the child has their own social worker.

The role of the social worker in fostering and adoption is to support the placement and provide a contact point for the services of the local authority, to ensure that the child's best interests are served and that the child's opinions are heard. Different social work teams may be assigned to the child and family, such as adoption and fostering team, post-adoption team, adolescent team or leaving care team.

Independent review officer (IRO)

The IRO has specific responsibilities for a looked after child in terms of action planning, reviewing and ensuring that statutory procedures have taken place. For instance, ensuring:

- the child is registered at a GP
- the child is registered at a dentist
- the child is seen by an optician if necessary
- regular appointments are made as necessary
- medical appointments are kept
- the child's views are heard
- actions from review meetings are followed through.

Supervising social worker

The supervising social worker has knowledge and understanding of the issues and demands associated with fostering and plays a supporting role, including the following:

- Making regular visits to the foster carer and staying in phone contact with them
- Arranging additional support
- Providing support at meetings
- Identifying training needs
- Helping to manage contact
- Maintaining records
- Arranging statutory visits and reviews
- Working alongside the child's social worker.

Child's social worker

The child's social worker has specialist knowledge of adoption and fostering, develops a relationship with the child and knows their history. They play a supportive role for the child, including the following:

- Maintaining visits, including statutory visits
- In relation to the child's identified needs, setting up statutory meetings and reviews – e.g. looked after child, team around the child, child in need, personal education plan and professionals meetings
- Maintaining records
- Assessing the needs of the child
- Involving appropriate departments – e.g. regarding referrals for disability, physiotherapy, occupational therapy
- Liaising with other agencies
- Identifying and providing appropriate support for the child and family

- Informing the family of training or support opportunities
- Arranging statutory medical checks.

The legal requirement is to respond to a request for an assessment of the family's needs. Requests for specific services, etc. may be considered after an assessment of the family's needs has been carried out and the needs of the family and child have been established.

Special educational needs (SEN) department

The SEN department in a school is responsible for assessing a child's level of need, working with an educational psychologist or other specialist professional to ensure that children have appropriate educational provision to support any special educational needs and disability (SEND).

Mainstream schools are expected to be able to support the majority of educational, developmental and behavioural issues with appropriate input from additional professionals. However, some children are still unable to manage mainstream schooling without specialist provision. In these cases, the level of need is assessed and incorporated into an EHCP (education, health and care plan).

Local authority provision for SEN and disability (SEND)

Under the SEND legislation which came into force in September 2014, local authorities have to publish a list of the services which are available to families of children with SEN and disabilities, which may include support groups, youth clubs, social learning groups and activities and support with schools. This is called the **local offer** and should be available via the local authority website.

To help families where there has been a recent assessment and diagnosis and to support families with issues in school, the local authority provides special educational needs and disability information advice and support services (SENDIASS). These are run by locally commissioned groups or charities and should be found via the local offer. The SENDIASS team are there to help families – for example, with information about the local offer, claims for benefits and grants, and information about local support groups, social groups and training. They can also support parents when liaising with schools or applying for an EHCP.

Child and adolescent mental health services (CAMHS)

CAMHS provide services for children and young people with emotional or behavioural difficulties as a result of mental health issues. Referrals are generally made via the young person's GP. CAMHS professionals make assessments, give specialist support and advice and provide therapeutic interventions. CAMHS teams include a range of professionals such as the following:

- Psychiatrists
- Psychologists
- Social workers
- Nurses
- Support workers
- Occupational therapists
- Psychological therapists
- Primary mental health link workers
- Specialist substance misuse workers.

Doctors

Typically, if we are talking about a visit to the doctor we mean a general practitioner working within the NHS or privately and able to manage a wide range of minor ailments or conditions at a local surgery. They may have the support of specialist nurses who carry out minor procedures or investigations – for example, taking bloods for tests. In emergency situations or where specialist knowledge is required, the GP may make a referral to the specialist department of a hospital where a consultant will continue the investigation and diagnosis and recommend and carry out treatment or surgical procedures if necessary. Once a patient is stabilized, they are referred back to their GP for day-to-day care.

Schools

In our experience many families find that school presents a number of challenges for them due to their children's learning styles, level of cognitive ability, ability to socialize and emotional management, and management of the school environment and organization, to name some of the most frequent issues. Many schools are now becoming more attachment aware; however, some are still struggling with how to manage children with developmental trauma at school. In some cases schools feel that if behaviours are only exhibited at home it is clearly the parental input that is at fault. Many schools have a policy regarding working in partnership with parents as this is recognized to be a very beneficial factor, so it is useful to acquaint yourself with this. The people who can be most helpful to you in school are listed below.

Head teacher or head of year

They should have some knowledge of attachment and be able to give clear guidance and direction to staff. This is not likely to be the person who has best knowledge of the child.

Special educational needs coordinator (SENCo)

This is the person with responsibility for any child with additional needs in the school. They should have some attachment awareness and be able to give guidance to class teachers about specific strategies. They are responsible for personal education plans (PEPs) for looked after children, keeping track of progress, maintaining evidence of actions, outcomes and achievements, and they may be able to instigate further assessments and call in additional professionals such as educational psychologists, speech and language experts or occupational therapists if needed. They may also be instrumental in applications for an education, health and care plan (EHCP) where the school is unable to meet the child's needs under School Action or School Action Plus. The SENCo also coordinates reviews of PEPs and EHCPs.

Higher level teaching assistant (HLTA) and teaching assistant (TA)

HLTAs implement recommended actions and strategies for individual children. This may mean that they are supporting more than one individual child in any given class. TAs give specific support in the classroom to one or more children.

You may find that an HLTA or TA is the person who best understands your child's needs and who becomes their secure base in school. Any disruption to this provision should be managed very carefully, with parents and children given advance notice and thought being given to how to support the child.

Class teacher

In primary schools the class teacher will be the person with most day-to-day interaction with your child, together with the HLTA or TA if applicable. They should be able to liaise with the primary carers for looked after or adopted children, perhaps by means of a home–school diary which allows the two to communicate well together and create a consistent and predictable home–school environment for the child. In secondary school this system is more complicated as there will be separate subject teachers for up to ten different subjects. In this case the young person's form tutor, who sees them every day and provides overall care, is the key person.

Home–school link worker (HSLW)

This is likely to be a peripatetic worker – i.e. they may have responsibility for several schools within a local area. The HSLW offers support, advice and local information to carers as well as providing support to the young people themselves. The HSLW can be instrumental in giving information and guidance to schools about specific topics such as bullying, attachment and SEN. They work with a range of agencies and their role within a local area means that they can provide continuity when there is transition between schools. The job title may vary – for example, they may be called a family support worker or a family liaison officer.

Virtual school head (VSH)

The Children and Families Act 2014 requires local authorities to have a VSH in charge of promoting the educational achievement of looked after children. Their role is to help schools identify the additional needs of the children in their care and make them aware of the support available. The VSH is also responsible for managing the pupil premium and tracking the children's progress, and works with schools and children's services on initiatives to support the education of children in care.

Designated teacher for looked after and previously looked after children

Every school has a designated member of staff to work with looked after children in the school. This person should have specialist training (but that is not a requirement), to enable them to better understand the complex needs of children in care.

Education, health and care plan – EHCP

The EHCP was introduced as part of the special educational needs and disability (SEND) reforms introduced in 2014. This plan both replaces and extends the old statement, recognizing the overlap between disability and some special educational needs and bringing all the necessary resources together. At the same time, a child with an EHCP is entitled to access the educational and medical and care services covered up until age 25. The individual would then be transferred to adult services if ongoing support was required.

Police

The police may become involved where a child has absconded, broken the law, caused a disturbance (including domestic disturbance) and if there are safeguarding issues. On occasions, the police may become part of the support for a family as part of a multiagency intervention.

Early Help

Under section 10 of the Children Act 2004 Local Authorities are responsible for promoting a joint responsibility to improve children's welfare and for ensuring that multi-agency training is undertaken that underpins the knowledge and skills required to achieve this. An Early Help assessment is an evidence based document with targeted actions to protect families from escalating circumstances which may lead to a statutory assessment under the Children Act 1989. Local Safeguarding Children's Boards have responsibility for setting out the process whereby the support is provided. (https://assets.publishing.service.gov.uk/government/uploads/system/uploads/attachment_data/file/779401/Working_Together_to_Safeguard-Children.pdf)

Early Help is the system by which families across the UK can receive support as soon as an issue first arises. The term Early Help refers to the point at which the support is offered, and does not imply that this is only available for young children – the service is in recognition that early intervention prevents situations from escalating and can be provided up to adulthood.

Early help services are available to improve outcomes for children and are flexible in how they are applied, for instance support may be given to improve the home environment by supporting the parents or to reduce risk by supporting the whole family. Reducing the risk to children is vital in order for them to develop emotional and social skills to engage in the community and within their relationships, and to do this families need a strong support network provided by family, friends and professionals; parents need to supported with issues of mental health; the family needs to be economically sound and they should be aware of help and support available within the local community. The programme may be home based, school based or may involve provision of a mentor to help the young person. (https://learning.nspcc.org.uk/safeguarding-child-protection/early-help-early-intervention)

Early help relies on:

- The provision of a Threshold Document by the safeguarding partners setting out the criteria (for example: https://lambeth-childcare.proceduresonline.com/p_threshold.html)
- Agreement and participation of parents and children
- Is multi-agency in nature
- Allows information to be shared (within GDPR and safeguarding guidelines) with consent of the family
- Takes the child's views into account
- Has established outcomes and actions and is reviewed
- Is flexible according to the changing needs of the family or child
- May be applied to families or individual children.

Family, friends and supporters

Although family and friends may wish to be supportive, the reality of the challenges faced by parents and carers of children who have suffered developmental trauma can be bewildering, especially when parents and carers choose to adopt therapeutic parenting methods as these may be misunderstood. In order to enable family, friends and supporters to form part of a supportive network to sustain the family, the following may be helpful.

Training

Where there is a strong commitment to support the family, it will be most beneficial for key supporters to take part in therapeutic parenting training to help them understand the child's behaviours and the reasons for the therapeutic interventions. There are also many books which can help develop this understanding. Training should provide an understanding of the causes of adverse behaviours and appropriate management strategies so that there is routine and consistency for the child. An excellent place to start for families wishing to understand the concepts of therapeutic parenting is *The Quick Guide to Therapeutic Parenting* by Sarah Naish.

Roles

It can help supporters if they are assigned specific tasks or supportive roles, and it is beneficial for the child if these become routine and consistent – for example, picking up the child from school on a specific day, taking the child out once a month, or providing babysitting (a chance for parents to concentrate on their own relationship) at regular intervals. Other things which may be helpful, depending on circumstances and availability, include help with housework, time for a chat, setting up an SOS telephone link, meeting for a coffee, going for a walk. Maybe what is needed most is a good listener. It is most helpful if the family is very specific about their needs.

Have a plan

Think about the following:

- What are your support needs? What would make a big difference to you? Make a list.
- Prioritize your most immediate support need.
- Match your needs with the most suitable person.
- What additional information do your friends and family need in order to better understand your situation?
- How might this be provided? (Training, books, video, attending a support group with you?)

CASE STUDY 11.1 – WORKING ALONGSIDE PROFESSIONALS

Gloria is a female child, ten years old and entering puberty. She has a late diagnosis of autism and is known to be emotionally dysfunctional and have an attachment disorder as a result of severe neglect. At school, Gloria is displaying some 'annoying' behaviours such as running up and down the classroom, distracting other children, being unable to focus. She is being bullied by some of the girls in her class who prevent her from interacting with the other children, meaning that she is isolated during break times. Her cognitive development is impaired, and she has an intervention for numeracy as she is unable to use basic number skills such as counting. She has had a speech and language assessment due to her inability to take in and process what she reads. She has extreme social difficulties and has been referred to CAMHS after an incident of self-harming in school. At home Gloria frequently acts out in inappropriate ways – shouting, throwing things around and behaving in an aggressive manner to her parents and siblings as her school life becomes more overwhelming. School put the family in touch with a family link worker who liaised between home and school, getting to know Gloria's history and helping the school to understand the issues the family was facing. She also gave the school information on bullying and insisted that the issue was resolved. This intervention (including her attending an appeal for a secondary school placement with the parents) enabled Gloria to complete her final year at her primary school, and provided Gloria with a friendly face and a place to air her worries. The family were supported by Nana on Father's side and two friends of Mum in the same school. They also felt very supported by the link worker, but very unsupported by the school, who they felt were not responsive to Gloria's needs.

		Numeracy
Diagnosis		Action Plus
CAMHS		Speech and language
Doctor		School/SENCO
	Gloria	
Social worker	Family link worker	Mum and Dad
Post-adoption team		Nana
		Siblings

Figure 11.1 Support system

In the above figure, JY is shown at the centre with primary support being Mum and Dad as the advocators, primary professionals in light grey and other support or actions in medium grey. This shows how a relatively simple situation (in adoption and fostering terms) can create nonetheless many interactions between the child, the family and the separate agencies.

12

Main Therapeutic Models

Whether you are a therapeutic parent yourself or a professional working alongside a family, it is useful to know about as many therapeutic tools as possible in order to manage the changing needs and abilities of children with developmental trauma. In this chapter we will examine some of the best known approaches.

Cognitive behavioural therapy (CBT)

The NHS website describes CBT:

> Cognitive behavioural therapy (CBT) is a talking therapy that can help you manage your problems by changing the way you think and behave.
>
> It's most commonly used to treat anxiety and depression, but can be useful for other mental and physical health problems.
>
> *(www.nhs.uk)*

CBT is based on the idea that our response to an event is part of a sequence:

Event ⟶ Thought ⟶ Feeling

This leads us to the idea that our thoughts about the event give rise to our feelings about the event, and therefore our responses. Clearly our thoughts and responses are linked to our experiences. This can also give rise to 'automatic thoughts', which can lead us into patterns of feelings about events which may be extremely unhelpful. In addition, these thoughts can lock us into a feedback loop which further entrenches our interpretation of the situation. This could be positive or negative in effect. I give an example below of how this might work within a family.

Cycle type	**Positive (securely attached child)**	**Negative (child with RAD or developmental trauma/ multiple moves)**
Event	Argument with Mum	Argument with Mum
Thought	I am so cross with Mum! She makes me so angry!	I am so cross with Mum! She does not like me, I can tell. Just like my birth mum!
Feeling	Anger – calming down	Anger – escalating
Thought	I made a mistake. I should apologize and make up. That will help me feel better. I love Mum, and I know she loves me	I know Mum hates me because I am horrible! Everyone hates me! I do everything wrong. I don't know what to do!
Feeling	Calming, thoughtful	Fearful, escalating
Thought	I will go and give Mum a cuddle and say sorry now. I know she will understand	I hate Mum! I hate this stupid house! Nobody wanted me anyway! Nobody ever wants me, because I am horrible!
Event	Finds Mum and makes up. Has a chat about what happened	Fearful feelings lead to angry outburst with aggression, involving additional members of family
Thought	That's better! I know Mum always loves me	Nobody likes me! I bet they are going to get rid of me now! I will be sent away again because I am horrible!

Feeling	Safe, secure with new understanding	Vulnerable, fearful, intense feeling of worthlessness
Looking forwards	Family continues to feel safe and feelings are contained	Family and child both feel at risk, scared and angry, feeding into further negative events

The 'automatic thoughts' which drive our feelings and responses are unique to us and our experiences, and CBT seeks to help us identify these thoughts and then develop a new narrative for ourselves to enable us to step away from the unhelpful patterns we have become set in. McKay *et al.* (2011) suggest this can be done by experiencing the type of 'limited thinking pattern' that best fits your way of thinking (filtering, polarized thinking, overgeneralization, mind reading, catastrophizing, magnifying, personalization) and then creating 'balancing statements' or 'alternative thoughts' to help you to step out of the negative cycle. McKay *et al.* describe a number of strategies which can be used to help create a new and more positive mindset.

Sarah Edelman (2002) explains that CBT focuses on the present instead of trying to make sense of the past. This kind of 'here and now' thinking or 'thought stopping' can be very useful for individuals with rigidity of thinking who tend to perseverate, such as those on the autistic spectrum.

RESOURCES

Edelman, S. (2002) *Change Your Thinking with CBT*. London: Vermilion.

McKay, M., Davis, M. and Fanning, P. (2011) *Thoughts and Feelings: Taking Control of Your Moods and Your Life*. Oakland, CA: New Harbinger Publications.

NHS (2020) *Cognitive Behavioural Therapy*. Accessed on 16 February 2020 at www.nhs.uk/Conditions/Cognitive-behavioural-therapy/Pages/Introduction.aspx

Dyadic Developmental Psychotherapy (DDP), (Dyadic Developmental Practice) (Dyadic Developmental Parenting)

From early 2000, Dan Hughes together with like-minded therapists developed the first ideas of attachment-based relational strategies which used John Bowlby's seminal work on attachment and Colwyn Trevarthen's ideas about intersubjectivity, extended and informed by new information about neuroscience and the role of attachment. This resulted in the emergence of Dyadic Developmental Psychotherapy and PACE (Playfulness, Acceptance, Curiosity and Empathy), which is a cornerstone of the model. As this work was extended and developed, Dyadic Developmental Practice and Dyadic Developmental Parenting also evolved.

DDP is a child and relationship-centred approach, recognizing that the extremely challenging behaviours which are often displayed by children who have been traumatized within relationships are their way of managing the high levels of fear that overwhelm them when they are parented, especially if the parent is using a standard parenting approach. This is because standard parenting approaches do not help the child with the fear of connection that they developed because of their traumatizing experience. Typically, these behaviours make it difficult to connect emotionally to their child.

DDP starts with the parents, explaining the approach, preparing them and exploring their feelings about parenting the child. If they are in a state of blocked care the therapist will work with them to move out of this state. This helps parents to remain empathic to the child. They also need help to adopt DDP-informed parenting (also called Dyadic Developmental Parenting), understanding and adopting the attitude of PACE and learning to provide this alongside supporting behaviour. The therapist helps the parents to explore the impact parenting the child is having upon them, learning to notice times when they become defensive towards the child and finding ways to move back into an open and engaged stance. This often involves exploring past relationship experience, including attachment history. The child is then brought into the process and enabled to explore their thoughts, feelings and fears in the safe relationship with their parents, which is facilitated by the psychotherapist.

Dan Hughes also introduces the affective-reflective dialogue (A-R dialogue). He states that 'AFFT focusses on helping family members to get to know each other from a basic stance of acceptance rather than evaluation. This understanding includes their strengths and vulnerabilities as well as the impact they are having on each other, for better or worse' (Hughes 2011, p.3).

The therapy is based on theories of attachment and intersubjectivity (how we understand and relate to each other). The process facilitates communication whilst remaining open to the experience of the other members of the family with therapeutic support in a safe environment. This enables new understanding to be achieved and incidents are redefined within a joint meaning for the family.

As a process, the therapy involves the following (with therapeutic support):

- Establishing a safe place to explore the issues
- Understanding intersubjectivity
- Understanding your own attachment history and noticing when a current experience with your child activates memories of past experience leading to defensive responding
- Establishing PACE
- Communicating
- Relating emotionally
- Reflecting on their experience as a parent and the child's experience
- Repairing relationship ruptures allowing the child to begin to understand that relationships can be resilient.

The outcomes are typically increased attachment and ability to sustain a healthy relationship. They will be better able to manage their emotions and relax so that controlling behaviours reduce. Their sense of safety and security within their family will be increased.

For further information, the most recent publication at time of going to press is: *Healing Relational Trauma with Attachment-focused Interventions* (Dan Hughes, Kim Golding and Julie Hudson).

RESOURCES

Bowlby, J. (1977) *Attachment and Loss, Vol. 1*. London: Pimlico.

Hughes, D., Golding, K. and Hudson, J. (2019) *Healing Relational Trauma with Attachment-Focused Interventions: Dyadic Developmental Psychotherapy with Children and Families*. New York: W.W. Norton.

Shell, D. and Becker-Weidman, A. (2005) *Creating Capacity for Attachment: Dyadic Developmental Psychotherapy in the Treatment of Trauma-Attachment Disorders*. Oklahoma City: Wood 'N' Barnes.

Trevarthen, C. (2005) 'Stepping Away from the Mirror: Pride and Shame in Adventures of Companionship. Reflections on the Nature and Emotional Needs of Infant Intersubjectivity.' In S. Carter, L. Ahnert, K.E. Grossmann, S.B. Hrdy *et al.* (eds) *Attachment and Bonding: A New Synthesis*. Cambridge, MA: MIT Press.

DDP Network: https://ddpnetwork.org

Eye Movement Desensitization and Reprocessing (EMDR)

When an individual experiences an extremely stressful event this can be encoded as implicit memory – in order words, the event itself is internalized as a feeling or state on behalf of the sufferer. The emotional link is very strong and a sensation such as a smell, a noise, an expression or a movement can in the right conditions be enough to trigger all of the stress of the original event. For some traumatized children, this replaying of emotional trauma is like a broken record, they are stuck in the cycle of their past experiences and find it hard or impossible to move past that point. For example, a child that has had multiple moves will live in daily expectation of the same thing happening and this fear will activate their trauma memories repeatedly – especially if they are feeling ashamed or stressed.

EMDR was developed by Dr Francine Shapiro in the 1980s. The therapy uses the patient's rapid eye movements to dampen the power of memories of past traumatic events. This has been shown to be useful for example in the treatment of PTSD. There are no therapeutic talking sessions and no medication; instead the therapist asks the patient to talk about a traumatic event, whilst following hand movements in front of the eyes. The effect of this is to produce alternating stimulation of opposite sides of the brain, helping re-integration of the neurophysiological system and reducing the emotional impact of the experience.

'As troubling images and feelings are processed by the brain via the eye-movement patterns of EMDR, resolution of the issues and a more peaceful state are achieved.' (EMDR-Therapy, http://emdr-therapy.com/emdr.html, accessed 05.05.17)

RESOURCE

Boulware, C. (n.d.) What is 'EMDR?' Accessed on 28 September 2020 at http://emdr-therapy.com/emdr.html

Play therapy

Play therapy is a technique whereby the child is encouraged by the therapist to communicate their experiences and feelings and explore these by use of a playful medium which may be play sand, clay, puppets, small world toys or colouring and drawing. The therapist then guides the child to make new meaning and understanding. This was discussed as an emerging technique in 1964 when Virginia Mae Axline wrote about her experiences in helping a child who was very cut off to reconnect with the world around him. This child was called 'Dibs' in her book *Dibs: In Search of Self* (1964).

Play is a natural form of communication for a child, and during play therapy the child is enabled to process their thoughts and feelings through interactions with their therapist. Parents are involved initially for the therapist to gain a picture of how things are and what the background to the challenges faced by the child (and the family) are. The parent is then encouraged to support the child to commit to the process (e.g. making sure appointments are kept) and to be open to conversations (if the child instigates these) about the therapy. Otherwise, parents are updated on the process by the therapist.

RESOURCES

Axline, V.M. (1964) *Dibs: In Search of Self*. Harmondsworth: Penguin.

British Association of Play Therapists (BAPT): www.bapt.info

Filial therapy

This play therapy was developed by Drs Bernard and Louise Gurney. In this therapy, Parents are trained to instigate therapeutic sessions with their child and to be the facilitators. This is the major differential with play therapy where the therapist facilitates the therapy and the parent is given progress reports.

Initially there is a parent training phase, after which there are firstly supervised parent–child play sessions. Finally the therapeutic sessions move into the home with support from the therapist in processing and making meaning of these sessions.

During the sessions parents learn how to structure play and how to 'follow' the child's lead in imaginary play – this is a highly effective tool to connect with your child and meet unmet needs as it recreates early bonding experiences. In addition the parent learns the art and value of empathic listening and how to set enforceable boundaries. This increases safety and trust from child to parent.

The outcomes include: Greater connection, trust and communication between parent and child; Parent gains understanding of the child and their behaviours and is able to implement strategies to reduce confrontation and stress; Children gain coping strategies; Behaviours reduce because parents come to an acceptance of their child and an appreciation of their abilities and the child who is being nurtured and supported by the process gains confidence and self esteem. Parents also feel empowered and regain confidence in their parenting capability (Filial Therapy, http://cfhplay.com/filial.html, accessed 08.05.17).

The importance of this therapy is that it places parents at the centre of the process, recognizing their special knowledge of their child and empowering them as the central core of a process which can enable the child to reflect on and gain a new understanding of experiences in a safe, non-judgemental and accepting environment. Evidence has shown that using this therapy the key central relationship is strengthened and that parents develop crucial skills to manage the challenges faced by the family.

> By training parents to acquire skills that enable them to grow in understanding and acceptance of the child as well as to sensitively and empathically respond to the child's communications a context is created in which the child's fears and anxieties related to earlier experience can be safely explored and expressed within a new special parent-child alliance. (http://filialplaytherapy.co.uk)

RESOURCES

Thomas, G. (n.d.) *Welcome to Filial Therapy*. http://filialplaytherapy.co.uk, accessed 08.05.2017.

Filial Therapy. http://cfhplay.com/filial.html

Theraplay

The Theraplay Institute defines Theraplay as 'a child and family therapy for building and enhancing attachment, self-esteem, trust in others, and joyful engagement. It is based on the natural patterns of playful, healthy interaction between parent and child and is personal, physical, and fun. Theraplay interactions focus on four essential qualities found in parent-child relationships: Structure, Engagement, Nurture, and Challenge. Theraplay sessions create an active, emotional connection between the child and parent or caregiver, resulting in a changed view of the self as worthy and lovable and of relationships as positive and rewarding' (www.theraplay.org).

In a Theraplay session, the therapist guides the family to create opportunities for connection, regulation and trust using a variety of activities which may be nurturing, challenging or fun. The therapist creates the safe environment where the family are able to interact and engage so that the child (and adults) feel secure and cared for. Theraplay may also be introduced by parents at home.

This therapy is extremely useful for creating connections and building trust with children who have low social and emotional functioning age, helping children to learn to trust.

RESOURCES

Myrow, D.L. (2013) 'Theraplay activities for older children and young teens.' The Theraplay Institute, www.theraplay.org/index.php/articles-about-theraplay/81-theraplay-and-adolescents/216-article-theraplay-activities-teens

The Theraplay Institute (1994) 'Home Theraplay activities for young children.' www.theraplay.org/index.php/articles-about-theraplay/83-theraplay-in-early-childhood/61-article-home-theraplay-activities-for-young-children

Dyadic Development Psychotherapy (DDP)

From early 2000, Dan Hughes together with like-minded therapists developed the first ideas of attachment-based relational strategies which used John Bowlby's seminal work on attachment, extended and informed by new information about neuroscience and the role of attachment. This resulted in the emergence of Dyadic Developmental Psychotherapy and PACE (Playfulness, Acceptance, Curiosity and Empathy) which is a cornerstone of the technique.

DDP is a child and relationship-centred approach, recognizing that the extremely challenging behaviours which are often displayed by children who have been traumatized are their way of managing the high levels of fear that overwhelm them when they are parented, especially if the parent is using a standard parenting approach. Typically these behaviours make it difficult to connect emotionally to their child.

DDP starts with the parents, explaining the approach, preparing them and exploring their feelings about parenting the child. This helps parents to remain empathic to the child. The child is then brought into the process and enabled to explore their thoughts, feelings and fears in the safe relationship with their parents which is facilitated by the psychotherapist. The outcomes are typically increased attachment and ability to sustain a healthy relationship. They will be better able to manage their emotions, and relax so that controlling behaviours reduce. Their sense of safety and security within their family will be increased.

RESOURCES

Becker-Weidman, A. "*Creating Capacity for Attachment – Dyadic* Shell, D (2005) *Developmental Psychotherapy in the Treatment of Trauma-Attachment Disorders*" DDP Network https://ddpnetwork.org, accessed 10.05.2017.

Attachment-focused therapy/ Attachment-focused family therapy

Aain, developed by Dan Hughes, this therapy uses the same basic principles as DDP in that it relies on PACE. In this therapy, Dan Hughes introduces the affective-reflective dialogue (A-R dialogue). He says that:

> AFFT focuses on helping family members to get to know each other from a basic stance of acceptance rather than evaluation. This understanding includes their strengths and vulnerabilities as well as the impact they are having on each other, for better or worse. (Hughes 2011, p.3)

The therapy is based on theories of attachment and intersubjectivity (how we understand and relate to each other). The process facilitates communication whilst remaining open to the experience of the other members of the family with therapeutic support in a safe environment. This enables new understanding to be achieved and incidents are redefined within a joint meaning for the family.

As a process, the therapy involves the following:

- Establishing a safe place to explore the issues
- Understanding intersubjectivity
- Organizing your own attachment history
- Establishing PACE
- Communicating
- Relating emotionally
- Reflecting
- Repairing.

RESOURCES

Hughes, D. (2009) *Attachment-Focused Parenting*. New York: W.W. Norton.

Hughes, D. (2011) *Attachment-Focused Family Therapy Workbook.* New York: W.W. Norton.

Life story work

Understanding our history is key to understanding ourselves and unlocking the reasons for the thoughts, feelings and self concepts that we carry with us. Biological children who have not experienced trauma have a narrative or story that is given to them from birth: It encompasses their family history, inherited characteristics such as eye and hair colour, height and body shape as well as skills and interests. It forms the backdrop of their identity and is a solid and secure base for them.

As we have discussed in this book, any child that has suffered trauma will have a disrupted story to some extent – some children from trauma have had a story told to them that confirms to them that everything is their fault – they are bad. Others may feel disposable – bouncing around the system until they are deemed to be independent at 18. These ideas need to be unravelled and placed in context in order for the child to e able to make sense of their past, be as comfortable as possible in their present and able to predict a future of their choosing.

Life story work enables children to start putting their early experiences into context so that they can create a narrative of their experiences that makes sense. As many young people struggle with their past and the feelings that emerge, but also have a need to understand their own roots and identity, especially as they approach adolescence, this can be a vitally important tool to help fill in the gaps and allow the child or young person to get a coherent sense of self. The therapist helps the child to fit the known pieces of their individual 'puzzle' together. Richard Rose states that

> everyone has a story: their perception of what, where, when, who, why and how. Our stories are what make us – we are, after all, what we

were. In acknowledging this simple truth, we can look to the future with acceptance of a healthier tomorrow. (Rose 2012, p.15)

RESOURCES

Rose, R. (2012) *Life Story Therapy with Traumatized Children.* London: Jessica Kingsley Publishers

UK Fostering (n.d.) *Life Story Work.* http://ukfostering.org.uk/life-story-work

Bibliography

Publication references

Adams, P. (2017) *Restraint and Physical Intervention in Foster Care*. Practice Note 63, CoramBAAF Adoption & Fostering Academy and the Nationwide Association of Fostering Providers (NAFP). London: CoramBAAF. Accessed on 14 February 2020 at https://corambaaf.org.uk/sites/default/files/Members%20Area/Resources/Practice%20Notes/PN63.pdf

Axline, V.M. (1964) *Dibs in Search of Self*. Harmondsworth: Penguin.

Bloom, S. L. and Farragher, B. (2010) *Destroying Sanctuary: The Crisis in Human Service*. Delivery Systems. New York: Oxford University Press.

Bourg Carter, S. (2012) 'Emotions are contagious – choose your company wisely.' *Psychology Today,* 20 October. Accessed on 17 February 2020 at www.psychologytoday.com/gb/blog/high-octane-women/201210/emotions-are-contagious-choose-your-company-wisely

Bowlby, J. (1988) *A Secure Base*. New York: Basic Books.

Bronfenbrenner, U. (1979) *The Ecology of Human Development: Experiments by Nature and Design*. Cambridge, MA: Harvard University Press.

Cook O'Toole, J. (2012) *Asperkids*. London: Jessica Kingsley Publishers.

Department for Education (DfE) (2013) *Early Years Outcomes: A Non-Statutory*

Guide for Practitioners and Inspectors to Help Inform Understanding of Child Development through the Early Years. London: DfE. Accessed on 11 February 2020 at www.foundationyears.org.uk/wp-content/uploads/2012/03/Early_Years_Outcomes.pdf

Edelman, S. (2002) *Change Your Thinking with CBT*. London: Vermilion.

Elliott, A. (2013) *Why Can't My Child Behave? Empathic Parenting Strategies That Work for Adoptive and Foster Families*. London: Jessica Kingsley Publishers.

Forbes, H. and Post, B. (2014) *Beyond Consequences, Logic and Control*. Boulder, CO: Beyond Consequences Institute.

Gardener, N. (2007) *A Friend Like Henry*. London: Hodder & Stoughton.

Gerhardt, S. (2004) *Why Love Matters*. Hove: Brunner Routledge.

Gerhardt, S. (2010) *The Selfish Society*. London: Simon & Schuster.

Golding, K. and Hughes, D. (2015) *Creating Loving Attachments: Parenting with PACE to Nurture Confidence and Security in the Troubled Child*. London: Jessica Kingsley Publishers.

Goleman, D. (1996) *Emotional Intelligence*. London: Bloomsbury.

Higashida, N. (2013) *The Reason I Jump*. London: Sceptre.

Hughes, D. (2009) *Attachment-Focused Parenting*. New York: W.W. Norton.

Hughes, D. (2011) *Attachment-Focused Family Therapy*. New York: W.W. Norton.

Hughes, D. (2013) *Building the Bonds of Attachment*. Lanham, MD: Jason Aronson.

Hughes, D. and Baylin, J. (2012) *Brain-Based Parenting*. New York: W.W. Norton.

Hughes, D., Golding, K. and Hudson, J. (2019) *Healing Relational Trauma with Attachment-Focused Interventions: Dyadic Developmental Psychotherapy with Children and Families*. New York: W.W. Norton.

Jakob, P. (n.d.) *Non-Violent Resistance.*

Keck, G. (2009) *Parenting Adopted Adolescents*. Colorado Springs: NavPress.

Laming, Lord (2003) *The Victoria Climbié Inquiry: Report*. CM 5730. Accessed on 17 February 2020 at https://assets.publishing.service.gov.uk/government/uploads/system/uploads/attachment_data/file/273183/5730.pdf

Luxmoore, N. (2008) *Feeling Like Crap*. London: Jessica Kingsley Publishers.

McKay, M., Davis, M. and Fanning, P. (2011) *Thoughts and Feelings: Taking Control of Your Moods and Your Life*. Oakland, CA: New Harbinger Publications.

Mitchell, J. (2007) 'Reflecting on chaos.' *Adoption Today*, June.

Mitchell, J. (2009) 'Riding in tandem.' *Adoption Today*, August.

Morgan, N. (2005) *Blame My Brain*. London: Walker Books.

Myrow, D.L. (2013) 'Theraplay activities for older children and young teens.' The Theraplay Institute. Accessed on 16 February 2020 at www.theraplay.org/index.php/articles-about-theraplay/81-theraplay-and-adolescents/ 216-article-theraplay-activities-teens

Naish, S. (2016) *Therapeutic Parenting in a Nutshell*. Amazon.

Naish, S. (2018) *The A-Z of Therapeutic Parenting: Strategies and Solutions*. London: Jessica Kingsley Publishers.

Naish, S. (2020) *The Quick Guide to Therapeutic Parenting: A Visual Introduction*. London: Jessica Kingsley Publishers.

Naish, S. and Dillon, S. (2020) *The Quick Guide to Therapeutic Parenting*. London: Jessica Kingsley Publishers.

NHS (2020) *Cognitive Behavioural Therapy*. Accessed on 16 February 2020 at www.nhs.uk/Conditions/Cognitive-behavioural-therapy/Pages/Introduction.aspx

Norris, V. and Lender, D. (2020) *Theraplay: The Practitioner's Guide*. London: Jessica Kingsley Publishers.

Norris, V. and Rodwell, H. (2017) *Parenting with Theraplay*. London: Jessica Kingsley Publishers.

Ottaway, H. and Selwyn, J. (2016) '"No-one told us it was going to be like this": compassion fatigue and foster carers.' Accessed on 12 February 2020 at https://research-information.bris.ac.uk/files/189522328/Compassion_fatigue_and_foster_carers_Final_report.pdf

Pelzer, D. (1995) *A Child Called It*. Florida: Health Communications Inc.

Perry, B. (1999) 'Memories of fear: how the brain stores and retrieves physiologic states, feelings, behaviors and thoughts from traumatic events.' The Child Trauma Academy. Accessed on 7 February 2020 at www.healing-arts.org/tir/perry_memories_of_fear.pdf

Perry, S. (2008) 'Mirror neurons.' BrainFacts.org. Accessed on 11 February 2020 at www.brainfacts.org/archives/2008/mirror-neurons

Post, B. (2009) *The Great Behavior Breakdown*. Palmyra, VA: Post Institutes and Associates.

Robinson, J.E. (2007) *Look Me in the Eye*. New York: Three Rivers Press.

Rose, R. (2012) *Life Story Therapy with Traumatized Children*. London: Jessica Kingsley Publishers.

Saunders, H. and Selwyn, J. (2011) *Adopting Large Sibling Groups*. London: BAAF.

Selwyn, J., Wijedasa, D. and Meakings, S. (2014) *Beyond the Adoption Order: Challenges, Interventions and Adoption Disruption*. London: DfE. Accessed on 12 February 2020 at https://assets.publishing.service.gov.uk/government/uploads/system/uploads/attachment_data/file/301889/Final_Report_-_3rd_April_2014v2.pdf

Shell, D. and Becker-Weidman, A. (2005) *Creating Capacity for Attachment: Dyadic Developmental Psychotherapy in the Treatment of Trauma-Attachment Disorders*. Oklahoma City: Wood 'N' Barnes.

Siegel, D. (2007) *The Mindful Brain in Human Development: Reflection and Attunement in the Cultivation of Well-Being*. New York: W.W. Norton.

Siegel, D. (2011) *Mindsight: Transform Your Brain with the New Science of Kindness*. Oxford: Oneworld Publications.

Siegel, D. (2014) *Brainstorm: The Power and Purpose of the Teenage Brain*. Gurgaon: Hachette India.

Siegel, D. (2015) *The Developing Mind*, 2nd edn. New York: The Guilford Press.

Siegel, D. and Hartzell, M. (2004) *Parenting from the Inside Out*. New York: TarcherPerigree.

Sunderland, M. (2006) *The Science of Parenting*. London: Dorling Kindersley.

The Theraplay Institute (1994) 'Home Theraplay activities for young children.' Accessed on 16 February 2020 at www.theraplay.org/index.php/articles-about-theraplay/83-theraplay-in-early-childhood/61-article-home-theraplay-activities-for-young-children

UK Fostering (n.d.) *Life Story Work*. Accessed on 16 February 2020 at http://ukfostering.org.uk/life-story-work

van der Kolk, B. (2005) *Developmental Trauma*. http://developmentaltrauma.com.au/tag/bessel-van-der-kolk

Verrier, N. (1993) *The Primal Wound*. Baltimore: Gateway Press.

Winerman, L. (2005) 'The mind's mirror.' *American Psychological Association 36*, 9, 48.

Websites

Autism

National Autistic Society, www.autism.org.uk

ADHD

ADDiSS (ADHD Information Services), www.addiss.co.uk

ACEs

CDC (Centers for Disease Control and Prevention), on Adverse Childhood Experiences (ACEs) – CDC-Kaiser ACE Study, www.cdc.gov/violenceprevention/childabuseandneglect/acestudy/index.html?CDC_AA_refVal=https%3A%2F%2Fwww.cdc.gov%2Fviolenceprevention%2Facestudy%2Findex.html

Aces Too High, https://acestoohigh.com/aces-101

Attachment

Bowlby, Alliance for Childhood – attachment, www.allianceforchildhood.eu/files/QOC%20Sig%204.pdf

PsychNet-UK
www.psychnetuk.com/x_new_site/DSM_IV/attachment_disorder.html

Attachment and Trauma Network Inc
What is Healthy Attachment?
www.attachmenttraumanetwork.org/understanding-attachment/healthy-attachment

Eating disorders

BEAT Eating Disorders, www.b-eat.co.uk

Puberty

BBC Science: Human Body and Mind
www.bbc.co.uk/science/humanbody/body/articles/lifecycle/teenagers/sexual_changes.shtml

Boundless
Physical Development in Adolescence
www.boundless.com/psychology/textbooks/boundless-psychology-textbook/human-development-14/adolescence-73/physical-development-in-adolescence-282-12817

Brain Facts
Neuroanatomy – Mirror Neurones
www.brainfacts.org/archives/2008/mirror-neurons

Brainworks, 'What is neuroplasticity?', https://brainworksneurotherapy.com/what-neuroplasticity

Bloom, S. L. and Farragher, B. (2010)
The Human Stress Response: What Does Everyone Need to Know?
Destroying Sanctuary: The Crisis in Human Service Delivery Systems.
New York: Oxford University Press. (pp. 102-106) http://www.mvbcn.org/shop/images/the_human_stress_response.pdf

Care Connection for Children
Transition Planning Checklist (my own suggestion of how a transition planning checklist might look like)
https://view.officeapps.live.com/op/view.aspx?src=http%3A%2F%2Fwww.chkd.org%2FuploadedFiles%2FDocuments%2FPrograms_and_Clinics%2FCCC%2520-%2520COMPLETE%2520Transition-%2520Guideline%2520Checklist.doc

Child Welfare Information Gateway
Sibling Issues in Foster Care and Adoption
www.childwelfare.gov/pubPDFs/siblingissues.pdf
01.2013

Children and Adults with Attention Deficit Hyperactivity Disorder (CHADD)
www.chadd.org

Children and Families Act 2014
Current legislation including SEND Provision
www.safeguardingchildrenea.co.uk/resources/summary-children-families-act-2014

Coping Skills for Kids
Brain and behavior changes
http://copingskills4kids.net/Changes.html#Brain_and_Behavior

C Wilson Meloncelli
HPA axis
www.cwilsonmeloncelli.com/hpa-axis

Compassion fatigue
www.bristol.ac.uk/sps/research/projects/completed/2016/compassion-fatigue-in-foster-carers

DDP Network
http://ddpnetwork.org/about-ddp/dyadic-developmental-parenting
https://ddpnetwork.org

Dyspraxia
http://dyspraxiafoundation.org.uk/about-dyspraxia/dyspraxia-glance

Early Childhood Mental Health – Trauma
https://dmh.mo.gov/healthykids/providers/trauma.html

EMDR-Therapy
What is EMDR?
emdr-therapy.com/emdr.html

EMDR UK & Ireland
(Professional Association of EMDR)
How Does EMDR Work?
http://emdrassociation.org.uk/whatis-emdr

Everyday health
Living with ADHD: Max's Story
www.everydayhealth.com/adhd-awareness/living-with-adhd-maxs-story.aspx

Every Child Matters Green Paper
www.gov.uk/government/publications/every-child-matters

EYFS Statutory Framework
www.foundationyears.org.uk/eyfs-statutory-framework/

Every Child Matters
www.gov.uk/government/publications/every-child-matters

The FASD Trust
www.fasdtrust.co.uk

Filial Therapy
http://cfhplay.com/filial.html

Foundation Years – development and outcomes

DfE Early Years Outcomes
www.foundationyears.org.uk/wp-content/uploads/2012/03/Early_Years_Outcomes.pdf

About Filial Play Therapy
http://filialplaytherapy.co.uk

Gestational Diabetes
www.mayoclinic.org/diseases-conditions/gestational-diabetes/symptoms-causes/syc-20355339

Help HER – Hyperemesis Education
https://helpher.org

Kendra Cherry, *Bowlby and Ainsworth: What is Attachment Theory? The Importance of Early Emotional Bonds*, www.verywell.com/what-is-attachment-theory-2795337

Live Science

Adrenal Glands: Facts, Function & Disease
www.livescience.com/59039-adrenal-glands

Maria Droste Counseling Center
The Psychology of Self Harm
www.mariadroste.org/2016/04/the-psychology-of-self-harm

Mason and Gupta
Siblings and Adoption – Reflections on Research and Experience
www.kcl.ac.uk/sspp/policy-institute/scwru/mrc/events2015/27Jan15-LMasonandAGupta.pdf

Max Planck Institute for Human Development
Isabel Dziobek
Differentiating Cognitive and Emotional Empathy in Individuals with Asperger Syndrome
www.mpib-berlin.mpg.de/en/research/concluded-areas/mprg-neuro-cognition-of-decision-making/decision-making-in-social-contexts/individuals-with-asperger

Mayo Clinic
Oppositional Defiant Disorder
www.mayoclinic.org/diseases-conditions/oppositional-defiant-disorder/basics/definition/con-20024559

McLeod, C.
Simply Psychology
Attachment Theory
www.simplypsychology.org/simplypsychology.org-attachment.pdf

McLeod, S.A. (2018, 21 May) Maslow's hierarchy of needs. Retrieved from https://www.simplypsychology.org/maslow.html

Myrow, David L. (2013) Theraplay Activities for Older Children and Young Teens
www.theraplay.org/index.php/articles-about-theraplay/81-theraplay-and-adolescents/216-article-theraplay-activities-teens

Medical News Today
Role of the Hypothalamus
www.medicalnewstoday.com/articles/312628.php

Mental Health Foundation
ADHD
www.mentalhealth.org.uk/a-to-z/a/attention-deficit-hyperactivity-disorder-adhd

NHS Choices
Developmental coordination disorder (dyspraxia) in children
www.nhs.uk/Conditions/Dyspraxia-(childhood)/Pages/Symptoms.aspx

NHS Choices
Foetal Alcohol Syndrome
www.nhs.uk/conditions/foetal-alcohol-syndrome

NHS Choices, Anorexia Nervosa
Kate's Story
www.nhs.uk/Conditions/Anorexia-nervosa/Pages/Realstorypg.aspx

NHS Choices, Bulimia
www.nhs.uk/conditions/bulimia

NHS Scotland
Information about Mental Health
www.moodjuice.scot.nhs.uk

NHS
Cognitive Behavioural Therapy (CBT)
www.nhs.uk/Conditions/Cognitive-behavioural-therapy/Pages/Introduction.aspx

National Institute for Clinical Excellence
www.nice.org.uk

Neonatal Abstinence Syndrome
Medline Plus
https://medlineplus.gov/ency/article/007313.htm

Neonatal Abstinence Syndrome – Scoring, Long-term effects
https://syndromespedia.com/neonatal-abstinence-syndrome-scoring-long-term-effects.html

NOFAS UK (National Organisation for Foetal Alcohol Syndrome UK)
www.nofas.org

NVR (Non-Violent Resistance)
Partnership Projects
www.partnershipprojectsuk.com

PTSD UK
www.ptsduk.org

Pathological Demand Disorder
www.pdasociety.org.uk

Piaget
Simply Psychology.org
www.simplypsychology.org/piaget.html

British Association of Play Therapists (BAPT)
www.bapt.info

Preeclampsia
www.mayoclinic.org/diseases-conditions/preeclampsia/symptoms-causes/syc-20355745

Psychology Today:
Narcissistic Personality Disorder
www.psychologytoday.com/conditions/narcissistic-personality-disorder

Raising Children
Teens (12–18 years)
http://raisingchildren.net.au/teens/teens.html

Science Direct
Hypothalamic-Pituitary-Adrenal Axis
www.sciencedirect.com/topics/neuroscience/hypothalamic-pituitary-adrenal-axis

Sensory Processing Disorder Website
www.sensory-processing-disorder.com/sensory-integration-dysfunction-symptoms.html

Special Needs Jungle – EHCP
www.specialneedsjungle.com

Special Educational Needs Support
IPSEA
www.ipsea.org.uk

Special Educational Needs Support
SOS!SEN
www.sossen.org.uk

Stanford Health
Neonatal Abstinence Syndrome
www.stanfordchildrens.org/en/topic/default?id=neonatal-abstinence-syndrome-90-P02387

Star Institute for Sensory Processing Disorder
www.spdstar.org
Staying Put guidance
DfE, DWP and HMRC guidance
https://assets.publishing.service.gov.uk/government/uploads/system/uploads/attachment_data/file/201015/Staying_Put_Guidance.pdf

Stress and Pregnancy (prenatal and perinatal)
www.child-encyclopedia.com/stress-and-pregnancy-prenatal-and-perinatal/according-experts/effects-prenatal-stress-child

Structure and Function of Nervous Tissue
www.ivyroses.com/HumanBody/Tissue/Tissue_Nervous-Tissue.php

The Best Brain Possible
How the Amygdala Hijacks Your Life
www.thebestbrainpossible.com/is-your-amygdala-hijacking-your-life

The Theraplay Institute
Home Theraplay Activities for Young Children
www.theraplay.org/index.php/articles-about-theraplay/83-theraplay-in-early-childhood/61-article-home-theraplay-activities-for-young-children

Opposition Defiance Disorder
NHS
www.nhs.uk/news/2013/03March/Pages/New-guidelines-on-child-antisocial-behaviour.aspx

Pregnancy Sickness Support website
www.pregnancysicknesssupport.org.uk

SEND Code of Practice 0–25
www.gov.uk/government/publications/send-code-of-practice-0-to-25

SENDIASS
https://cyp.iassnetwork.org.uk

Teleos Leadership Institute
Chris Allen Thomas
Emotional Empathy and Cognitive Empathy
http://blog.teleosleaders.com/2013/07/19/emotional-empathy-and-cognitive-empathy

Thinkuknow
www.thinkuknow.co.uk

Thoughtco
What Does the Brain's Cerebral Cortex Do?
www.thoughtco.com/anatomy-of-the-brain-cerebral-cortex-373217
Pituitary Gland
www.thoughtco.com/pituitary-gland-anatomy-373226

van der Kolk, Bessel
Developmental Trauma
http://developmentaltrauma.com.au/tag/bessel-van-der-kolk

Verywellmind – Arlin Cuncic
Amygdala Hijack and the Fight or Flight Response
www.verywellmind.com/what-happens-during-an-amygdala-hijack-4165944

The Urban Child Institute
Baby's Brain Begins Now: Conception to Age 3
www.urbanchildinstitute.org/why-0-3/baby-and-brain

Journal of Natural Science, Biology and Medicine
Mirror neurons: Enigma of the metaphysical modular brain
www.ncbi.nlm.nih.gov/pmc/articles/PMC3510904

Child Development Media
Mary Ainsworth and Attachment Theory
www.childdevelopmentmedia.com/articles/mary-ainsworth-and-attachment-theory

Developmental Trauma Disorder, Bessel van der Kolk
Psychiatric Annals; May 2005; 35, 5; Psychology Module
www.wjcia.org/conpast/2008/trauma/trauma.pdf

UN Convention on the Rights of the Child
www.unicef.org/crc

YouTube

Hand Model of the Brain
Dan Siegel
www.youtube.com/watch?v=gm9CIJ74Oxw&t=8s

'Flipping Your Lid'
Dan Siegel
www.youtube.com/watch?v=G0T_2NNoC68

Dan Hughes on empathy
www.youtube.com/watch?v=rM1seYXN1Nc

Sarah Naish
www.youtube.com/results?search_query=therapeutic+parenting+sarah+naish

Subject Index

Author Index

The A–Z of Therapeutic Parenting
Strategies and Solutions
Sarah Naish

£16.99 | $24.95 | PB | 344PP |
ISBN 978 1 78592 376 0 |
eISBN 978 1 78450 732 9

Therapeutic parenting is a deeply nurturing parenting style, and is especially effective for children with attachment difficulties, or who experienced childhood trauma. This book provides everything you need to know in order to be able to effectively therapeutically parent.

Providing a model of intervention, The A–Z of Therapeutic Parenting gives parents or caregivers an easy to follow process to use when responding to issues with their children. The following A–Z covers 60 common problems parents face, from acting aggressively to difficulties with sleep, with advice on what might trigger these issues, and how to respond.

Easy to navigate and written in a straightforward style, this book is a 'must have' for all therapeutic parents.

Sarah Naish is an adoptive parent, director of Inspire Training Group, which delivers training on attachment issues, founder of the National Association of Therapeutic Parents and author of the hugely popular Therapeutic Parenting Books series.

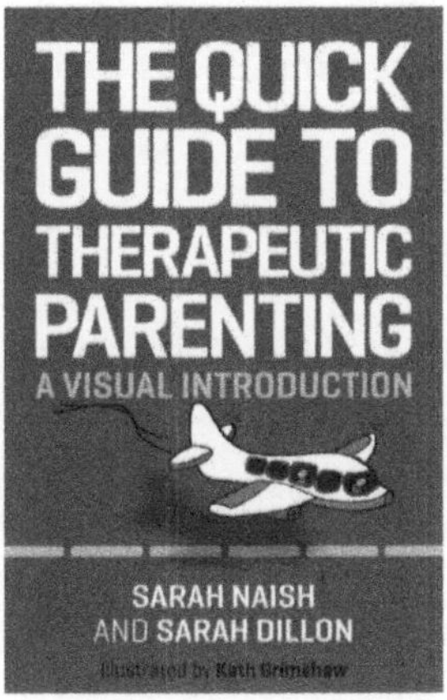

The Quick Guide to Therapeutic Parenting
A Visual Introduction
Sarah Naish and Sarah Dillon

£13.99 | $17.95 | PB | 256PP |
ISBN 978 1 78775 357 0 |
eISBN 978 1 78775 358 7

Therapeutic parenting is not your usual parenting style. It's a special, specific way to raise kids who have experienced trauma in their past, and requires a lot of commitment and determination – this is about far more than love and care.

But where do you start?

This book is the ideal first step for anyone who wants to understand how therapeutic parenting works. It offers simple summaries of the key ideas behind it, fully illustrated throughout with informative cartoons and graphics. Over 40 different issues are covered, from dysregulation and fear, to setting boundaries and parenting in the midst of trauma.

The perfect introduction for new therapeutic parents, family members, teachers or other adults who need to help support you and your child, this Quick Guide will also be a source of inspiration for more experienced parents.

Sarah Naish is author of bestselling parenting guide The A–Z of Therapeutic Parenting. She is an adoptive parent, founder of the National Association of Therapeutic Parents, director of Inspire Training Group and author of the hugely popular Therapeutic Parenting Books series. She lives in Gloucestershire.

Sarah Dillon is a Founding Committee Member and Therapeutic Lead of the National Association of Therapeutic Parents. She is also a therapist, specialising in attachment difficulties, complex and developmental trauma, and spent much of her childhood in the care system. She lives in Derby.

Sarah Dillon spent much of her childhood in foster care, and is now an attachment therapist and Panel Chair.

Jane Mitchell is an adoptive parent, and specialises in training around attachment, developmental trauma and related neuroscience.